HOW TO BUILD A THRIVII
FEE-FOR-SERVICE PRACTIC

D0803891

"Dr. Kolt provides an excellent resource for those b those facing the challenges of a new healthcare marketplace. This is a welcome and much needed resource to enable therapists to maintain the integrity of a caring practice while also being successful in business. This is a gift to her profession."

— Reverend Richard Bowyer
Campus Minister, Wesley Foundation at Fairmont State College

"Reading Dr. Kolt's book is like having a mentor hold your hand and walk you through the practice development and marketing process step by step. It's time for graduate schools and internship programs to teach students these skills and this is the ideal text. Dr. Kolt's book is also an excellent resource for experienced psychologists who want to improve or reinvent their practices."

— Michael Brickey, Ph.D., ABPP

"There is real value here for those who want a detailed map on building and maintaining a therapy practice."

— William Meyers
Former editor, APA Division 42, Independent Practitioner

"This book is for every psychologist who wants to have a more profitable practice. Well written, with essential information for psychologists who want to grow their practice. Want an ethical and successful practice that you control? If so, this book is for you. Dr. Kolt's book will not only help you obtain an ethical profitable practice, it will lead you through a path of self-discovery and provide a toolbox for obtaining your professional dreams. Dr. Kolt's book is a fascinating exercise in personal development in the service of professional growth. As any good psychologist should, Dr. Kolt helps you to clarify your own practice vision and then guides you to a custom plan for getting what you want. Not easy, but she has really done it. I love the motivational aspects of this book. Dr. Kolt not only gives you the tools needed to build your practice to your own specifications, she helps you defeat your own demons in the process. The amount of practice building help in this book is truly astounding. Dr. Kolt guides you through the options to develop a personal practice building plan, and then overcome the barriers to its achievement."

— Judith Steward, Ph.D.
President-Elect Designate, APA Division of Independent Practice

"After reading this book mental health practitioners will not only relinquish traditional resistances to marketing, but they will be left with a sense of professional obligation to inform the public about the benefits of the practices! Dr. Kolt understands the pressures and challenges that face professionals in today's market economy and demonstrates how to turn this awareness into a successful practice. After galvanizing her readers to action, Dr. Kolt then provides them with practical step-by-step information and exercises designed to ethically and professionally integrate business and marketing strategies into independent practice. *How to Build a Thriving Fee-for-Service Practice* will not be collecting dust on a shelf. This book is an indispensable resource which practitioners will reach for again and again."

— Noemi Balinth, Ph.D.
President-Elect, New York State Psychological Association

"Dr. Kolt's book should be required reading for every psychologist or therapist launching a practice. Built on a solid foundation of proven marketing techniques, she provides the reader with both the tools to build a niche market practice and the confidence to achieve success. This book is *the* course in building a practice—and a career in psychology—that most doctoral students never receive."

— Judith E. N. Albino, Ph.D.
President, California School of Professional Psychology

"Dr. Kolt's optimistic and yet inspirational and clear ideas put building a psychotherapy practice back into focus. It is a must T.D.R. (Therapists' Desk Reference) for every clinician."

– Richard J. Kay, M.A.
President, Michigan Professional Psychology Association

"Changes in the health care delivery system have made it difficult for psychologists to practice ethically and autonomously. Nevertheless, like me, there are many experienced and new clinicians who see independent practice as the way in which they want to serve the public. Kolt's book provides all of us with useful and creative ways in which we can successfully meet the goal of a rewarding practice which meets the myriad needs of the American people."

– Dorothy W. Cantor, Psy.D.
Former President, American Psychological Association

HOW TO BUILD
A THRIVING
FEE-FOR-SERVICE
PRACTICE

HOW TO BUILD A THRIVING FEE-FOR-SERVICE PRACTICE

Integrating the Healing Side with the Business Side of Psychotherapy

Laurie Kolt

San Diego, California

ACADEMIC PRESS

San Diego   London   Boston   New York   Sydney   Tokyo   Toronto

Academic Press
a division of Harcourt Brace & Company
525 B Street, Suite 1900, San Diego, California 92101-4495, USA
http://www.apnet.com

Academic Press
24-28 Oval Road, London NW1 7DX, UK
http://www.hbuk.co.uk/ap/

Library of Congress Catalog Card Number: 99-61536

International Standard Book Number: 0-12-417945-2

PRINTED IN THE UNITED STATES OF AMERICA
99 00 01 02 03 04 EB 9 8 7 6 5 4 3 2 1

To all of the powerfully effective and caring therapists who touch lives through the gift of their work . . .

and to all of the clients that need to know how to find us during the toughest or most important hours of their lives.

CONTENTS

2 CHOOSING A STRATEGIC SPECIALTY

3 DEVELOPING YOUR MARKETING PLANS

4 HOW TO DO SEMINARS, WORKSHOPS, WRITING, AND LARGE-SCALE PROJECTS

5 GIVING PSYCHOLOGY AWAY

6 ANATOMY OF A SMALL BUSINESS

7 STARTING A NEW OFFICE OR RELOCATING

8 PRACTICE MANAGEMENT TRACKING AND STATISTICS

9 MOTIVATIONAL BLOCKS TO PRACTICE SUCCESS

FOREWORD

As we enter the 21st century, it is vitally important that all mental health practitioners appreciate the magnitude and breadth of the rapid changes occurring within our nation's health care industry. Dr. Kolt's book provides practitioners with ways to adapt their approaches to building a practice and to adjust to such changing demands and expectations.

Consumers, the media, and those who ultimately "pay the bills" are demanding that their practitioners provide the services they want in a highly cost-effective and personally convenient fashion. Practitioners bemoan the advent of managed care—proclaiming, often with good reason, that economic considerations often override clinical concerns. However, managed care is not a new phenomenon. It existed in the days of the Great Depression and became the keystone of President Richard Nixon's health policy agenda. During the 1990s, containment of escalating health care costs became a major public issue. We have seen a fundamental change in who is the ultimate health care decision maker and how decisions are made about which services will be rendered under what conditions to individual patients.

Without question, these are radical changes. Yet, as licensed health care professionals, we have both a professional and a societal responsibility to provide proactive leadership. We must be responsive to patient and consumer demand, and affirmatively shape their expectations. We must be visionary. We must not be reactive or merely self-serving. This is no easy task, but a responsibility for which very few health care practitioners have any formal training or guidance. Dr. Kolt has made a unique and valuable contribution that will help those who have been in practice for years, as well as students and persons just entering practice.

From a public policy perspective, psychology is a relatively young profession. We have definitely matured in stature, and our numbers have expanded dramatically. In 1977, which was also the year of President Carter's Commission on Mental Health, there were approximately 25,000 licensed health care psychologists. Today there are more than 81,000, with a growing future. A decade ago, the American Psychological Association governance established the Committee for the American Psychological Association of Graduate Students (APAGS)—this is the future of our profession. Today, APAGS has 64,000-plus members. Legislatively, psychology is included in a great many federal and state statutes.

However, one can no longer reasonably hold onto the myth that psychology is the exclusive provider of quality mental health care. Increasing numbers of other disciplines have laid claim to possessing quality mental health expertise. Society's health care experts "used to" talk about the four core mental health disciplines: psychology, nursing, social work, and psychiatry. Today, the U.S. Public Health Service points to an even wider range of practitioners, including those in such fields as professional counseling and marriage and family therapy.

The environment or the marketplace in which psychological care is provided is qualitatively different than it was "in the old days." Mental health is steadily becoming an integral component of today's health care system. Psychologists are practicing in a world entirely different from the one in which many were trained. It is a new world with its own language, culture, and expectations. The health care arena is truly interdisciplinary. Dr. Kolt's 19 years of experience have helped her adapt to these changes and equipped her to provide leadership and vision in this new environment. It is just such qualities that make this book essential reading for today's practitioners.

Prestigious national think tanks, including the Institute of Medicine, have concluded that it is possible for health care providers to develop objective standards of "quality of care." Dr. Kolt provides clear and practical models and procedures for equipping a practitioner to confront such issues as the following:

- How do practitioners survive in the midst of unprecedented changes over which individual clinicians appear to have little control?
- How do dedicated clinicians, extraordinarily skilled in the theory and technique of helping people, also develop the skills necessary

to see the bigger picture and ensure that their practices remain economically viable and professionally rewarding in today's uncharted waters?
- Where are the future markets that would welcome and benefit from quality psychological expertise?

These are some of the complex issues that very few of our training programs have ever addressed. Dr. Kolt's text is innovative in helping practitioners as well as educators understand these issues.

Over the years, I have been personally involved with the governance of organized psychology and our nation's public policy development. I have become increasingly impressed by the extent to which an individual can make a real difference in the policies adopted by national bodies and in the lives of ordinary citizens. Dr. Kolt joins the ranks of those making a real difference by sharing her leadership, vision, and expertise in this book.

Psychology truly has much to offer society. Nearly every pressing societal problem possesses a significant behavioral or psychological component. The key is for us, as practitioners, to act as the "learned profession" that we are. We must design a future that is compatible with our advanced training, professionalism, and dedication. This book emphasizes that psychology possesses no limits other than those that are self-imposed. With the right tools and perspective, the 21st century should be extraordinarily exciting, challenging, and rewarding.

Patrick H. DeLeon
President, 2000
American Psychological Association

PREFACE

I remember very clearly when I became interested in helping our profession overcome the threats of managed care and the fears of losing our practices. In the summer of 1993, the San Diego Psychological Association (SDPA) presented an "unusual" daylong seminar on how changes in the health care industry would trickle down to psychotherapists. The SDPA had invited Tom Schwab of the Los Angeles consulting group Schwab, Bennett and Associates to speak at the seminar. Until then, my practice had run like a dream. It was thriving and fulfilling, and I made a respectable income. I also liked the idea that I was helping people. When I heard his premonitions of drastic and negative changes coming because of managed care, it honestly did not concern me very much. In fact, it made me feel creative, and the entrepreneurial side of me thought, "So how can I get around these new obstacles and maintain my practice the way *I* want it?"

At the time I heard Mr. Schwab speak, I had taken a couple of years off from practicing to start a family. Despite no longer *having* a practice, I envisioned that I would *"just build it again,"* with more refined business and marketing strategies. And I was right. My practice took off as expected and quickly began to soar.

It never occurred to me that the events Mr. Schwab forecasted could stop my new practice from thriving. But in the restroom during one of the breaks, I was shocked by what I heard. Several of my colleagues were immobilized and depressed and even talked about retiring from the field. Some of them were former graduate school classmates and incredibly good therapists. I remember thinking, "People like them need to stay in the field!" I was convinced that many ways existed to build and sustain my new practice, even as the landscape of the profession began to change.

For the past six years, I have been committed to helping our profession retool and find new ways to reach clients and patients that need our services. Since then, I have written many articles, chapters, and training manuals on practice development, as well as coached and mentored clinicians in 43 states, the Virgin Islands, and four foreign countries. In my workshops, I have seen practitioners come in viewing business and marketing as ego dystonic ventures. Yet, they have left with hope, enthusiasm, and clarity about specific plans to create fulfilling practices that thrive and also serve more people. The ideas and skills presented in this book are geared to reach this same goal.

The psychotherapy profession desperately needs role models for our future. We all hear the horror stories and see many skilled clinicians struggling to survive within the changing health care system. We need new visionary leaders to show us how we can create thriving, rewarding practices that combine the highest ethical standards, the greatest compassion and respect for our clientele, and the best rewards that practicing psychotherapy offers.

Our profession is a resilient one, and I am pleased that new mentors are emerging who can help build growth and revitalization into our profession. This book provides a thorough step-by-step plan to renew your practice and to build a better psychology. In this spirit, I offer this book as a blueprint to revitalizing your practice or, in some cases, building your first practice during these changing times.

Laurie Kolt

ABOUT THE AUTHOR

Laurie Kolt, Ph.D., is an award-winning and nationally respected practice-building consultant. She is a frequently invited presenter for continuing education workshops, seminars, and keynote addresses for national, state, and local therapy organizations.

The author of numerous training manuals, she has written over 100 articles on practice development and goal setting. Her work has also been featured in the *APA Monitor, Psychotherapy Finances,* The APA *Independent Practitioner,* ACA's *Counseling Today,* The APA Division of Psychotherapy *Bulletin, Practice Management Monthly,* and the *San Diego Daily Transcript.*

Dr. Kolt strives to be accessible to individual practitioners. She distributes a practice newsletter, provides training through her website at http://www.kolt.com, and works one-on-one with clinicians across the country.

Dr. Kolt has a thriving practice in San Diego, California, and has been in private practice for 19 years. She is a clinical and organizational/industrial psychologist, marriage and family therapist, and career development researcher. Through her consulting firm, Kolt Consulting, she has been instrumental in building practices across 43 states and 4 countries.

1

PRIVATE PRACTICE IN TRANSITION

People who care about helping others have historically been drawn to the profession of psychotherapy. We enjoyed the autonomy, satisfaction, income, and flexibility of our work. The role of psychotherapist made us feel proud and also humble. It provided us with a window into the hearts and lives of many people, from many walks of life. Like a stone thrown into the water, we made our impact on the world by helping people grow and change, so they could, in turn, make their own positive impact on their families, workplace, and communities.

A CYCLE OF CHANGE

But now, our profession is in a full cycle of change. We need to let go of the idea that it is stable and predictable. There is no question about it: the image of "the good old days," when you could graduate from school, hang up your shingle, network with a few people, and your private practice would just kind of *develop itself* is long gone. Yet in reality, it was never that simple. Successful practitioners figured out how to promote their services. Through trial and error, they learned how to make their practices grow.

Private practitioners with consistently full caseloads have always known that business and marketing skills were a part of operating a practice. Successful therapists *planned* their practice growth.

Despite the lack of training in graduate schools, the need for business, marketing, and public relations skills has never been greater. With the changes in health care today, they are essential ingredients to sustain a practice that bypasses the restrictions of managed care. It is still very possible to sustain a rewarding practice where you are in control. We can still enjoy the best of our profession.

Yet, before we can completely achieve these goals, we must understand the changes within psychology. Anger, fear, and even denial have kept some of us from moving past what has seemed like the demolition of our profession. But our profession is resilient. We can transform it into a revitalized version that is honest, lucrative, confidential, and once again rewarding. Understanding the journey from where our profession was born and to where our new opportunities lie is the key to this renewal. This new perception also demands that we realize that it is not just psychotherapy that is changing. *We* must change, too.

BUILDING YOUR IDEAL PRACTICE

Building your ideal practice today requires two main ingredients. One is to embrace change and know that part of our practice success lies in a personal journey into the self. We must break through our own barriers, get out of our comfort zones, and breathe new life into our careers. Private practitioners have always been "small business owners," but few of us have integrated the true meaning of the term into our selves. Let yourself imagine that this can be fun, creative, and even exhilarating, and you are on the way to reaffirming your position in the field. With sound business and marketing skills, clinicians today can maintain the benefits of doing psychotherapy that many now dream of.

Second, we must learn to see the fresh and abundant opportunities before us. Imagine what it would feel like if you were convinced that the vast majority of the public believed strongly in the value of psychotherapy? Dr. Martin Seligman, President of the American Psychological Association (APA), captured part of this wider vision in his welcoming message to the APA National Convention in San Francisco in 1998.

> Psychology is not just the study of weakness and damage, it is also—or should be—the study of strength and virtue. Treatment is not just fixing what is broken, it is nurturing what is best within ourselves. And by focusing on our strengths and virtues rather than our deficits and the wounds, I believe we have the opportunity to effectively prevent many of the problems we have spent the past 50 years trying to cure. (Seligmen, 1998, xxv)

The APA's 1998 President of the Independent Practice Division, Sandra Haber, made the following insightful observation.

> Practitioners need to set aside the conventional idea that no one wants to pay for therapy. Instead, watch what people do with their discretionary income. They spend money on things they believe will make their lives better, from big-ticket items like vacations, houses, and plastic surgery to smaller perks such as movies, restaurants, and premium ice cream. (Rabasda, 1998, p. 38)

Imagine what would happen to the profession of psychotherapy if the public at large saw therapy as a useful way to spend their discretionary income. Other leaders go even further and feel that it is our opportunity as well as our responsibility to catch onto it. Alice Rubenstein, 1998 President of the Psychotherapy Division of APA, suggests that clinicians "think of marketing as their public service responsibility" (Rabasda, 1998, p. 38).

Across the country practices are in crisis, yet there are also people who make their practices thrive. I invite you now to walk with me, while I show you how to change your perception about the strength and health of your practice and where it can go.

BUSINESS TRAINING IS CREATIVE AND FUN

The surprising news is that adapting traditional business skills to building a clinical practice can be creative and fun. They can bring the enthusiasm and entrepreneurial spirit out of you that little kids with lemonade stands have always enjoyed (Kolt, 1996). They will give you an opportunity to reach out and touch the people who truly need your services. These skills will also help your practice *thrive!*

This book is designed to inspire you. It will help you see business as fun, creative, and even enjoyable. Many practice development ideas are outlined that encompass the strict requirements of our profession without compromising effectiveness in bringing in new clients. The book will guide you from your ideal practice vision through the "how-to" steps to success. Chapter after chapter will contain solid training to help you not only survive, but thrive in the highly competitive market place. Several learning formats including examples, worksheets, business forms, flow charts, paper-and-pen exercises, and even assignments in the *real world* will expose you to essential materials and ideas.

CHALLENGES AND OPPORTUNITIES

Over the last several years, practitioners have faced serious external and internal challenges. Managed care has stripped away our sacred responsibilities to our clientele. As a result, some therapists have left the field rather than compromising their integrity and respect for their clients. Seminars in short-term therapy have included training in doing "two-session rape recovery sessions" as one chilling and sad example. For therapists who work within the managed care system, control of our practices has changed hands, while we endured plummeting income, reduced satisfaction, and endless paperwork.

Challenges for students and the newly licensed are very real. Today, there are more therapists and seemingly fewer clients. It is also not unusual for graduate school debts to reach $100,000. Many managed care panels will not let newly licensed people join their ranks, shrinking the pool of clients that new professionals can attract.

People have always hoped to have a strong fee-for-service practice, but newly licensed as well as seasoned clinicians are questioning whether the profession is dying. It is not dying. It is changing. And for many of our own visionary leaders, it has the potential to reach tremendous levels of expansion, not extinction. Now is a time to hang on. Pull out your patience and perseverance. There are vast opportunities right in front of us. Commit to learning the new skills you need to make your practice succeed. Read this book cover to cover and commit to retooling your practice. Here are some points to consider:

- The public needs to hear much more about how and why therapy benefits their lives. It is our responsibility to communicate this message.
- To really reach the masses, we cannot just leave this task for our highest or most visible leaders. We must all communicate the message and filter it into our individual communities.
- When we eliminate the stigma and old stereotypes about seeing a therapist, an unlimited stream of clients from our world's peak performers to those with the deepest levels of grief will come and see us.
- Today, it is a necessity to know how to promote *your work:* not *you,* but the service that you provide. Part of what holds practitioners back from exploring marketing and public relations is the discomfort with "marketing themselves." We need to stop viewing "ourselves" as the focal point and start seeing "our services" or more importantly, "the value of our services" as the issue.
- Understand that the qualities that make you a competent clinician do not necessarily make you a successful businessperson.
- Therapists tend to be process oriented, introspective, and focused on caring about others, whereas successful business owners tend to be individualistic, high-energy, results-oriented risk takers.

- Our profession now demands new avenues of continuing education. Allow this book, workshops, and other training avenues at your national, state, and local levels to expose you to critical business and marketing skills tailored to our profession.

Business courses have never been taught in our graduate schools. Perhaps they will start to be taught now. For those of you with an entrepreneurial spirit, learning these skills will be creative and fun. Yet for others, the idea of "going business" may make you skeptical and concerned that you will have to "sell out."

ALL PROFESSIONS CHANGE

The therapy profession is not alone in this. All industries change over time. One way to dispel widespread therapist reactions of anger, powerlessness, and accompanying immobilization, is to understand that all segments of our culture are changing rapidly. In the late 1980s, the United States economy changed substantially. Despite American business' embrace of Peters and Watermans (1982) *In Search of Excellence,* one by one, businesses began to reorganize, merge, and lay off many people. The domino effect led to more companies feeling the financial pinch and more quality employees finding themselves out of jobs. For many loyal career people, they also found themselves out of a profession as well. Downsizing was scary, painful, and hit the majority of towns across America.

Imagine being an engineer, accountant, or a graphic designer 20 years ago. If they did not to adapt to computers, they were destined to go the way of the dinosaur. We do not have to flock blindly like sheep in the direction of managed care. But we do have to climb up high enough to see the reality that all industries change over time. When was the last time you used a mimeograph machine, or washed the white walls on your tires? Remember the pony express?

Whether you look at the effects of the industrial revolution, the information age, or any other evolution in our world, change seems to roar ahead. Those who are open to change can adapt and survive. Those who allow themselves to be overwhelmed, don't. When computers were introduced into the workforce, older or more conservative engineers, graphic designers, and people in virtually all professions were faced with a tough dilemma. Force yourself to grow or perish.

Our profession faces that same dilemma today. We need to grow and adapt and not find ourselves frozen with fear or anger. We need to look for new opportunities and new applications of our work, and new ways to build our practices. We need to *relax into change* to get beyond adamant defiance. Every psychotherapist is challenged today to find practice strategies to maintain their integrity and ensure their economic survival.

HOW AND WHY PRIVATE PRACTICE IS CHANGING

During the national economic upheaval of the 1980s and 1990s, the field of psychotherapy was pulled into focus. National health care became too expensive for the average family to afford. Too many loopholes left innocent people without coverage. Stories filled the national news and the Senate floor about laid-off people left with no insurance to cover the medical care for their young children. In the 1970s, Senator Ted Kennedy was one of the earliest to push for reform, particularly national health care, as a solution. With time, some health-care reform was inevitable.

Medical expenses were growing at an astronomical rate. Although the largest costs occurred during the last 2 weeks of a person's life, all of health care was suspect. Issues such as high physician incomes, rising malpractice settlements, and the public's demand for the best care as well as expensive medical tests put the whole system under a microscope. When President Clinton entered office, one of his first agenda items was to study and "fix" the health-care problem in America. With that focus, bureaucratic experts and consultants spent enormous amounts to time and money to control health-care dollars, only to find that that no easy solution existed. Mental health was dragged into the examination process, sometimes incidentally due to its ability to bill Medicare and other insurance companies.

Few health-care dollars were actually spent on outpatient psychotherapy. If anything, inpatient psychotherapy was a more substantial drain. The psychotherapy profession was not the root of the problem, but it had three things working against it.

1. We were too inexperienced in the business and political arenas to address the national concerns adequately.
2. Our 1970s psychotherapy styles led to an air of mystique, perhaps faddishness, to our profession, that it was "weird" or for "crazy" people. The public did not see the value of our work as essential.
3. Because our work was highly confidential, many of the people who knew the real value of it could not speak about it openly.

Medical Necessity

When we began to receive the right to bill insurance whenever we could document a "medical necessity," we gained some things and lost others. We gained the right to be elevated to the position of traditional health-care providers working with "patients" within the medical model. For clinicians specializing in treating patients with serious illnesses, such as cardiac care or cancer, this recognition increased the legitimacy of our work.

The split between the medical model and adjustment disorder or life span-oriented therapists was accentuated by the use of the term *patient* versus *client*. For those who worked with normal, healthy people who were dealing with life transitions, this added a complication. Individuals were not comfortable entering therapy if they had to view themselves as sick or weak. They felt uneasy being put into a diagnostic category that could follow them around for life. Job security screenings, life insurance applications, and general privacy rights could be jeopardized. As a result, this negative public perception made therapy less desirable to a large portion of the population.

The Evolution of Private Practice

A look at the long-term evolution of clinical practice puts things in an even clearer perspective (Strickland, 1998). The origin of psychology can be traced to the Greek philosophers. Plato and Aristotle made early attempts to understand what the mind really *was*. Thousands of years later, psychology incorporated the perspective of behavior with the "science" of psychology, emerging about a century ago. In 1892, a consortium of philosophers, physicians, educators, and early psychologists formed the APA. The interest in "child guidance clinics" in the 1920s continued the trend towards intervention (Black, 1949). During World War I, the field was mobilized into action when psychologists administered the first intelligence tests to distinguish officer candidates from the rest of the 1.75 million recruits.

With this new role, a new chapter of growth in the field of applied psychology emerged. World War II served to refine the role of psychologists to include the treatment of "battle fatigue." President Lyndon Johnson's community mental health center movement in 1963 opened the door for many more to join the ranks of psychotherapists. Despite these advances, years passed before psychotherapy began to move toward becoming a part of mainstream society.

The practice of psychotherapy is now about a half-century old. Once licensure was established and practitioners began to gain autonomous recognition under insurance programs, the profession took another monumental turn (APA, 1987). Although receiving increased levels of parity with other health-care providers, psychotherapists began to rely on insurance payments for a large portion of their income. For a period, therapy was accessible, practitioners were paid well with few complications, and independent practices flourished.

Since then, the evolution of our field has turned down a more difficult path. Psychotherapy, now a part of the health-care system, is referred to as a "commercial product." Many therapists have difficulty being referred to as a "provider" by health-care administrators and business executives. Therapists resent this transition from doing important work that helps people, to being reduced to a "worker bee." Organizations such as The National Coalition of Mental Health Professionals and Consultants, Inc., led by President Dr. Karen Shore, have formed in protest of what is perceived as unfair, unethical, and even immoral constraints on our work. California psychologist, Phyllis Watts, is an advocate of divorcing ourselves from the managed care system in order to allow the soul of the profession to remain intact.

> The values of managed care fundamentally differ from those of psychology. We are being encouraged to develop our primary relationship with the managed care company, rather than the client. From their perspective, the relationship between psychologist and client is tangential. Yet the most prevalent consistent finding in outcomes research is the importance of the relationship, irrespective of theoretical orientation. (Watts, 1996, p. 15).

Arthur Kovaks is another perceptive advocate for building practices that are free of managed care and center on the life span.

RECLAIMING OUR IDENTITY

Don Lindskoog (1998) advocates that leaders in the field have often confused or merged the profession of psychology with medicine, sociology, and religion. The profession struggles to define a single image of itself. Internal turf battles between the different licensed professions contribute to the fragmentation. A united front is needed now to educate the public about the value of therapy. It is important that we remove the problems that reside *within our ranks*. We need to view the challenges that we face as *separate from us*. Then, we can gain a wider perspective and develop new solutions.

THE CHALLENGE OF CHANGE

We hear all too often about therapist-saturated communities, managed care stresses, reduced caseloads, and our colleagues' fears and frustrations. We clearly need to reinvent our profession. Knowledge can reduce stress while we attempt to do new things. Yet some question whether business skills are inappropriate for the sensitive nature of a therapist's work. Fearful of appearing like "ambulance chasers," they wonder if there can be any formula to attract clients that is ethical, tasteful, and effective. This book will demonstrate a model of practice development that integrates the healing side of our profession with the business side, in a manner that is both palatable and effective.

WHAT HOLDS PRACTITIONERS BACK?

We can all agree that there are new challenges in the health-care system. We can also agree that managed care has changed how many therapists do their work. But it is time to stop "agreeing" that our profession has radically changed. It is time to start taking the initiative and responding with creativity and determination to push past the barriers to success. YOU make a big difference in whether your practice thrives, struggles, or just putters along.

Like the deer with huge, staring eyes, standing frozen in the middle of the road, the approaching car will kill your practice if you don't move fast. Fear, inertia, and lack of direction will not save your practice from extinction. But *you* can.

When you have a client who is dealing with a major life transition, what do you do? You help him or her process the change so he or she can gain strength, clarity, and become empowered to move on. You get the deer to breathe again, move again, and get off the road so it can survive.

As a therapist, you need to practice what you preach. You need to get mobilized so you can walk off the road and do what it takes to make your practice thrive. Develop new levels of confidence, vision, and sound business tools, and you will be armed not only with the necessary ingredients to make your practice come alive, but you can make it soar.

Start today by revisiting your goals and dreams about why you chose to be a therapist. What did you want to experience and achieve? How can you explain concisely to others the value of psychotherapy? What specialties are you passionate about pursuing? This book will walk you through the steps to develop realistic goals to reach the vision you have for your own practice.

You will discover that there is a way to build a thriving practice *without* compromising your ethics, your integrity, or your love of your work. If you believe this, things will begin to change.

FIFTEEN ATTRIBUTES OF A SUCCESSFUL, HIGH-VOLUME PRACTITIONER

1. Has *specific* and *written* practice goals
2. Maintains a low-anxiety lifestyle
3. Is optimistic about the future of their profession
4. Enjoys life
5. Is physically relaxed
6. Has practice systems in place to run it efficiently
7. Is energized, alert, and focused
8. Is open to change and growth
9. Has confidence
10. Is in control
11. Operates with the highest standards and integrity
12. Feels it is comfortable and legitimate to make money

13. Is willing to step out of their comfort zone
14. Feels a sense of civic responsibility to use his or her skills to improve their community or society
15. Embraces the fun, playfulness, and rewards of being a small business owner

SOME THOUGHTS YOU MIGHT HAVE

How hard will this be?

You can do it. Mental toughness is not inherited, it is developed over time. With clear goals, focus, consistency, and self-discipline, you can build your practice bigger than you ever have before. Don't fall into the trap of going all out, expecting big results quickly, and then becoming discouraged. You need to approach practice building like you would a marathon instead of a sprint. Getting through graduate school took many years and hard work. So give your practice the necessary time and effort to really flourish. Today, business and clinical practice are not mutually exclusive. Make the shift in your mind and develop a new strategy, a new mindset, and mobilize yourself into action. Then enjoy the process and rewards of a practice that thrives and satisfies you!

I have been in the field for 25 years. I don't like the idea of marketing.

What you have going for you is experience, confidence in yourself as a professional, and probably community contacts. However, you have a distinct disadvantage over graduate students and newly licensed clinicians. You have to change what you have been doing for a long time. Retooling may involve getting past inertia, anger, or even fear of the unknown. For some seasoned therapists, creating a ritual about moving into this new role may help. For others, making a short-term commitment to wholeheartedly try it can get you moving in the right direction.

I just received my license. I don't know a thing about private practice. How do I begin?

Congratulations on a job well done! If you can get through graduate school, get all of your supervised hours in, *and* pass the licensing exam, you can accomplish a lot! Stay in that mindset and start building your ideal plan. Don't worry if you aren't completely sure what you want your practice to be like. It is much easier to alter your course than to generate the initial momentum. Look for role models. Adopt ideas from others who do things you like.

Your advantage is that you don't have to abandon old ways and retool an existing practice. You do not have to complain about the good ol' days and remember how private practice used to be. Your energy can steer you clear of this negativism. Keep the student work ethic and you will find yourself moving forward.

I'm working in a community agency and would love to transition into private practice. What is a good plan?

You have experience, confidence, and community connections on your side. What you need to learn are business and marketing skills to become a successful small business owner. Your best strategy may be to rent space in an established clinician's office so you have someone to ask questions of and to observe as a model of how a private practice can be run. This book will also give you the up-to-date basics.

Start to open your mind. See new opportunities to grow your career. Einstein said that you cannot solve a problem from the perspective in which it was created. Allow yourself to see a new perspective openly and without censorship. Imagine that you are holding your practice in your hand right now, as if it were a beautiful vase. Take a look at it from the angle that you always have. Now turn it slightly. Notice how shadows enhance the beauty of what you see. Keep rotating it slowly and become aware of the different angles and lines. New shapes and ideas will be visible now. These can lead to new ways to understand what your practice can be.

The Chinese symbol for crisis is also the same symbol for opportunity. If you can accept that your profession is changing and relax into it, new approaches will seem clearer. Now is a time to seek solutions, eliminate fear, and focus on what you want to create. Do not focus on competition between therapists or even therapy professions. Imagine that there are plenty of clients for everyone who knows the keys to build their practice. Be flexible and creative. Get ready to grow. The following exercise will help you begin.

EXERCISE: YOUR IDEAL PRACTICE: A GUIDED VISUALIZATION

Get a piece of paper and a pen. Close your eyes and relax. Imagine what your ideal practice would look and feel like.

For the next few minutes, give yourself the luxury of looking at what you would like to create. Don't let your mind focus on frustrations or fears about managed care, therapist-saturated communities, graduate school debts, or how some people say there are fewer patients to go around.

Remember why you chose this profession in the first place. Open your mind right now. Let yourself become introspective.

Imagine how your practice has grown and developed over the last 5 years. You truly enjoy your work and you find it both intellectually stimulating and rewarding in many ways. See, hear, feel, and experience this part of your ideal practice of the future.

Here are some questions to address on a separate piece of paper:

1. What do you enjoy most about your work? (• the people • using your analytical skills • variety • flexibility • helping others change • etc.)

2. What does your office look and feel like? (• high tech and contemporary • cozy and relaxed • group or solo practice • support staff • computerized)

3. Describe your clients and work hours. (• your specialties • number of clients seen per day • days you work • etc.)

4. From where do your referrals come? (• long-term relationships with professionals • ongoing marketing plans • managed care • community involvement • past client referrals • etc.)

5. How much money do you make? (• average fee per client • yearly revenues and net income • other employment (nonprivate practice) • etc.)

6. What percentage of your clients are managed care?

- 75% managed care, enjoy short-term, results-oriented work, comfortable partnering with managed care
- 50% managed care/cash practice
- 75% cash practice, enjoy long-term or psychodynamic work • don't like managed care
- 100% cash practice, enjoy maximum autonomy, creativity, and control over your practice • etc.

7. Describe your lifestyle (Work hours vary or are stable • Is family a big part of your life? • Are you in the middle of a strong career building mode? • enjoy traveling & leisure time • etc.)

8. How would you feel if you achieved all of these goals?

9. What changes will you have to make to really go for it and make the vision of your ideal practice a reality?

10. Are you willing to do all that it will take to achieve these goals.

What you have written is a blueprint for your practice business goals. The last two questions are the most important ones. If you can develop a strong commitment to work hard at all the steps to build your practice, you can achieve your goals. Some of your hard work may include getting past inertia, fear of failure, or doing new things that feel uncomfortable. However, if you are willing to do what it takes, you may be surprised that it may not be as hard as you think. The biggest goal is to make a paradigm shift. Getting out of your comfort zone is a normal part of the identity transition from viewing yourself as a therapist to owning the reality that you are also a businessperson.

CRISIS VERSUS OPPORTUNITY: SHIFTING YOUR ATTITUDE

Now that you have begun to identify a realistic vision for your practice, you can begin to develop the skills to get there. Imagine that you have a tool belt on. The rest of this book can give you knowledge, perspective, and "how-to" skills to fill your tool belt. Here is a summary of the tools you have added up to now:

- Your "ideal practice vision" is your initial tool.
- You have added the ability to be flexible, strategic, and opportunistic.
- You have decided to focus on cooperation and collaboration, rather than competition with your peers. There is truly enough work for all of us.
- You have dispelled any ideas that business skills need to be intimidating, unethical, or dry.
- You know the paralysis that can result from complaining or stepping into fear.
- You understand that you have both an opportunity and a *responsibility* to educate the public about the value of your services. You can learn to reach out to your community in the way that fits your unique style.
- You have decided to allow your practice development to be creative and playful. Remember the glee in the eyes of little children with lemonade stands.

ASSIGNMENT: UNDERSTANDING A BUSINESS MINDSET

Are You an Entrepreneur?

Successful small business owners are classically viewed as entrepreneurial. Although there is no single demographic profile, there are some traits and life experiences that contribute to their interest and success in their work life. What molds and motivates entrepreneurs is captured in the following quiz by Dr. Joseph R. Mancuso, founder and president of the Center for Entrepreneurial Management, Inc. (Mancuso, 1998).[1]

As you take the quiz, notice how some questions relate easily to the psychotherapy "business" and others appear foreign. Remember that all businesses have a common thread of purpose, structure, needs, and goals. Stretch your thinking to see how *all* the questions can tell you about yourself and your work as a psychotherapy business owner.

[1] Reprinted with permission of Dr. Joseph Mancuso (1988).

The Entrepreneur's Quiz

1. How were your parents employed?
   A. Both worked and were self-employed for most of their working lives.
   B. Both worked and were self-employed for some part of their working lives.
   C. One parent was self-employed.
   D. Neither parent was self-employed.

2. Have you ever been fired from a job?
   A. Yes, more than once
   B. Yes, once
   C. No

3. Are you an immigrant, or were your parents or grandparents immigrants?
   A. I was born outside the United States.
   B. One or both of my parents were born outside the United States.
   C. At least one of my grandparents was born outside of the United States.
   D. Does not apply

4. Your work career has been:
   A. Primarily in small businesses (less than 100 employees)
   B. Primarily in medium-sized businesses (100–500 employees)
   C. Primarily in big businesses (over 500 employees)

5. Did you operate any businesses before you were twenty?
   A. Many
   B. Few
   C. None

6. What is your present age?
   A. 21–30
   B. 31–40
   C. 41–50
   D. Over 50

7. Your highest level of formal education is:
   A. Some high school
   B. Finished high school
   C. Bachelor's degree
   D. Master's degree
   E. Doctorate degree

8. What would be your primary motivation in starting a business?
   A. To make money
   B. I don't like working for someone else

C. To be famous

D. As an outlet for excess energy

9. Your relationship to the parent who provided most of the family's income was:

A. Strained

B. Comfortable

C. Competitive

D. Nonexistent

10. You find the answers to difficult questions by:

A. Working hard

B. Working smart

C. Both

11. If you were at the racetrack, which of these would you bet on?

A. The daily double—a chance to make a killing

B. A 10–1 shot

C. A 3–1 shot

D. The 2–1 favorite

12. The only ingredient that is both necessary and sufficient for starting a business is:

A. Money

B. Customers

C. An idea or product

D. A combination of motivation and hard work

What the Answers Say about You

Add the appropriate number of points for each answer below. Each answer is followed by examples about traditional businesspeople. After Dr. Mancuso's responses, I have added some comments that relate more directly to our profession.

Question 1

$$A = 10, B = 5, C = 5, D = 2, E = 0$$

It's only natural that a child who has grown up in a home where at least one parent is self-employed is likely to try his hand at starting a business. Examples are Fred Smith of Federal Express, New York real-estate tycoon Donald Trump, and Howard Hughes.

Dr. Kolt: How does this relate to therapists? Certainly two self-employed parents would provide role models of a consistent career path. Since the entrepreneurial personality style would be dominant in the family, that would be a plus. At this point in time, most therapists grew up in a generation where women worked primarily in the home and one entrepreneurial parent was more likely to be seen if any.

Question 2

$$A = 10, B = 7, C = 0$$

Steven Jobs and Steven Wozniak went ahead with Apple Computer when their project was rejected by their employers, Atari and Hewlett Packard. When Thomas Watson was fired by National Cash Register in 1913, he joined the Computer Tabulating-Recording Company and ran it until a month before his death in 1956. He also changed the company's name to IBM.

Dr. Kolt: In our profession, we are more likely to be connecting and rapport-building people. We are less likely to be perseverant or obstinant visionaries. Although we don't need to be obnoxious, many of us could use more entrepreneurial zeal.

Question 3

$$A = 5, B = 4, C = 3, D = 0$$

America is still the land of opportunity and a hotbed for entrepreneurship. The displaced people who arrive on our shores can still turn hard work and enthusiasm into successful business enterprises. Though it is far from a necessary ingredient for entrepreneurship, the need to succeed is often greater among those whose backgrounds contain an extra struggle to fit into society.

Dr. Kolt: My doctoral dissertation examined success, identity, and mentoring variables of career women in male-dominated professions (Kolt, 1982). When the study was completed, the literature mentioned that having a foreign-born parent was quite useful for another reason. *Nondominant people* (like immigrants, women in male-dominated professions, and even therapists viewing themselves as business owners for the first time) entering the *dominant culture* (the business world) learned an important thing from their foreign-born parent (Astin, 1969).

They saw that there is more than one way to think and be. They did not just have the Mexican, European, Vietnamese, or American cultural mores to live by; they saw two versions of life values and goals. Many first-generation Americans can assimilate into American culture faster than their parents because they are more successful and resilient in blending the two worlds. By integrating two cultures, they learned how to be more independent in their thinking. That creative ability to see beyond a norm can generalize throughout life and allow them to be bold, innovative, and therefore more adaptable to necessary change.

Until recently, therapists have been told that marketing is inappropriate. More of us are beginning to ask why. We are able to see new, creative, and ethical ways to reach clients and get them into their offices. This flexibility without abandoning ethics is a key to building a practice today.

Question 4

$$A = 10, B = 5, C = 0$$

It has been said that "inside every corporate body, there's an entrepreneur struggling to escape." However, small-business management is more than just a scaled-down version of big-business management. While the professional manager is skilled at protecting resources, the entrepreneurial manager is skilled at creating them. An entrepreneur is at his best when he can still control all aspects of his company.

Dr. Kolt: A therapist usually works with a single client at a time or in a small system like a family. We tend to be oriented to a smaller number of people. However, we also need to be thinking about larger numbers of people. We need to envision how to reach our target market in our community. Can you envision having hundreds or thousands of people hear your message and that the ones who are ready for therapy will call you? We also need to look nationally to mobilize Americans to see the value in seeing a therapist. The public needs to understand that any family can be touched by rape, a heart attack, cancer, divorce, or even simple depression and can *benefit* from our services.

Question 5

$$A = 10, B = 7, C = 0$$

The enterprising adult first appears as the enterprising child. The paper route of today could be the Federal Express of tomorrow.

Dr. Kolt: Think back to your childhood for times that you may have had the entrepreneurial spirit. Did you have a lemonade stand, cut lawns, sell Girl Scout cookies, or put on neighborhood carnivals? Can you can go back in time and rekindle that free and fun spirit? When you bring it out again, your practice will grow.

Question 6

$$A = 8, B = 10, C = 5, D = 2$$

Recent research puts the highest concentration of entrepreneurs in their thirties, although there are always exceptions. Computer whiz Jonathan Rotenberg is just such an exception. In 1978, Rotenberg's advice was solicited by the promoter of an upcoming public computer show. After conferring several times on the phone, the promoter suggested they meet for a drink to continue their discussion. "I can't," Rotenberg replied. When asked, "Why not?" Jonathan answered, "I'm only 15."

Dr. Kolt: Although many people rise to success at a relatively young age, others point to the fact that some of our greatest thinkers and achievers came into their own after the age of 40. There is something to be said about letting go of what you are "supposed to do" and following your own path. It is often down that type of path that many of us produce our best ideas and work.

Question 7

$$A = 2, B = 3, C = 10, D = 8, E = 4$$

The question of formal education among entrepreneurs has always been controversial. Many have never finished high school, not to mention college. Polaroid's founder, Edwin Land, has long been considered an "entrepreneur in a hurry" because he quit Harvard in his freshman year to get his business off the ground.

Dr. Kolt: Advanced training in clinical work is important in our field. But also consider that a strong emphasis on research-oriented education may slow down your entrepreneurial mindset. If you need a scientifically validated method of proof that each practice development idea will work for your practice before you proceed, you may go the way of the dinosaur. Yes, validity factors are always essential ingredients, but don't let this be your only mindset. You also need a balance of dreaming, pulling your dreams down to earth, and even shooting from the hip when your instinct says your good idea is timely.

Question 8

$$A = 0, B = 15, C = 0, D = 0$$

Entrepreneurs don't like working for anyone but themselves. While money is always a consideration, more often than not, money is a by-product of an entrepreneur's motivation rather than the motivation itself.

Dr. Kolt: The independence of private practice does attract a certain type of therapist. We do it for independence, love of people, and love of our work. Many successful private practitioners also feel quite good making a lot of money, too.

Question 9

$$A = 10, B = 5, C = 10, D = 5$$

Past studies have always emphasized the strained or competitive relationship between the entrepreneur and the income-producing parent (usually the father). However, our study revealed that a surprising percentage of entrepreneurs had what they considered to be comfortable relationships with their income-producing parents. We think it's directly related to the changing ages and educational backgrounds of the new entrepreneurs. The new entrepreneurs are children of the sixties, not the children of the Depression. In most cases they're college educated. The entrepreneur's innate independence has not come into such dramatic conflict with the father as it might have in the past.

Dr. Kolt: Other variables can pull a person in the direction of becoming a therapist. Some people are attracted to the field because they, or someone they love, has gone through a painful life experience. Some entered the field to heal themselves through their professional training and work. Some because they loved working with a particular population, such as children or couples. They understand them and feel a calling to help them. Others feel that doing therapy is a natural fit because they intuitively know what loss, depression, or anxiety feel like, and how to navigate through them to the other side.

Question 10

A = 0, B = 5, C = 10

The difference between the hard worker and the smart worker is the difference between the hired hand and the boss. What's more, the entrepreneur usually enjoys what he's doing so much that he rarely notices how hard he's really working.

Dr. Kolt: It's true that engaging in hard work that one loves can propel a person to accomplish great things. When more therapists learn to view practice development in this way, they will get lost in the passion and joy of building it. Get caught up in the rewarding feeling of this and your motivation will soar!

Question 11

A = 0, B = 2, C = 10, D = 3

Contrary to popular belief, entrepreneurs are not high risk takers. They tend to set realistic and achievable goals, and when they do take risks they're usually calculated risks. If an entrepreneur found himself in Atlantic City with just $10 in his pocket, chances are he'd spend it on telephone calls, not in slot machines.

Dr. Kolt: We are not great risk takers, but then we are not structured, methodical people who dive into goal-setting habits either. If you set realistic and achievable goals, you can make your practice thrive! And what's even better, you can reap the rewards for a long time.

Question 12

A = 0, B = 10, C = 0, D = 0

All business begins with orders, and orders can only come from customers. You might think you're in business when you've developed a prototype or after you've raised capital, but bankers and venture capitalists only buy potential. It takes customers to buy products.

Dr. Kolt: Getting clients to come to see us is key to a thriving practice. Yet they need to do more than come, they also need to pay us the kind of money that allows us to pay our bills, have a successful lifestyle, and make psychotherapy a rewarding career. Clients are the key—not just clinical training, hard work, or even marketing plans. This is why outreach and promotional projects are so important. We can't be so narcissistic as to think that they will come just because we are good at what we do.

Score	Your entrepreneurial profile
125–135	Successful entrepreneur
115–124	Entrepreneur
105–114	Latent entrepreneur
95–104	Potential entrepreneur
85–94	Borderline entrepreneur
Below 84	Hired Hand

Dr. Kolt: If you did not score over 115, don't drop into a deep depression. I have had a good practice since 1980. I have a foreign-born parent, bought a franchise when I was 30, ran several small business ventures as a kid, and get lost in the passion of my work as a practice-building consultant. But I did pretty lousy on this quiz. There are some differences between "traditional" businesses and the mindset of business owners who gravitate to our profession. Keep in mind that the quiz was not designed specifically for us. Yet the quiz will help you stretch further and understand what molds and motivates common types of entrepreneurs.

No one has studied private practitioners adequately as a subset of what makes a successful entrepreneur. That would make a great dissertation topic. It would also make a terrific grant proposal for one of our national organizations to pursue.

If you can dream it, you can do it.

—*Walt Disney*

2

CHOOSING A
STRATEGIC SPECIALTY

ARE YOU A GENERALIST OR A SPECIALIST?

Many therapists consider themselves generalists. Perhaps, like your colleagues, you work with depression, anxiety, and stress. You probably see individuals, couples, and families. Yet, what sets one therapist apart from the others are the specialties they enjoy, as wells as their unique knowledge and training in certain clinical areas.

For example, not everybody works with cardiac patients, posttraumatic stress disorders, gay and lesbian issues, or executive coaching. Each specialty has a unique volume of research, clinical issues, and knowledge base with which many generalists would not be familiar. If your loved one needed a therapist in one of these areas, would you want them to see a generalist? Would all generalists know the terminology, most effective treatment strategies, and cultural issues from an insider's perspective?

Many of us are generalists, but we tend to develop specialties that parallel our interests. The beauty of our profession is that we can work in the field for decades and not get bored or unchallenged. After working in a particular specialty for a period of time, we can change specialties without having to change careers. Our specialty interests can parallel our own interests, new societal needs, and even subjects we have experienced personally. If you have used the internet, you may know a bit about how an internet addiction can come about. If you have lost a parent or gone through a divorce, you understand these particular versions of grieving and loss quite well. With the pursuit of research, literature, and advanced training, you can become a specialist in virtually any area that you can imagine, and do so with enthusiasm and commitment.

When you develop expertise in a specialty, you are superbly poised to design programs that capture the essential ingredients for successful therapy. Since you choose the area of emphasis, you are likely to enjoy your work, do it well, and attract more new clients. You are also in an excellent position to reach out to that segment of the public that needs your specialized services and educate them about the value of therapy.

HOW TALKING LIKE A SPECIALIST WORKS

You may still feel like a generalist, even a highly competent one, but the public needs to understand what you do and how you can help them. The value of the job titles, "psychologist," "clinical social worker," "marriage and family therapist," and so on, do not tell the public anything *specific* about what you do or why seeing you would benefit them. If someone sitting next to you asks you *what you do,* don't say, I'm a psychotherapist. Here are some better things to say:

- I am a marriage counselor who works with couples whose marriages are in trouble and need help to get back on track.
- I do career counseling and work with people who are switching careers and aren't sure what an ideal career transition might be.
- I'm a psychologist and I work with women and couples who are struggling with infertility.
- I work with people who have physical health problems like cardiac disease and need to reduce stress and slow down.

When you say these kinds of things, you are inviting them into a conversation. They may say, "Oh, my friend Mary has been trying to have a baby for so long and she is really sad." That can flow into a conversation about how depression is a common and natural symptom of infertility. You can then explain that it is also isolating to see others with young kids, and that it can be hard for couples to know how to effectively support each other. You may want to mention that seeing a therapist for infertility is common these days. This translates into, "You don't have to be sick or weak to see a therapist, just normal." You might also add, "Therapy can really help individuals and couples turn the emotional struggles of infertility around."

If the person asks how they can get Mary to contact you, you can give them your card and simply have Mary call you for a brief chat on the phone. When she calls, it is your job to establish rapport and help her feel a sense of hope in her life challenge. Mary may be very glad her friend struck up a conversation with you if she enters therapy and gets help. But she may never have the chance to know that you are out there if you answered that initial question regarding what you do with a general response like, "I'm a psychotherapist." As you are probably aware, for some people this sort of statement may conjure up old stereotypes about therapy that may immediately shut them down. Try to prevent this by inviting them in to a conversation about "people" that relates to your work. Help them become involved and interested. What can ensure is an opportunity for them to be intrigued and learn more about why people are the way they are. They can also learn more about what you do, and possibly whether they or their loved ones can benefit from your practice.

Here is another example: If you tell someone you work with people who have eating disorders, the person may say, "Oh, that is so weird when people actually want to throw up!" You can then begin the education process by saying something like, "It may sound weird, but what is usually the case is that they come from troubled families, and it's an attempt to find one part of their lives over which they feel they have control. They may have felt alone, helpless, and even developed a poor self-image. They may not like what they see in the mirror. Society has been hard on women about the need to be thin and 'perfect'. But for these people, getting help is crucial because such disorders can lead to some extremely serious health problems."

Again, inviting people into an educational conversation can help them see that getting help is important. But they won't know that unless they *understand.* If they know only that you are a psychotherapist, the conversation may go nowhere. They may even sit next to you and feel uncomfortable. Old notions and biases about therapy (or therapists) may come to mind, in which case they will not open up to the depth of a conversation that may ultimately make a difference in someone's life. Your caring, educational, and productive conversation will open their own minds about the value of therapy. Even if they don't tell their friends about you, they may themselves enter therapy some day because they have a clearer picture about who therapists are and a general sense of the benefits they can reap.

So, developing a mindset that you are not a generalist but a *specialist* is good for the public and good for your practice. One of the things that we often like about our profession is that we learn about all kinds of people, lifestyles, life challenges, and life triumphs. Everyone else has these interests, too. As you learn to talk in "people terms" about your work, you will see that you can easily move into educating others about that clinical specialty and even about mental health issues in general.

CHOOSING A CLINICAL SPECIALTY

A clinical specialty should be something that really holds your interest. Choose a specialty that energizes you, as opposed to one that drains you. If the topic is depressing, heartbreaking, or just not that interesting to you anymore, you will not have the passion and drive to build it to its maximum potential. Look at your caseload over time and see which types of clients and clinical areas have been the most stimulating, worthwhile, and enjoyable. In other words, be prepared to marry it, and have it as a constant companion in your business life for a significant period of time. What are some specialties to choose from? Table 2.1 should help. Also, page through the *Diagnostic and Statistical Manual of Mental Disorders* 4th ed. (*DSM-IV*) for more ideas.

TURNING YOUR CLINICAL SPECIALTY INTO A MARKET NICHE

A market niche is not based on clinical expertise. It is based on consumer needs and preferences regarding services they are willing to purchase.

A market niche is a business term that describes a clinical specialty. Sophisticated consumers today are more likely to seek out a specialist, if they can find one. How will they find you? Start by learning the skills to pick a strategic clinical specialty. Then learn how to let the public know about it, and you will increase your referrals in that area.

When choosing a clinical specialty to turn into a market niche, you will want to consider much more than your training, clinical experience, and personal tastes. Assuming that you want to be able to work with lots of clients in this area, you need to also address the reality of how you will get them into your office. Review your clinical specialty top choices and select the ones that can be most effectively transformed into a marketing niche.

One way to begin this process is to survey the needs of your community. When you know who is out there and what they need, you will begin to see which specialties will transform into market niches more successfully. If you have lived in your community for many years, this will be an easier job. But if you have just moved to town, there are still many avenues you can pursue to get good information. Your goal is to acquire information to build the strategy you'll use to grow your practice. Here are some general points to consider:

- Is your community a large metropolis or a small town? Different specialties and different approaches will work best if you assimilate your plans into the cultural context of your community.

TABLE 2.1   The Top 125 Market Niches

Adolescents	Ethnic and cultural populations
Adoption	Ethnic specialty
Anger and aggression	Family therapy
AIDS	Family-run businesses
Aging	Fear of flying workshops (contract with
Alcoholism and alcohol abuse	airlines)
Anxiety	Feminist therapy
Attention deficit disorder (ADD)	Forensics (testing, testifying, jury selection)
Behavior modification	Gay, lesbian, bisexual, and transsexual
Breast cancer	people
Burnout	Geri-psychiatric services
Cardiac psychology	Giftedness
Career counseling and planning, testing, job	Grief and bereavement
reentry	Group psychotherapy
Child abuse	Groups for perpetrators of domestic
Child loss/sudden infant death syndrome	violence
Child therapy	Habit cessation (smoking, gambling, etc.)
Chronic physical illnesses	Health psychology and education
Church-run workshops	Homelessness
Clergy screening	Hotline counselor training classes
Coaching	Human resources
Colleague supervision	In-home therapy
College students	Incest
Competency evaluations	Infancy
Corporate consultation	Infertility
Couples	Inherited wealth
Critical incident debriefing	Leadership development
Cults	Life transitions
Custody	Male impotence issues
Death and dying	Managed care
Dentists (Dental anxiety, TMJ)	Marriage
Depression	Media (TV, newspaper, and magazine
Developmental disabilities	columns)
Disabled population (physical disabilities)	Mediation (divorce)
Disease management (HIV, diabetes,	Medical rehabilitation
cancer)	Menopause
Divorce/family mediation	Mental health professionals needing help
Divorce recovery workshops	Military psychology
Divorcing dads	Mind/body
DSM-IV—look at all diagnostic categories	Mood disorders
Domestic violence	Motivational speaking
Dual-career couples	Neuropsychology—assessments and
Dual diagnosis	treatment
DUI diversion classes	No-cost support groups
Employee Assistance Program evaluations	Nuclear personnel screening
and assessments	Outplacement services
Eating disorders	Pain control and management
Eye Movement Desensitization and	Panic disorders
Reprocessing (EMDR)	Parenting

(continues)

TABLE 2.1 (*Continued*)

Pastoral psychology	Serious illnesses
Performance evaluation	Sex addiction
Personal injury	Sex offenders
Pet death	Sexual dysfunction
Phobias	Singles
Physically handicapped	Social security (vocational rehabilitation)
Premarital counseling and testing	Social skills
Premenstrual syndrome	Sports psychology
Police psychology	Step-parenting
Pregnancy	Stress reduction
Preschool and day care issues	Suicide
Prostitution rehabilitation	12-step therapy groups/interventions with
Psychoimmunology	families
Psychosomatic disorders	Values and moral behavior
Rape	Weight management
Religious/spiritual counseling	Wellness/early intervention services
School counseling	Worker's compensation
Services for severely and persistently	Zoology (just kidding!)
mentally ill	

- How many kids, senior citizens, people from other cultures, or representatives of other significant groups are in your community? This information can help you identify unusual market niches or underserved populations.
- Is your community saturated with therapists or are many clients available for your work? This will affect how you target your marketing plans and which specialties will have a sizable need for your services.
- What are the major industries in your area? This can point to specific problems, challenges, and needs for which some specialties are best suited.
- Are people moving in or out of your town?
- What is the average income range for community members?

MARKET NICHE SPECIALTIES

The following examples of market niche categories are only the beginning. When you develop the skills to think creatively about how to build your practice, your mind will easily turn ideas into clinical specialties and specialties into market niches. If you are unclear about how to think in terms of market niches, the following examples will help.

Attracting Direct Pay and Cash Clients

We are all aware of the extra paperwork, as well as reduced autonomy and income that results from working exclusively with managed care. You can increase your income substantially by selecting specialties that tend to draw in the most people who either do not have managed care insurance or do not want to use it. When you develop this type of practice, you will regain some of the freedom and autonomy to control your life and your career. Keep in mind that you can still choose to take some managed care clients or continue to have a sliding scale with a cash practice. The decision to build a cash practice is not about making money only to get rich. When you are economically successful, you can pick and choose which special clients or community projects you can volunteer to serve. Here are some specialties and ideas that help you focus on clients who will pay you cash.

Types of Clients

- High-profile or nationally prominent people in your community who may want to maintain the strictest level of confidentiality, such as sports figures, newscasters, politicians, prominent businesspeople, entertainers, and so on.
- People who do not want a "mental health diagnosis" on record for work, security, or personal reasons.
- Wealthy people
- Personal injury victims—people who pay you directly and get reimbursement from an injury caused by another party or by nature. Examples include people emotionally or physically injured by house fires, car accidents, plane crashes, and so on.

Clinical Areas That May Bypass Insurance

- Infertility
- Forensic psychology
- Group therapy
- Coaching
- Seminars or workshops
- Mountain retreats
- Business consulting
- Writing books
- Audio- or videotapes
- Therapy-related product sales—for our industry (billing software, psychological tests, etc.)
- Therapy-related product sales—for the public (such as, The Ungame, calendars with daily psychological sayings to promote better living, seminar workbooks, etc.)

Capitalizing on Unusual Market Niches

Infertility Clients

I would highly recommend going into infertility as a specialty for any therapist. Coping with infertility is a relatively new specialty, yet a significant emotional issue for millions of couples today. It is an opportunity to assist people in an area where few therapists are expert (Kolt, 1997).

Infertility Background Information

As this generation's career women work longer before settling down to raise families, women in their mid- to late 30s are discovering that they may be unable to have children with ease. During the course of their care, either partner may experience "roller-coaster emotions" from excitement and anticipation, to repeated frustration (Kolt, 1997a). Research has shown that depression, isolation, anxiety, and feelings of "not being in control" are commonly seen in people coping with infertility. Several studies also show that the severity of depression parallels those of a person coping with a life-threatening illness, such as cancer or AIDS (Kolt, Slawsby, & Domar, 1999). Add to this the stress of spending tens of thousands of dollars on medical intervention, and you can see why infertility has become a much-needed psychological specialty.

Several national articles have been published covering my work in how to develop an infertility practice (Glider, 1995; Morrissey, 1996; Rabasca, 1998). As a result, I have heard from therapists from all over the country and know it is a hot topic because they have been very passionate and eager to get more information so they, too, can start an infertility practice. Some of the calls have come from therapists who already work with couples, women's issues, grief and loss, or other areas that are related to infertility issues. Some of the therapists have had personal experiences with infertility and expressed excitement at the prospect of helping others who are going through similar crises and, at the same time, building their own practices.

I am happy to share this personally rewarding, lucrative, and unique specialty with others. In the correspondence I received from therapists wanting to begin this specialty, I have been repeatedly struck by how many have opened their hearts through letter and e-mail. Here is just one touching example:

> My spirituality was in limbo because I struggle with understanding what my genuine mission, my purpose is all about. This article hit me between the eyes! Please pardon my rambling, but I cannot contain my enthusiasm in learning more about this timely and sensitive issue.

HEALTH PSYCHOLOGY SPECIALTIES

Cardiac Care Psychology

Cardiac psychology[1] is a specialty that should be in great demand. With the large amount of Americans at risk and the exorbitant medical costs involved, this is a significant national problem. Given the tremendous documented benefits of psychological intervention, we need to increase awareness of the valuable role that therapists can play. The public needs to know how we can help with the recovery, rehabilitation, and maintenance phases of care. Indeed, this is one instance in which seeing a therapist can help save lives.

This specialty is particularly well suited for someone familiar with the medical system and interested in learning about cardiac care. The available literature on the subject will tell you a lot about the common profile of cardiac patients. Many will be middle-aged, career-oriented men who are driving themselves too hard. Various defenses—anger, hostility, a sense of urgency, or even depression—can make it hard for some of these clients to look squarely at their problems. Some may not be compliant with necessary lifestyle changes to diet, nutrition, and smoking habits. Others may have heart disease in their families or have even had a series of heart attacks.

If they have just had a heart attack, it may serve as a wake-up call. You can be the person who helps them reframe their crisis as an opportunity to reevaluate their lifestyles and ultimately *live life* with more richness and quality. This reframing can be transformed into an effective marketing emphasis that your potential clients are ready to hear.

The psychology of cardiac care is a wide-open field for therapists to develop a successful and rewarding practice. Developing a market niche in cardiac care can provide you with an opportunity to assist people in an area where good psychological experts are scarce. Even in regions that are oversaturated with therapists, cardiac care is an untapped avenue that is ripe for professional growth.

Trauma Patients or Serious Illnesses

The need for psychologists working with serious illnesses is growing rapidly. Perhaps you or someone you know has encountered a serious illness. The majority of Americans can identify with this difficult emotional, as well as physical, life challenge. Medical conditions that are life threatening span many areas: strokes, multiple sclerosis, kidney disease, cancer, heart disease, liver disease, lupus, AIDS, and emphysema are some common examples.

[1] From: Kolt (1998a).

Imagine what a person so afflicted is experiencing, feeling, and needing. Then ask yourself how they will know that you are out there and what will make them interested enough to pick up the phone and give you a call.

Initially, you may want to specialize in one particular disease so you can learn the terminology, disease progression, and treatment options your clientele will be facing. I suggest you start small to simplify and keep your level of competence high. You can get good medical information on-line through AOL's health options or going to a website such as healthgate.com. Once you are competent and experienced in one disease area, you may want to move into another specialized population or develop "general psychoeducational, mind/body, or cognitive behavioral interventions" that can span a wide range of health problems. These additional services can target couples, family, career, body image, pain management, and countless other life areas that are impacted by a serious disease.

Breast Cancer

Breast cancer is receiving increasing national attention. From the deaths of prominent people like the mothers of President Clinton and Rosie O'Donnell to Linda McCartney, people are coming out and talking about the disease. Many towns across America sponsor "breast cancer find-a-cure runs," and even art exhibits by breast cancer patients. Recent pharmaceutical discoveries have also received national attention and served to inspire hope that a cure will be developed soon. For all these reasons, breast cancer is a timely and important specialty (Kolt, 1998b).

If a woman has been diagnosed with breast cancer she may feel overcome with worry and fear. With special training, you can help women and their families deal with the fear, as well as the accompanying feelings of depression, guilt, and self-doubt. You can also offer assistance in coping with chemotherapy and even help with pain management. Therapists can help with the immediate fear factor of getting through treatment, and they can also address long-term recovery issues, such as worries about recurrence, feelings of loss and grief, changes in sexuality, body image adjustment, and infertility concerns.

Information included in this section was adapted from (Haber et al., 1998) *Breast Cancer: Talk To Someone Who Can Help,* The Brochure Project, a joint venture of the Divisions of Psychotherapy and Independent Practice of the American Psychological Association (APA). It is an excellent and vast project that has produced a professional-looking breast cancer brochure, along with clinical information and marketing ideas for psychologists.[2]

---

[2] To find out about this or other brochure project titles or to order brochures, call 602-854-8950.

COMMON MARKET NICHES WITH A SPECIAL PERSPECTIVE

Couples and Parenting

Parenting is the only job that people don't go to school to learn or take some specialty training to master. Given the incredible importance of raising the people we love most and the people who will be leading our world into the new millennium, it is obviously a very important job. It is a position essential to the fabric of our community, our society, and our world. So, why not pursue the idea that everyone should take an Intro-to-Parenting Course? Effective tools with which to nurture the growth of our next generation can include the following:

- preparing emotionally for a new life when you are expecting a baby
- the unique stresses of today's dual-career couples
- understanding and supporting your child's major life milestones
- handling family frustration and conflict
- understanding how your family-of-origin issues affect your new family
- helping children make healthy choices about sex, drugs, peer pressure, and self-destructive opportunities
- guiding kids through divorce
- building your child's self-esteem and confidence
- goal setting and success
- dealing with the "empty nest"
- coping with a middle-age transition or crisis
- being caught in the middle: the "sandwich generation"
- healthy aging today
- how to deal with disappointment or loss
- when a child or spouse dies

These ideas are contemporary and presented in "people terms." Can you see how the public can identify with them? They would make great group, workshop, seminar, article, and media topics in your community. Many therapists do family work. But most don't know how to reach out into their communities and relate to the public *in their words* and capture their hearts and struggles, so they feel ready to enter therapy.

Divorce

With about 50% of American marriages ending in divorce, this specialty should be in great demand. It seems like people everywhere are getting divorced, and divorce certainly is a painful life transition. Grief, loss, anger, hurt, regret, and resentment are just some of the volatile issues that can overwhelm even the healthiest person. Helping kids cope is another important aspect of divorce that can be addressed by therapeutic intervention. From individual and family therapy to divorce recovery workshops, there is plenty of work out there for therapists that know how to reach these potential clients. Helping people walk through the tough feelings and then switch gears to redefine themselves and begin a healthy new chapter can be gratifying work.

NEW AND TIMELY MARKET NICHES

Baby Boomers

Do you want to take up a new market niche that you may already know intuitively? A specialty that you may understand from your own personal experiences? Then consider having baby boomers as a market niche.[3] Born between 1946 and 1964, this segment of society spans 76 million people. This age group has moved through the population like a pig swallowed whole by a python and has been a prominent force in shaping both American culture and the business world. By the year 2010, two-thirds of the U.S. population will be 50 or over. They are a huge group to be reckoned with and they have money to spend.

Read through the following list of baby-boomer characteristics and ask yourself how YOU could adapt your therapeutic skills and services to address their needs. Here is a sampling of baby boomer demographic variables (Kolt, 1997b):

1. They are more likely than either younger or older adults to have dependent children at home.

2. Despite delayed marriages and high divorce rates, nearly two-thirds are currently married.

3. About six million of them are now grandparents, and this number will increase fourfold in the next 10 years.

4. They are at the peak of their careers and labor force participation. Many are earning their top salaries now.

5. They are less likely than younger adults to change their marital status, although some will be dating for the first time in their lives.

6. Born after World War II, they tend to be more individualistic and skeptical, less happy with the status quo, and they may reject authority.

7. They are not good at saving money, and they are notorious for buying on credit.

8. They work harder, have less leisure time and more stress in their lives.

---

[3] The information on baby boomers was originally written by Dr. Kolt and published as Baby boomers as a market niche, Practice Builder Column. *Practice Management Monthly,* June, 1997.

9. They list continuing education as a high priority in their lives.

10. They are more active, healthy, and vital than previous generations their age. Yet as they head past "50 plus" years, they will inevitably come to experience a physical decline in their bodies.

Companies with foresight have already made moves to capture this emerging market. McDonald's has put millions of dollars into a marketing campaign to target baby boomers with a new hamburger. The developer of Clearasil, the "pimple cream of the baby boomers' generation," has recently acquired Grecian Formula hair coloring to follow their sales dollars into the future.

Lots of money can be made by businesses with an eye on baby boomers, including therapists. If you want to be one of them, take a few minutes to consider the following questions. Who is more equipped than we to understand what the psychological issues and life transitions of baby boomers? Think about their family stage, career issues, body-image challenges, financial status, personal goals, and their midlife development process and compare them with your own.

EXERCISE: CHOOSING YOUR MARKET NICHE

This exercise will help you focus on which specialties could make good market niches for you. Remember what you wrote down in your Ideal Practice Vision exercise in chapter 1. Your specialty should be in line with those goals too.

- Start by listing several potential specialties.
- Add new specialties to your list as you think of them.
- Cross out the ones that are no longer a good fit.
- You should be left with the best specialties to pursue from a clinical, practice-building, and business perspective.
- Use the comments section to elaborate on any responses.
- Open up and think creatively. Know that you are in the process of growing your career.
- Relax and enjoy the exercise!

Possible clinical specialties or market niches   *Comments*

1. _____   _____
2. _____   _____
3. _____   _____
4. _____   _____
5. _____   _____
6. _____   _____
7. _____   _____
8. _____   _____

1. **What issues or clinical populations are you passionate about? List the reasons.**

_____

_____

_____

_____

_____

_____

2. **What do you know intuitively and enjoy?**

_____

_____

_____

_____

_____

3. **What topics or populations did you pursue for your thesis, dissertation, practicum, or internships?**

_____

_____

_____

_____

_____

4. **What is timely and needed in your community?**

_____

_____

_____

_____

_____

5. **With what type of clientele or in what clinical areas have you done your best work? Why?**

_____

_____

_____

_____

_____

_____

6. **What specialties would allow you to use your natural talents and interests?**

_____

_____

_____

_____

_____

_____

7. **If you review the _DSM-IV_ and The Top 125 Specialties (Table 2.1), what diagnostic categories are the most interesting?**

_____

_____

_____

_____

_____

_____

8. **Can you see any transference or countertransference concerns with any of your potential specialties? If so, can they be ethically resolved or managed?**

_____

_____

_____

_____

_____

_____

9. **Which specialties have ample referral sources to sustain your practice? List as many referral people, community groups, and organizations as you can for each specialty.**

_____

_____

_____

_____

_____

_____

10. **Which specialties have the right mix of managed care versus cash practice clients that you want?**

_____

_____

_____

_____

_____

_____

11. **Can you make the kind of income that you want to make with the specialties you have listed?**

_____

_____

_____

_____

_____

_____

12. **What specialties will allow you to live the lifestyle that you would like to live?**

(e.g., no crisis intervention work when you have an infant at home. If you like to work in long spurts with time off, psychological testing can provide that, etc.)

_____

_____

_____

_____

_____

_____

13. **What kind of training would you need to become current and competent in this area? How would you gain this knowledge?**

(e.g., doing your dissertation or thesis in the area, doing a review of the research and literature, continuing education classes, reading books, the internet, supervision, professional organizations, etc.)

_____

_____

_____

_____

_____

_____

14. **Are you willing and able to put in the time now?**

_____

_____

_____

_____

_____

_____

15. Can you see yourself becoming a community expert in this area? How would it _feel?_

_____

_____

_____

_____

_____

_____

16. **Which specialties fit into your _practice vision_ and _long-term goals?_**

_____

_____

_____

_____

_____

_____

17. **Which specialty is your BEST choice to turn into a market niche _right now?_ Circle the specialty on the top section of your worksheet.**

_____

_____

_____

_____

_____

_____

18. **Are you willing to do everything it takes to build a thriving practice in this specialty?**

_____

_____

_____

_____

_____

_____

ASSIGNMENT: RESEARCH YOUR MARKET NICHE

After reviewing your best options for a market niche, select the one that you are ready to begin first. Even if you are not ready to begin the specialty, do the exercise now to keep your momentum going.

Before you develop any promotional plans, you will want to review the clinical and research information published in the area. Block out 2–3 hours and go to the local university library to update your knowledge base in your clinical specialty. You will want to obtain copies of essential abstracts, book reviews, and other relevant information to become clinically competent in your specialty. You can also obtain the information by accessing it through the Internet.

The initial goal is to copy all relevant information and compile it in a three-ring binder. You can review it when you are ready. Plan to continually add new information to your binder whenever you find any, whether your sources be scholarly, pop cultural, or media-related in nature.

DEVELOPING YOUR MARKETING PLANS

MARKETING FOR THERAPISTS: EXPLORING THE OPPORTUNITIES

According to Dorothy Cantor, Psy.D., past President of the American Psychological Association (APA), "A recent study conducted by the APA revealed that 84 percent of Americans believe psychological health plays an important role in overall health, but more than two-thirds don't know how to find help for emotional needs" (APA, 1996, p. 1). By teaching therapists how to promote the value of their work, the public is educated about the worth of psychotherapy. Thus, more clients in need will know that help is available and where they can get it.

There is incredible value for all parties when psychotherapists get comfortable with marketing their skills and services. Here are some examples of what it can do.

Benefits to Your Community

- Shapes and heals your community
- Helps and heals people you will never know you reached

- Gives useful tips to people
- Lets new referral sources know you are out there

Benefits to the Practitioner

- Creates name recognition
- Increases credibility and expertise status in your community
- Gets you massive exposure, often at no cost to you
- Extends your practice by donating your time in a public forum
- Builds your network of colleagues and referral sources
- Brings in referrals!

Our comfort and skills in marketing for our profession have changed dramatically. Until recently, it was rare for an ethical and professional health-care provider to even think about marketing. When attorneys challenged their own profession's ethical guidelines and won, they were one of the first professions to experiment with marketing their practices.

Each psychotherapy profession has strict guidelines, based on things like (a) not promising unrealistic results or other things that cannot be guaranteed; (b) not overstating one's credentials or experience; and (c) not appearing "cheap" or unprofessional. Slowly, we have begun to grow to see that we not only need to market our practices to stay in business, but we can do it in tasteful and ethical ways. As we begin to realize that so many people can benefit from our work, we can begin to understand what APA President of the Division of Psychotherapy, Dr. Alice Rubenstein meant when she said, "it is our responsibility to market our practices," (Rabasca, 1998, p. 38). The current APA President Dr. Martin Seligman made it a theme of his 1998 presidency to help the profession focus on not just the people who are "ill," but on the majority of the population, who can benefit from prevention or guidance in the rough times that all of us face. As more therapists understand the humble mission that this implies— and not fear that ego gratification, money, or fame is at the root of good marketing—more therapists will find meaningful and effective ways to reach out to the public so they know how we can help and where they can find us.

To Whom Can You Promote Yourself?

- Professionals such as doctors, attorneys, teachers, and so on.
- Schools, businesses, organizations and groups
- The general public
- Managed care

What Is Marketing for Us?

An important component of marketing *in our field* is to let people know how *we can help them*. Various defenses including fear, anger, denial, and even low self-esteem can keep people away for a long time. They may not know that they have a problem, or be ready to deal with it . . . until they go to a seminar or read an article that *speaks to them*. For example, a rape survivor who withdrew and became depressed may finally find the courage to call you after she reads your article in the paper about the stages of rape recovery. A man attending your seminar may learn that feeling over-whelmed by the death of his wife is normal and he is not alone. This type of acknowledgment can take him to the next step of wanting to let go of the pain, anxiety, grief, or other emotional issues that he has struggled with. Whether you want to develop your skills for seminars, writing, networking, workshops, media work, or other ideas to reach the public, you need to develop a *thorough plan* to let people know *what* you do, *how* you can help, and *how* they can reach you.

Would you be willing to stretch and grow to make it happen? If the answer is *Yes,* then the work to get there may not be as hard as you think. Often the happiest and most successful business owners get lost in the playful side of business. The first step is to develop a simple system to contain your structure as you let yourself be flexible and creative in building your plans to reach the public.

EACH OF US IS UNIQUE

Each of us is a unique person and therapist, and as a result you will need to design different program and marketing plans. Although the basic template is the same for everyone, you need to take into account who you are, your unique practice goals, and the demographics of your community in order to be most effective. Your personality, business skills, and market niche will dictate whether your marketing vehicles will be networking, public speaking, workshops, radio/TV exposure, or professional writing.

Choose the ones that you intuitively enjoy and have experience in. But don't rule out others just because you have not tried them or they make you uncomfortable. With the proper information and training, new marketing avenues can effectively help build your practice. One of the toughest chal-lenges for therapists in a building phase is in *implementing* their plans. Consider hiring a practice-building specialist to help you refine your goals or provide knowledge, mentoring, and pacing so you are able to execute a solid marketing plan successfully.

Develop a Practice-Building Mindset

To maintain a solid practice today, it is very important to develop a *practice-building mindset* (Kolt, 1997a). Think creatively about how you can educate the public about important clinical issues related to your specialty. By doing this, you are accomplishing two things: (a) providing a valuable public service to your community, and (b) getting massive community exposure, often at no cost to you, which can brand you as an expert in your field.

Ask yourself these questions:

1. Am I up to date on the current clinical and research knowledge to feel *confident* and provide *competent* services?
2. *Who* is my target clientele (gender, age, issues, etc.)?
3. *What* do they need and feel inside?
4. *How* can you provide what they need (therapy, a seminar, or a workshop, etc.)?
5. *Why* do they need to see *you?* (What do you do that is unique or special?)
6. *How* will you reach them? (And what referrals sources will also send them to you?)

Three Keys to Developing Your Market Niche Specialty

1. Set up a file to collect everything from research information to newspaper articles on your specialty.
2. Look for subsets of referral sources, and you may uncover new and creative ideas.
3. Think in terms of creating regular exposure with your referral sources so they remember you.

Developing Your Practice-Building Binder

Practice development is both a creative project and a complex one. One of the biggest challenges people face is not their understanding of how to promote their work, but rather how to stay organized and follow through to completion. Most psychotherapists are busy people and often work in several settings. A full and successful private practice is often a therapist's dream, but devoting the time it takes to create one is another issue. Creating a practice-building binder will help you to (a) think through your plans thoroughly, (b) set up timelines and track your progress, (c) help you spot any fears or motivational blocks, and (d) keep you motivated (Kolt, 1996b).

This easy and flexible system simply starts with a three-ring binder. Your practice binder is an organized place to keep vital practice information. It is portable, allowing you to carry it from home to office to "corporate retreat." It will increase your effectiveness at monitoring your progress toward your important goals. After you use it for a while, you will appreciate how it organizes and manages your growth—and leads to greater levels of practice success.

Step One: Buy Your Binder

Buy a three-ring binder with a clear, plastic cover. Put tabs in it and label each tab for a subset of your practice-building plan. Assemble the information on the important practice-building topics below. Plan on reviewing and refining your plan regularly, especially during the first year of serious practice building and throughout your career.

Step Two: Personalize Your Tabs

Here are common tab titles. Start with these or create your own. The goal is to have subject areas that are important to track or organize timely information.

1. Practice goals and statistics including your practice vision exercise, number of new patients, average fee per hour, income, expenses per project, etc.
2. Business identity (business card and letterhead designs, office brochures, newsletters, flyers, and other promotional materials)
3. Information on your clinical specialty/market niche (goals, expenses, project planner, results)
4. Project #1 (example: your specialty brochure)
5. Project #2 (example: an article you are going to write)
6. Project #3 (example: a workshop or seminar you are planning)
7. Project #4 (example: networking plan with a referral source group)
8. Mailing lists (new business acquaintances, people attending your event, etc.)
9. Marketing (samples of general ideas you like from brochures, speaking engagement titles, flyer designs for events, etc.)
10. New referrals (categorized by referral source category)

Step Three: Make a Motivational Cover

Personalize your cover with photographs—people or things that have meaning and make you feel successful and happy in your life. Your family, your dream house or a well-deserved vacation are good examples. Your cover should help center you, motivate you, and inspire you. It will remind you why you are committed to working hard to reach your practice goals.

Step Four: Set up Regular Times for Your Projects

As you develop your practice plans, you will be absorbed in many aspects of your project. Set a regular time for reviewing your goals as well as project execution. For example, once a week on Thursdays for 2 hours may keep you moving forward. When first starting your practice, you should probably devote more frequent and larger chunks of time to executing your idea.

Plan on visiting your practice-building binder quite thoroughly at least twice a year. Your birthday and the first of the year can be great times to sit down and do some reflective analysis and creative planning. Sit down by yourself with no distractions. Continue to review your goals and the timelines in which you would like to achieve them between now and retirement. Include areas such as your job title and responsibilities, income progression over time, types of continuing education you will need, things to watch for in monitoring the changes in your industry, and ways you can measure your progress and successes.

Plan on adding new tabs to further organize and systematize your practice expansion and changes when you are in an active phase of growth and development. For example, you may have one tab labeled "Infertility seminar." Initially, you may be simply gathering information for your seminar and placing it in this section. But when you actually begin the real preparation, a separate binder with new tabs may work better. This "subset" of your practice-building binder may include tabs such as speech, handouts, your specialty brochure, promotions, follow-up, referrals, and seminar analysis.

Once you experience success in one vertical area, then you can begin with another. For example, if your specialty is infertility issues, and you have attracted the attention of medical doctors, you can begin a similar plan with midwives and adoption agencies.

TWENTY MARKETING IDEAS TO BUILD YOUR PRACTICE

Marketing is a vehicle to reach the population that can benefit from your services. The following marketing questionnaire lists many examples. Look through the list and notice which ones would work well to attract the attention of potential referral sources or new clients. Keep in mind that some marketing vehicles may not be appropriate if the clients who comprise your specialty have boundary issues or are less functional. Some marketing avenues are directed to reach the public, whereas others are aimed at getting referrals from professionals.

Marketing Component Questionnaire

Use column A to check off the marketing methods that are ethically and psychologically appropriate for your chosen specialty. Use column B to check off the methods that you already have experience with. Use column C to check off the ones that you would like to do if you could get good training to learn to do them well. Transfer this information onto your annual marketing exercise in the next section.

A	B	C	
1. _____	_____	_____	Creating a brochure
2. _____	_____	_____	Networking
3. _____	_____	_____	Holidays or seasonal projects
4. _____	_____	_____	Seminars and workshops
5. _____	_____	_____	Tasteful flyers
6. _____	_____	_____	Newsletters

7. _____	_____	_____	Open houses
8. _____	_____	_____	Advertising
9. _____	_____	_____	Press releases
10. _____	_____	_____	Speaking at conventions
11. _____	_____	_____	Offering continuing education courses for your colleagues or referral sources
12. _____	_____	_____	Keynote addresses or more formal public speaking
13. _____	_____	_____	Health screening (such as depression, ADD, breast cancer, etc.)
14. _____	_____	_____	Being interviewed by newspapers
15. _____	_____	_____	Writing articles for newsletters or newspapers
16. _____	_____	_____	Writing a book for the public
17. _____	_____	_____	Radio interviews or talk shows
18. _____	_____	_____	TV news appearances or talk shows regarding your specialty
19. _____	_____	_____	Giving psychology away
20. _____	_____	_____	Assessing current or old client base

Choosing the Right Way to Communicate

The activities you choose will reflect your personality, your specialty, and how long you have been in practice in your community. Some specialties lend themselves to a more casual form of communication through marketing. Others focus on more formal or corporate-like approaches.

For example, if you are a people person and enjoy networking, send a specialty brochure and an introductory letter to strategic potential referral sources. Follow up with a phone call to meet face to face, and then schedule quarterly mailings to remind them of your services.

If you are comfortable with public speaking, but not with talking one on one with referral sources, your approach may be to do seminars directly for the public.

If you specialize in downsizing corporations or career development, a different approach is needed. A high-quality brochure with good graphics could be an excellent component of your marketing plan. Your target referral sources could include universities, large corporations, and industries experiencing hard economic times.

Although all 20 marketing projects will be discussed below, the first half will be covered in more detail here. Chapter 4 will provide training, examples, and worksheets to develop the second half of the list.

Creating Your General Office or Specialty Brochure

In today's world of private practice, you want to appear as competent and professional as possible (Kolt, 1996a). A brochure gives your practice an established and respected image. Create a comfortable and informative piece that makes the reader feel as if you are walking them through it, panel by panel. It should touch them, so that they say to themselves, "Hey, this therapist really knows what I am dealing with." It should convey caring, competence, and trust.

Where to Send Your Brochures

When you send introductory letters to your referral sources, a quality brochure will get you noticed. You do not want your mailing to be placed in the junk mail pile. A good brochure raises you above an "amateur status" and will open doors.

Also send your brochure to professional organizations. Brochures are especially useful for nontherapy organizations; the layperson then has a chance to read about your engagements. Also send them to your former clients.

Whenever you have a new client, attach your brochure to the intake papers. It will give them the opportunity to know more about you before they see you. It can reduce any nervousness many new clients experience, and it can also increase trust and rapport, which will get their therapy off to the right start. Leave plenty of brochures in your waiting room. Clients will take extras for friends or co-workers who need a therapist.

Start Your Brochure with Your Mission

Developing your brochure can be a fun and rewarding process because you need to affirm your purpose and what you believe in.

Relax, sit back, and grab a pad of paper. Get back in touch with why you entered the field in the first place. Then answer:

1. What do you want to accomplish with your clients?
2. What is your philosophy about therapy and what do you believe in?
3. How would you describe the value of therapy?
4. What would you tell a new client about the benefits of therapy?
5. How can you make them trust you and be ready to become motivated?

Now, restate your mission in a succinct way. When you have written something that feels right, consider it "your story" and be prepared to tell it as often as you can. The general public and even referral sources often ask therapists what they do. They may ask you to describe what therapy is really all about. By telling "the story," you are developing a clear message that educates the public about the value of what you do. It can be a very effective marketing tool. If all therapists begin to do this, it can raise the value of your profession in the eyes of the public.

Next, try to put yourself inside the head of a potential new patient. *You want to convey a message of hope.* You want to create an opportunity to develop rapport and trust, even before you speak with them. Next, imagine that you are a referral source reading it for them. You want to be brief and professional, yet you want them to see that you are an approachable and caring person.

Why Should They See You Now?

People come in when they feel that an immediate problem is affecting their lives. They need to know what the benefits of seeing you are likely to be. They don't want to read a lengthy dissertation or a lot of psychological jargon. Reach into their hearts and let them know you care and tell them that you can help.

Creating Your Title and Tag Line

Your front panel should grab their attention. Include a picture or a phrase that has immediate impact. Very often, you will find that you won't come up with the right title until you have completed your brochure. It may jump out at you after your ideas are refined and in place.

Your Brochure Layout

The Inside Panels. The first inside panel can state the prevalence of the problem and again convey a message of hope through therapy. If you ask questions, it will engage the reader. The middle panel can describe your program development. Individuals, couples, family, and group therapy formats can be mentioned along with some specific examples in a succinct, easy-to-read format. Bullets work well to help the reader's eye flow down the page.

The third inside panel is an excellent place to write your biographical information. You can include where you graduated from, how long you have been in practice, significant awards, memberships, academic positions, relevant research, or other things that distinguish you as an expert. Don't make it too wordy or too aloof, but leave them feeling confident that they are in good hands.

The back panels will allow you the flexibility to make a personal statement about therapy. This may be the perfect spot to state your story in layman's terms.

Here is an example:

> Dealing with fertility challenges can be a difficult road to go down. It is our belief that with information, support and understanding, you can down it with less emotional stress and you can eventually move on, feeling loving an whole in the family that you create. (Kolt, 1997c, p. 34)

The back panel is also a good place to mention other relevant information, such as your speaking engagement topics or information about your location or hours. Mention something they can get for free if they call you. Whether it is a free audiotape, a list of books and resources, or a complimentary initial appointment, make it easy for them to make the first call.

If you have extra copy that doesn't fit in, don't toss it out. Use it for a client fact sheet that you hand out in therapy or turn it into a handout for a speaking engagement.

The Importance of Graphics.   After you have created a wonderful message and have effective wording, don't stop there. Cheap paper or poor design can lessen the impact you have worked so hard to create. Pay special attention to the graphics and visual impression.

Several companies produce redesigned, four-color, brochure stock. If you choose to do the brochure on your own, this is the most cost-effective, yet impactful, option. Be sure your paper weight is not less than 38 pounds or it will look flimsy. A font size smaller than 12 points will be hard to read. Be sure to have several bold headings and use bullets to convey your

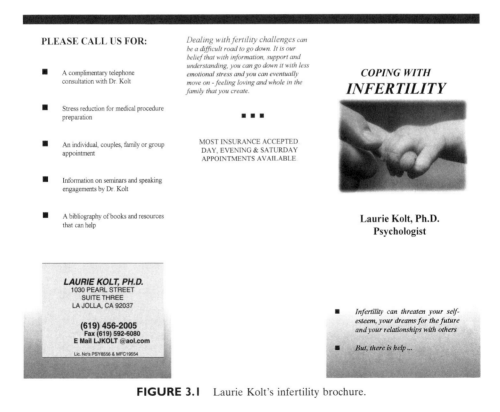

FIGURE 3.1   Laurie Kolt's infertility brochure.

points. A slightly larger phone number is easier to find on the page, but make sure that it is not screaming out like a billboard.

Proofread Until It Is Perfect

Spelling and grammar errors will dilute your impact. If you wrote the piece, you should not be the only proofreader. Have colleagues and also nonprofessionals read it and give their impressions. They can tell you if you are conveying what you want to say.

The enclosed infertility sample pulls at the heartstrings with a moving picture and the title, "Coping with Infertility" (Figure 3.1). At the bottom of the front panel, the message continues to convey understanding, sensitivity, and most importantly, hope.

> Infertility can threaten your self-esteem, your dreams for the future, and your relationships with others.
> But there is hope . . . (Kolt, 1997)

In Figure 3.2, panel one develops rapport by describing common emotional issues and reminds the potential client that they are not alone. The

---

FERTILITY CHALLENGES

■ *Over five million couples in America experience some type of fertility challenge.*

The pain of infertility can enter the deepest part of your being and can remain there. Embarking on this unique journey to *finally* begin your family can include many tests and medical procedures. During the course of your care, you or your partner may experience "roller coaster emotions" from excitement and anticipation, to repeated frustration.

Research has shown that depression, isolation, anxiety and feelings of "not being in control" are common symptoms when dealing with infertility. For many, psychotherapy and stress reduction training can greatly reduce these symptoms.

■ *It's important to know that you are not alone. And it's important to know that others understand.*

PSYCHOLOGICAL SOLUTIONS

INDIVIDUAL COUNSELING
■ Longing for a child
■ Grieving & loss
■ Depression, anxiety & stress

COUPLES COUNSELING
■ Keeping your marriage on track
■ Working together with patience, support and love
■ Enhancing communication & understanding

GROUP COUNSELING & EDUCATIONAL SEMINARS
■ Knowing you are not alone
■ Stress reduction & coping skills
■ Living "life" during infertility

STRATEGIES TO GAIN CONTROL
■ Learning stress management skills
■ Reviewing information and options
■ Creating a plan of action

HANDLING FAMILY, FRIENDS & CO-WORKERS
■ Dealing with people who mean well but just don't understand
■ Baby showers & pregnant friends
■ The internet, advice givers & myths

MOVING AHEAD
■ Weighing medical choices
■ Being pregnant after infertility
■ When to take a break or stop
■ Considering other lifestyle alternatives

LAURIE KOLT, PH.D.

Dr. Laurie Kolt is a Psychologist and a Marriage, Family & Child Counselor. A Phi Beta Kappa graduate from the University of Wisconsin in Milwaukee, she earned her Ph.D. at The California School of Professional Psychology in 1982. She has maintained a private practice in the San Diego area for 19 years.

Dr. Kolt has published extensively on the subject of infertility and has presented papers at The American Psychological Association national convention on the topic. She has spoken locally and nationally on related issues including stress reduction and infertility, coping with the emotional roller coaster and how to keep one's marriage strong during infertility.

Dr. Kolt is also a national trainer on assisting other clinicians in developing clinical practices in infertility across the nation. She has also served on a U.S. government subcommittee representing women's needs.

FIGURE 3.2   Laurie Kolt's infertility brochure.

middle panel describes issues so a client can learn more about what the can expect to address in therapy.

The second sample front panel has a crisp yet positive theme. The title of Figure 3.3 reflects this: "The New American Family: Challenge and Hope." You want to find the right wording that reflects your approach. Modify the structure if it feels right to you. To draw the reader in, Figure 3.4 begins with a question: "Is building a happy stepfamily proving harder than you thought?"

The third sample, shown in Figures 3.5 and 3.6, is a general practice brochure. The questions on the bottom of panel 3 (Figure 3.5) also draw the reader in. In panel one, beginning with "Everyone goes through life challenges," is meant to be an explanation of what therapy is in people terms. It is geared to high functioning people interested in help with life challenges and reaching resolutions effectively. Note how the placement of infertility under Psychotherapy Services in the first panel of Figure 3.6 is played down for other potential clients and referral sources. The biographical information is also more broad and general.

Professional help from someone who understands firsthand.

Jean Huber is a specialist in the problems faced by The New American Family. Her interest in this area was sparked by her own experience in a stepfamily setting. She also conducts professional seminars and workshops on family issues.

A Phi Beta Kappa psychology graduate from Columbia University, she earned her Master of Social Work degree at New York University and is a Certified Social Worker.

If you could use sympathetic, informed help with your situation, please call for:

- A complimentary telephone consultation
- An individual, couples, family, or group appointment
- Information on seminars and workshops by Jean Huber
- A copy of her audiotape, "The New American Family"
- A list of books and resources that can help.

Jean Huber, CSW
26 West 9th Street, Suite 9E
New York, NY 10011
(212) 243-0707

Answers to some questions you may be asking.

Convenient daytime, evening, and Saturday hours are available to fit your schedule. You can usually arrange to have a first appointment within three days. And we can work together to review the terms of your insurance, which may cover the cost of counseling.

Jean Huber, CSW

The New American Family: Challenge and Hope

FIGURE 3.3   Jean Huber's stepfamily brochure.

The pressures on a family are greater today...especially if you're remarried.

Today's busy schedules leave us less time for family bonding. Mass media and entertainment flood us with images of a world where values are relative and often undesirable.

All families feel these pressures. But second- and third-marriage families can be especially vulnerable.

Relationships in "remarriage" families are more complex than in first-marriage ones. Family members are not always sure of their roles. Old allegiances linger in the background.

As the stress of modern living bears down, children are more likely to develop behavior problems, while their parents are prone to frustration, anxiety, and other troubled feelings.

If you see this pattern in your family life, it's important to know that you are not alone...and that you can do something to gain control.

Proven ways to help your family be all that it can be.

Often, people have simply not been prepared for the complexities of remarriage. Fortunately, landmark studies have shown that the right kind of counseling can equip you to handle them...to make your family happier, smoother-functioning, and more resilient under pressure. These proven solutions include:

Couples Counseling
- Nourish your couple relationship
- Create a "parenting team" to deal with family issues
- Support one another in front of the children
- Learn how to work out financial matters together
- Strike a balance between family time and couple time.

Individual Counseling
- Put the past behind you for good
- Reduce anxiety
- Develop realistic expectations
- Learn to communicate your needs more clearly
- Separate your feelings from your behavior.

Group Counseling
- Share with others who face similar issues
- Gain perspective on your own situation

- Find out what is "normal" in remarriage families
- Get to know the common problems they experience.

Strategies to Gain Control
- Determine who is to discipline whose children
- Work effectively with your former spouse
- Family meetings to resolve conflict, enhance appreciation
- Focus on the most important issues and accept limitations
- Create new family rituals and holiday traditions.

Helping the Children
- Common issues for children at home and at school
- The impact of remarriage on children at different ages
- Help children talk about their feelings instead of acting out
- Effective parenting of children in remarriage families.

For the Parent without Custody
- Structure successful visits
- Continue to build your parent/child relationship
- Deal with feelings of loneliness, loss, powerlessness, and guilt.

FIGURE 3.4   Jean Huber's stepfamily brochure.

Your Investment: How Much Does a Brochure Cost?

A good brochure can range from $40.00 to several thousand dollars. The most cost-effective way is to purchase quality, four-color, 38-pound brochure stock and write your own copy. If you have access to a laser printer and print it yourself, the full job may cost you considerable time up front, but it can cost as little as $40.00. A midrange brochure can cost between $1,200 and $2,000. A large group practice that uses fancy graphics, extra color, and unusual sizing or folding can run several thousands of dollars. The costs go down per brochure, but can increase considerably with large quantities made for mass mailings.

Deciding on a Consultant

You need to be willing to spend some money to bring in more clients that will pay for your services. Because it takes money to make money, you need to decide how much of an investment is right for you. What's

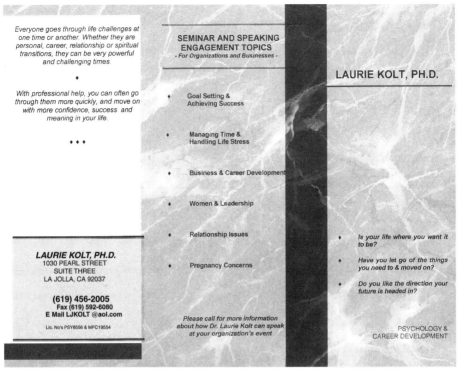

FIGURE 3.5   Laurie Kolt's general brochure.

the best way to produce an impactful, effective, and quality brochure? Here are some tips:

The whole project can be done by you if you

- are a great "brochure-type" writer,
- are proficient on the computer,
- have access to a laser printer,
- can find a good quality, predesigned stock.

Consulting fees will be $100–$400 if

- you want someone to walk you through the components and steps to produce your own brochure,
- you need help refining your mission, conveying your message, and doing it succinctly yet effectively.

Costs will be over $400 if

- you feel out of place in the marketing arena,
- you don't want to take the time get too involved,
- you want high-tech graphics, and
- you want someone to manage the entire project.

PSYCHOTHERAPY SERVICES
- Individual, Couples, Family & Group Therapy -

♦ Life Transitions:
Identity Issues, Relationship
Loss & Career Development

♦ Depression, Anxiety & Stress

♦ Pre-marital Counseling,
Couples Conflicts &
Coping With Divorce

♦ Pregnancy, Miscarriage.
Infertility & Adoption

♦ Rape, Incest, Spousal Abuse

♦ Building Self-Esteem,
Motivation & Confidence

CAREER DEVELOPMENT

♦ Choosing or Changing Careers. Finding
Work That You Love & Preparing For
Career Success

♦ Resumes and Interviews. Key Rules
That Make or Break Your Chances of
Getting Hired

♦ Handling Your Job Hunt. Getting
Organized, Developing Confidence &
Eliminating Fear of Rejection

THE GOAL SETTING PROGRAM
*"How High Would You Dream...
If You Knew You Wouldn't Fail?"*

♦ Clarify Personal & Career Goals

♦ Key Steps To Building A Small
Business. Strategy and Development

♦ Building Actions Plans and
Motivation to Achieve Success

♦ Resolve Obstacles and Fear of
Success or Failure

LAURIE KOLT, PH.D.

Dr. Laurie Kolt is a Psychologist, Marriage & Family Therapist, Career Counselor and a consultant to businesses. With her unique blend of training, she assists people in individual, relationship and work related concerns. She began her career in 1976 when she counseled suicide hotline callers during college.

Dr. Kolt received her bachelor's in psychology and graduated *Phi Beta Kappa* from the University of Wisconsin in Milwaukee. She earned her doctorate at CSPP after completing internships at the YWCA Battered Women's Shelter, Family Counseling Center and working with troubled youths and gangs in Logan Heights. She also trained in career development at SDSU and UCSD. After completing her dissertation on variables that produce career success, she earned her Ph.D. in 1982.

Dr. Kolt has been featured on numerous TV newscasts and is currently the co-host of *Perspectives*, a national radio talk show. She is a national public speaker and the author of over 100 magazine and newspaper articles, regarding personal and career success.

In addition to this, Dr. Kolt has also received multiple awards from The American Psychological Association for her work in promoting national programs that educate the public about the value of psychological services. She has also served on a U.S. Congressional subcommittee representing key psychological and career issues that effect women's' lives.

Her business consulting company, *Kolt Leadership Group*, has provided goal setting, leadership development, management training and small business development to companies across the country for the past 15 years.

FIGURE 3.6 Laurie Kolt's general brochure.

I recommend that you spend at least a nominal amount to have a professional refine and rework your ideas. Do not surrender the job completely to another person. Ask to see some other brochures the consultants has created. Make sure that they are experienced in the field of psychotherapy, because our clientele have more sensitive issues and needs. Your brochure needs to "talk to them" and develop rapport with them. It needs to be sensitive and professional to be effective. You want to feel proud of your brochure, comfortable with it. It needs to reflect *you*.

Networking

Developing a dynamic referral base may come easy for some people and is difficult for others. Before you embark upon this, you should be up-to-date and knowledgeable about your market niche and familiar with the marketing options available to you. You have begun to establish a professional image through your specialty brochure. This is a good point to begin interacting with your referral sources. The following four-step plan will help you structure your plans to meet your new referral sources. If you are comfortable with networking you will enjoy this. Use the following structure to meet referral sources.

Write a one-page introductory letter detailing succinctly (a) who you are, (b) the importance of how a therapist can complement the work that they do, and (c) end it with a request for a brief meeting.

1. Include a copy of your specialty brochure.

2. The goal of the letter is to meet in person. People are more likely to refer to someone that they know and in whom they have developed a sense of trust.

3. Unless you have a lot of free time, I recommend that you send out only 10 per week.

4. Follow up with a summary and thank-you letter after you meet.

5. Set up a year's worth of future mailings to send on a quarterly basis. If your specialty is serious illnesses, an announcement of a group you are starting for serious illnesses, a related article you have written, or an upcoming speaking engagement are good examples of things to include in quarterly mailings. The purpose of the quarterly mailings is to remind them that you are a visible community expert to whom they can refer clients.

Be sure to talk with the office staff; they can turn into reliable referral sources with patients. Before you leave, ask them if you can leave some brochures (with your name and phone number on the back) in the waiting room for patients to pick up. After your initial contact, plan to mail something to them every quarter.

Sample Introductory Doctor Letter

Date

Dave the Doctor, M.D.
9844 Name of Street
Suite 301
La Jolla, CA 92037

Dear Dr. Dave,

As a [psychologist, counselor, social worker, etc.] I provide psychotherapy for patients undergoing [your specialty] tests and procedures. When you have a patient who is experiencing emotional stress from any of these issues, please consider referring them to my office.

• I provide individual, couples, and group counseling as well as seminars at my office. I could also do this at your office, upon request.

• My office is located in [your location] and is easily accessible by [transportation, freeways, etc.] from all parts of the county. My patients describe my office as warm, comforting, and professional, with plenty of [parking].

• I have been active in [the clinical area] since 1986. My experience includes [teaching, doing psychotherapy, and writing] about [your clinical area]. I have conducted research on [if you have a related dissertation, thesis, research publication, etc.] and served on a [committee, board, etc.] addressing the needs of [clients in your specialty].

A large part of my practice is based on referrals. And like most doctors, to trust someone with your patients, you probably have more comfort and confidence when referring patients to people you know. In order to foster a good working relationship with you, I would like to come to your office next week for a brief visit. I look forward to speaking with you soon.

Sincerely,

Laurie Kolt, Ph.D.
Psychologist, M.F.C.C.

New Referral Source Call Backs

Personal Preparation before Making Your Calls

If you are a natural at networking, the next step should be easy and enjoyable. For other therapists the idea of making calls to professions that they have never met is uncomfortable. What you are about to embark upon is *not* telemarketing or sales calls. You are not selling an unneeded product. You are a community expert who is ethical, competent, and has done your homework. You are reaching out to parallel professionals to create a win-win-win opportunity. The purpose of your next move is ultimately to work in a collaborative effort with other professionals so you can both provide complementary and additional resources for your clientele. It will also help both of you reach more clients who need your services. You deserve to benefit from the value of what you have to offer.

The following information will help you get comfortable making multiple calls to people you have sent information to.

- Remember . . . that you are a competent, ethical professional. You are calling this person because you have an important service that complements their care. You would like to make them aware of what you do and how you can help them provide a higher quality of care.
- You will not sound like a stereotypical cold caller if you allow yourself to settle into a confident mindset. Keep focused on the fact that you believe in what you do. You are one health-care colleague speaking to another.
- Make your calls in a quiet, private place so you can get comfortable and get in the right frame of mind. Relax, close your eyes, take a couple of deep breaths, and switch gears. Get in touch with the good work you do and the lives you have touched. Feel proud of your talents, your skills, and your desire to serve others.
- Develop affirmations and visualizations and use them to gear up for your calls. "Warm up" for about five or ten minutes before you make your first call for the day. Like a professional athlete, you need to stretch, practice, and visualize yourself going through all the key steps in your peak performance. Get confident, focused, and open so you can convey your best impression over the phone.
- Consider tape-recording your calls so you have feedback on how you come across. Having a mirror in front of you will help you "smile" and "look at someone," which will make you sound more friendly and natural.
- By reaching out to doctors, you are helping more people, because their patients can truly benefit from what you do. Stay focused on allowing this to be a positive experience. Use your commitment to

serving others and your practice goals to reach more people with your good work.
- Allow yourself to reach out through the phone lines. Let your best, most genuine self come through. Know that not all people will be open to your message this time, for a variety of reasons that have nothing to do with you. But the ones who are receptive will be there. So make a personal connection with each person, and anticipate meeting some very nice and interesting people as a result of your calls.

Referral Source Call Backs: Phone Script and Sample Meeting Organizer

INTODUCTORY LETTER MAILED ON _____ *CALL DATE:* _____

Script

(Goal: Set up a face-to-face appointment)

"Hi, [name—if they give it] this is [your name], is Doctor [name] available?"

If not there: "Do you know when s/he may be free? Can you have them return my call? Our number is 452-7600. Thank you."

If the doctor is there: "Hello, this is [your name]. I would like to speak to Dr. [name] please."

"Hi, this is [your name]. I'm the [MFCC/social worker/psychologist] who sent you the [specialty] brochure and information on the [specialty] counseling that I do. I'm calling to follow up on that and to ask if you have any questions. Is this a good time to talk briefly?"

"I'd like to come down to your office, so we can both have a chance to meet each other. How does that sound to you?"

"Great. What days and blocks of time look best for you?
Let's see, I could make it at [date and time]. Great, I'll look forward to seeing you. Bye."

Sample Appointment List to make

Appointment date	Met	Doctor visit list
_____	____1.	Marsha Infertility Doc, M.D. 581-HELP 3023 Street Name, Ste. 203 San Diego, CA 92109
_____	____2.	Samuel OB/GYN, M.D., Ph.D. 625-BABY (Office hrs: 9:30–4:30) 4150 Somewhere Road La Jolla, CA 92037—Also Poway: 673-1000

Preparing to Meet New Referral Sources

Even if you are a seasoned therapist in your community, you may find yourself feeling nervous or insecure when you begin marketing your practice. Remember that you possess many skills and assets. When you send out your introductory letters, like the samples here, plan on mailing about 10 per week. If you send them all out at once, you may become overwhelmed

---

MEETING ORGANIZER

DOCTOR VISIT LIST

Apnt. Date	Met	Name/Address/Phone

_____ ☐   Name/Address/Phone

Comments:

_____ ☐   Name/Address/Phone

Comments:

_____ ☐   Name/Address/Phone

Comments:

_____ ☐   Name/Address/Phone

Comments:

_____ ☐   Name/Address/Phone

Comments:

FIGURE 3.7   Meeting organizer.

with so much scheduling and work, that you can't perform at your best, causing your existing caseload responsibilities to suffer. The meeting organizer in Figure 3.7 can help you stay organized.

After you have created a letter that you feel good about and that fits you, mail it so it arrives on a Tuesday, Wednesday, or Thursday. Mondays are usually busy, "catch-up" days, and Fridays are filled with thoughts about the approaching weekend. Plan to call each referral source in 2–3 days. It is best if you can speak to them directly. If necessary, schedule your meeting through their secretary or office manager.

It is a good idea to take a trip to their office before the day of your visit to be sure you can find it. This also gives you the chance to check out the atmosphere and see what you can learn about them. As a therapist, you can translate lots of things into Rorschach cards full of useful information about who they are and how to develop rapport, so you can begin to develop a good relationship with them.

On the Day of the Visit

When you go to the visit, dress professionally and wear something that makes you feel good. Be sure to bring along your business cards and brochures. If they have a waiting room or reception area, you can make some additional observations about their work and their philosophy. Look for areas of common interest to increase rapport. Prepare to educate them about your work and the value it holds for their clients.

Most people have stereotypic images of what therapists are like and what we do. Dispel any myths in an interesting and respectful manner. Imagine how interested you would be talking to an astronaut and learning what it is really like to venture into space. Help them get intrigued by the journey into"inner space" that we guide our clients through. If you can normalize your work and at the same time, make it profoundly interesting, you will have an ally who values and respects what you do.

Don't forget to ask them questions about their work so you can determine how you can help them. Can you give them some tips on how to deal with a patient who bursts into tears? Can you help them with clients who irritate them? How about suggesting things they can do that will build their practice or business?

Be sure to talk with the office staff because they can turn into reliable sources with clients. Before you leave, ask them if you can leave some brochures (with you name and phone number on the back) in the reception area for clients to pick up. After your first contact, plan to mail something to them every quarter.

Quarterly Mailings

After you have created a specialty brochure and met with potential referral sources, they need to keep you in mind. At quarterly intervals, mail them something that will serve this purpose. Set up planned quarterly mailings for at least a full year.

If your specialty is cardiac care, good examples can include the following:

1. Stress-reduction workshops
2. An announcement of a group for spouses
3. A copy of a professional article that you wrote about how cardiac care is effected by psychological interventions
4. An invitation to your office open house
5. An occasional "FYI" copy of any article that relates to their work that your ran across, or other thoughtful mailings can serve the purpose.

When they have a referral client, you want them to think about you. Don't forget that you can send out Christmas or Hanukah cards as an additional reminder that you appreciate them and that you care about their business referrals. Another quarterly mailing can be the following professionally developed card (Figure 3.8) that fits into a standard envelope

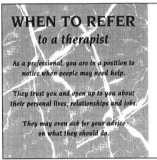

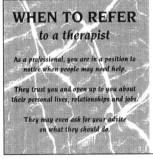

FIGURE 3.8   When to refer card.

and reminds them that they probably know people that could use psychotherapy.

A few of them may start referring to you right away. You may even have the opportunity to send a referral to some of them as the next interaction. Eventually, you will see how many will become good referral sources. Allow it to take time. Your best referral sources may not materialize for quite some time. Remember that good marketing takes time, so stay committed to your quarterly mailings and other outreach activities.

Don't get discouraged if all of your efforts do not bring in referrals very fast. You are *building momentum,* and you are proving to your referral sources that you are a stable, competent force in the psychological community. Chapter 9 is devoted to the issue of keeping yourself motivated and on track with your goals. This important chapter can help you if you feel that your practice development is going too slowly or you are in a slump. Marketing works. Once you have gone through a complete cycle of practice building, from the planning through execution and coming full circle, you will truly understand how the process works.

Eventually, you will have your referral sources building momentum in your practice. With time, you will have the opportunity to develop several good, working relationships. It is a great idea to give referrals to them too, so you both feel a balance in the relationship. With time, you will get to know each other, and some may even turn into good friends!

Holiday or Seasonal Projects

There are many holidays or seasons that can relate to your market niche. Clinicians who specialize in educational issues or kids know that the back-to-school time in the fall is a great time to connect with your referral sources. From new students or troubled students, to countless related opportunities, this is a good time to network.

Valentine's Day is another good opportunity to promote your *"how to find your ideal mate"* seminar or three-session premarital counseling program. Both of these could also get good local visibility for you through newspaper or local television coverage. Let them know about your work and why it is timely and important. Father's Day and Mother's Day can bring up parenting issues, and the list goes on.

Let your fall holiday greetings bring in referrals too! The fall holiday season is a great time to reflect on your practice successes and feel grateful about the referrals you have received. In that spirit, did you know that you can also put your genuine holiday energy to work—so it can also build your practice? If you start your plans during the quarter before the fall, you can integrate these projects into your autumn schedule. Here are a few tips:

1. Send Christmas, Hanukkah, or holiday cards to all of your past and current referral sources. Go to a store that stocks plenty of good cards and find a box that reflects you. Enhance your business image by matching the color combination of your cards to your office stationery. If you add an insert or a flyer of an upcoming workshop you are offering, your full presentation will tie together nicely.

2. Create your mailing list now, especially if you don't already have it in a computerized program. Address the envelopes by hand and select a unique holiday stamp. When you are in a reflective mood, sit down with your stack of cards and write each person a special note. A good generic example is, "Thank you for the trust you have shown in my office and for your referrals throughout the year." Here is another example: "Wishing you a happy and healthy holiday season. From the psychology office of Dr. Laurie Kolt."

3. Consider tailoring some messages in a special way. What do you like about each referral source? Do they really care about helping others? Have they gone to bat to get your bill paid? Which sources have referred clients who you have really enjoyed?

4. Don't forget to send cards to professional organizations, self-help groups, your attorney, accountant, doctor, and others who know you professionally. Everyone is a potential referral source, especially if you are in their mind. If you have done a speaking engagement for an organization, why not put a low-cost display ad in their December newsletter to remind them about you?

Seasonal marketing is an excellent idea to pursue. You can promote a *"start the new year with our goal-setting workshop"* as a January practice-building idea. In June, when kids get out of school, let your referral sources know that you appreciate them. A card expressing thankfulness for their trust and confidence in you at the end of the school year adds a nice note of closure. Then when the new school year begins in the fall, a phone call saying hello can continue to build your relationship.

When your mailing list is complete, it will take no time at all to add new referral sources and organizations. At some point, your system will run so well, you can venture into sending office newsletters. They will require more time, graphic design, and planning. By writing strategic articles, you can tailor them to the season, your specialities, or your referral source's needs (Kolt, 1996a).

Holiday cards and other mailings can give your practice the edge. They are a creative vehicle to making your practice thrive. If your mailings are professional, sincere, and tasteful, they can keep your name in the forefront of your referral sources' minds. And for those of you who have not discovered it yet, writing can be real fun!

Seminars and Workshops

Many therapists enjoy doing seminars or workshops. They are a creative opportunity to rework your clinical skills and go beyond one-on-one therapy. Designing your workshop involves many components. Smaller scale presentations can be given in your own office or in the office of a primary referral source. For example, if you specialize in divorce, a monthly *"coping with divorce"* seminar may be helpful for the clients of the attorneys you know, and also for your practice. If you want to go further or bigger with public-speaking ideas, they can be very fun, exhilarating, and useful in reaching large groups of people. In Chapter 4 we will go through the steps in designing and implementing successful seminars and other speaking engagements.

Tasteful Flyers

Professional-looking flyers are a great way to advertise a group or workshop in your office as well as in your community. Place a small stack in your waiting room for clients to see. A popular topic seminar might do well with flyers in your community. If your target population is teens or college students, this casual approach can fit into the culture of your potential clients quite well. The people who need your services may find your flyers stapled on a student bulletin board. Done professionally, yet casually, you can successfully reach clients at a very low cost.

Newsletters

The primary purpose of a newsletter is to communicate and educate. A good newsletter will take your research, clinical, or theoretical knowledge and transform it into a language the layperson can identify with. You want your newsletter to *change them, move them,* or even at times, *provoke them.* Why shouldn't they do all they can to create a more fulfilling and balanced life? Your newsletter is also a vehicle to reveal your competence, which is an important factor when a person chooses a therapist.

What Newsletters Can Do

1. They build a preestablished relationship. People get to know your ideas. They provide an opportunity to build important rapport.

2. They enhance the perception that you are an expert in your community. You may be the most competent therapist in your clinical area, but if *they* do not know it, they may go to someone else.

3. They allow you to talk one-on-one, and at the same time, it gives you the opportunity to reach many people with a single effort.

4. They keep your ideas and your name in the minds of people who need your services as well as for people who may know someone who does. This ongoing communication creates name recognition so when a person (or someone they know) is ready to get help, they are more likely to think of you.

5. They provide a forum to talk about your philosophy of mental health and optimal well-being. Your readers may say, "Hey, I didn't know that a psychotherapists could help me with that."

6. They create a competitive edge. A professional image with good writing and ideas conveys competence.

7. They support other communication or services. For example, if one of your articles is about how dual-career parents juggle multiple roles and stresses, they may say, "Hey, he is talking about us!" In the same issue, you can let them know about your next couple's seminar. Provided there is enough true substance in the newsletter and it does not appear to be self-serving, you can gain credibility, educate, and give them a chance to learn and grow.

Planning Your Newsletter

Producing a regular newsletter is not a small task. It takes planning, thought, money, and coordination. A good newsletter can help your practice, but a poor one can be frustrating, time consuming, and even keep people away. In our age of information overload, it seems that everyone has a brochure, newsletter, or website. So how can your newsletter stand out? Remember that the main goal is to *communicate and educate*. Begin a discussion with people in a way that brings them in, helps them become involved, and also lets them see how they can go further. Make sure your writing is in "people terms." It should be clear, crisp, and succinct. Good writing is a pleasure to read and invites the reader to pay attention. Get into the mindset of your reader. If it is a newsletter for teachers, coaches, and other educators that deal with kids, then write about what they want to know. What are key motivators for kids? What are typical and not-so-typical symptoms of kids having emotional trouble? How can they enlist parents to help? The ideas are endless.

Graphics and design can also make a significant statement about your practice. They can make your newsletter look disorganized or uninteresting, and that will reflect upon you. It can also create a professional image that implies competence and caring. Four pages will be ideal. A feature article on the front cover can be continued on an inside page to bring the reader in. The front cover should also have a table of contents or the highlights of your issue. A good mix of information can include tips, "short-takes" on a subject, or even a question and answer forum to encourage interactive participation. Never allow advertising and maintain your neutrality on controversial issues.

You only get one chance to make a good first impression! For this reason, expect to spend time planning your concept and your first issues. I also suggest that you get a graphic designer involved in the early stages to develop a template that fits your image and content. Consider having a logo or a recognizable cover page banner that readers will recognize over time. Good design will encourage readers to pick up the newsletter, and it can help drive your message home. Be sure to have each issue thoroughly proofread.

Assess Your Newsletter Effectiveness

Over time you can track your calls and referrals from the newsletter. Other forms of visibility including your other marketing projects will continually remind people about the value of your work. Your newsletter will give you the advantage of spaced repletion during the time when some people are building their need—or courage—to give you a call. In chapter 7 we will cover tracking your newsletter referrals more thoroughly.

Newsletter Questionnaire

1. List the main purpose of your newsletter.

(e.g., To educate the public about issues within your area of expertise.)

_____

_____

_____

_____

_____

_____

2. What message do you want to convey?

(e.g., Everyone goes through tough times but with psychotherapy, they can get through them quicker, with more wisdom, and move on more effectively.)

_____

_____

_____

_____

_____

3. What other purposes do you have for producing a newsletter?

(e.g., to educate the public about general psychological health; to establish community name recognition and credibility)

_____

_____

_____

_____

_____

4. Who is your target audience?

(e.g., attorneys, doctors, parents, past clients, corporations, etc.)

_____

_____

_____

_____

_____

_____

5. How often do you want to send your newsletter out?
(e.g., monthly, quarterly, or seasonally)

_____

_____

_____

_____

_____

6. What image do you want to project?
(e.g., friendly, successful, professional, etc.)

_____

_____

_____

_____

_____

7. How much time and money will you need to invest in your newsletter?
(Consider the quantity you will mail, the cost of the paper stock and stamps, possible design or word-processing fees, data input into a mailing label program, etc.)

_____

_____

_____

_____

_____

8. **What timelines will you create for the next year's scheduled your mailings?**

(1) Choose four distribution target dates based on key practice projects you want to highlight, seasons, holidays, or other relevant events. (2) One month before distribution, decide on the theme and begin writing articles. (3) Three weeks before distribution, have the newsletter input into the correct format. (4) Two weeks before distribution have two people proofread it thoroughly. (5) One week before distribution, buy stamps and paper (or give it to a secretary or mailing house) and add new names to your mailing list. Send a copy to yourself in the mailing and review it like a potential client or referral source.

_____

_____

_____

_____

_____

_____

Open Houses

Open houses are a good opportunity to bring attention to new referral sources. They can also bring together old friends, colleagues, and people that you want to thank for referrals. A holiday theme can make it festive, such as during the Christmas or Hanukah season. If your market niche is kids, an end-of the-school-year open house can be a great place to let go, reflect on the year, and get more personal with the professionals you may have had contact with by phone.

Don't forget to plan some food and entertainment. Have plenty of practice brochures as well as program flyers in your reception area so they can still be in a referral mode. It is also a good time to let them know that your practice has a wider scope than just the clinical specialty they are familiar with. If you are a heath-related clinician, but you also do couples counseling, they may know of a neighbor or friend who needs your services.

Advertising

Direct Mail

Direct mail advertising can also be a good avenue for promoting workshops, groups, and even therapy product sales. If you have produced a stress reduction or guided visualization tape, you could do a mailing to all relevant referral sources and past clients to let them know about how to order one. A workbook you designed for a workshop on how to stop smoking could also be sold to the public. The "Rituals of Letting Go and Saying Good-Bye" booklet that you wrote may be great reading for people who are going through divorce or the death of a loved one. The public, as well as funeral home directors or divorce attorneys may pass your flyers along to those who can benefit.

Done well, direct mail can be a cost-effective way to deliver your message to precisely the people whom you most want to impact. It can also project a poor professional image, cost lots of money, and bring in no new clients. To increase your success rate, get a good list. Your message is important, but getting your mailer into the right hands is even more essential.

The yellow pages can be an excellent local way to assemble your names. Infertility doctors are listed under endocrinologists, OB/GYNs, and urologists. Family law attorneys will be listed under attorneys. If you want to expand beyond your current geographic drawing area, or you are moving your practice to a new community, use national directories. Here are some Internet lists that can be useful: http://www.bigyellow.com and http://www.bigbook.com.

Yellow Pages

There are many conflicting opinions about spending money on advertising in the yellow pages. People who can afford, as well as understand, the value of therapy are unlikely to seek a competent therapist through the yellow pages. If you needed open heart surgery, would you look in the yellow pages to find the best surgeon? You would more likely ask a trusted person such as a friend or your family doctor.

However, in a rural or small community where the pool of available help is smaller, the yellow pages may be a more logical source. Also, discrete or unique specialities, such as sex therapy, infertility "coming out," or even divorce clientele may not feel comfortable asking someone they know for help.

The real question becomes, will any ad you pay good money for ultimately pay for itself and more? You can experiment with different ad sizes, placement, and text and then track the income they generate for the year. Many therapists find the free one-line listing provided by the telephone company to be sufficient, and they spend their marketing dollars on other avenues.

Press Releases

When you have a special event, a press release will let your community know. Press releases are also an excellent way to get widespread exposure at no cost to you. When should you notify the media? Any time you think you or your practice is involved with something that is of interest. Examples include the following: workshops, seminars, keynotes, receiving an award, moving to a new facility, receiving statewide or national recognition, when you have published a book, and when you are offering a new service or program, having an open house, or forming a community advisory board. Think about how you can tie the subject of your seminar into something timely or in the news. Your local media will often find it interesting to have a local angle on national events.

How to Write a Press Release

A press release should ideally be one page. Start with something that will quickly attract attention. The title should be catchy such as, "Pathological Internet Use: Psychologists Examine Who Is Hooked On the Net And Why?" (Fizel, 1997). At the top on the right or left side, write the name, address, telephone, and e-mail information for a contact person. If you have more than one page, write "-more-" centered at the bottom page one. End the last page "###" centered. It will give your press release a more professional look.

Speaking at Conventions

Speaking at a convention on your clinical area of expertise can add credibility and visibility to your practice. People will assume that if you could put together a proposal that has been accepted, you and your topic must have merit. Although you must still prove yourself, you will have a forum of people who could advance your career. You should probably not attempt to present at a convention without a successful history of presenting workshops, seminars, or speaking in similar forums. You should be polished, impressive, and present effectively.

Speaking at a state or national convention can catapult your name and your work up to a national level. Although you should not count on this making you a household name like John Gray and his "Venus and Mars" phenomenon, there are times that your work may bring in calls from around the country.

For example, at the APA National Convention in Chicago in 1997, press releases were submitted to the media room at the convention. All of the local, national, and even international media browse through the press releases and presentation information. Then they decide what fits with their audience. From *The Boston Globe* to the *Los Angeles Times* and the major network news, topics with a timely or interesting slant are picked up for national consumption.

The press room had copies of a presentation by psychologists, Blake Sperry Bowden, from the Cincinnati Children's Hospital Medial Center, and Jennie M. Zeiz, from DePaul University. The press release on their work was titled, "Frequency of Family Meals May Prevent Teen Adjustment Problems" (Bryan, 1997). Although it was a bit wordy for the general public, the topic proved to be of interest to the media. What researchers found was that the well-adjusted teens—those less likely to do drugs, less likely to be depressed, more motivated at school, and had better peer relationships, ate with their families an average of five days a week compared to nonadjusted teens who only ate with their families three days a week.

The very next morning, the national morning talk show, *The VIEW* with four women cohosts led by Barbara Walters, spent a considerable amount of time talking about the study. Raquel Welch was a guest on the show and joined the conversation. The five women chatted about the dismantling of the American family by our fast-paced society, the stress of dual-career couples, and the difficult world that today's teens live in. They talked about their own childhood memories of the ritual of sitting around the dinner table and compared it to the flurry of rushing and schedules today. From personalizing the information to expanding it to "what's wrong in America today," the story received excellent, personal, lengthy, and effective coverage of Bowden's and Zeiz's work.

Offering Continuing Education Courses

Offering continuing education (CE) courses can be done for your clinical colleagues and even for your referral sources. If you specialize in forensic psychology, you may want to present a workshop on issues such as the psychology of personal injury, family law, or jury selection. If you get heavily involved with CE seminars, you will find that they can become lucrative income sources in their own right. You can expand your market niche to include "other therapists" and teach CE classes at the state or national level on your topic. CE convention and symposium speaking would be a natural extension of this type of work.

You can provide CE seminars to other professionals who are potential referral sources. In this way, you will be defining the classes as a subset of your specialty marketing plan. For example, if your specialty is infertility, you could provide CE seminars to endocrinologists, urologists, OB/GYNs, primary care physicians, midwives, nurses, and other related health-care professionals. Your course could cover (a) what the psychological variables are that impact women and men coping with infertility, (b) how psychological interventions help, (c) what the health-care professional can do, and what not do, to make the experience easier on the couple, (d) how low stress and psychotherapy can increase patient compliance with medical treatment plans.

You can bet that they would perceive you as an expert in your field after they attended your CE class. And with a little extra networking and quarterly contacts, they will think of you when they have referrals. In fact, part of your CE class can cover common psychological symptoms their clientele may experience and how they will manifest them. Spotting symptoms and helping them get to a trained professional helps them provide better patient care.

Your expert status can also open doors for writing in the local American Medical Association (AMA) journal and speaking at their monthly meetings. You can also think about branching out to medical doctors with other specialties and teaching them about rapport building, how stress impacts disease, and other relevant topics that have more generic medical interest. Can you see how one marketing vehicle can spiral into bigger and wider groups that can refer to you?

Keynotes

After you have had good success with general public speaking in seminars or workshops, you may be interested in speaking at formal events. What are some examples? A national sorority alumni luncheon coordinator may invite you, as an expert on the career development of women, to give a luncheon speech. An end-of-the-year PTA event may want a speaker on "What's working right with kids today." Your local Funeral Directors Society may want a therapist who specializes in death and dying or loss issues to remind them of the rituals of grieving and "saying good-bye." They may tell you that they are looking to freshen up their services and understanding about how they can make a huge difference to the grieving families who are their clients.

Can you see how you will be viewed as an expert? Can you imagine how you can begin a new level of networking with them that already begins with you as an expert with credibility?

Health Screening

Health screenings are opportunities to reach into your community and help assess potential problems and give people guidance. Here are several of the many examples: depression, anxiety, breast cancer, eating disorders, helping people quit smoking, and ADD. Multidisciplinary screening can team up mental health professionals with others such as coaches, teachers, or medical personnel.

If you get involved on the ground floor of a screening, you can get considerable exposure in your community. This can naturally lead to widespread respect and exposure for you in the eyes of many people and organizations. Some of them may have money to spend on pet projects and opportunities that can really put you in a position to use your talents creatively (see chapter 5 for more information).

Newspaper Interviews

Being quoted in the newspaper can give you exposure to large numbers of people in your community. Perhaps you can get a feature article about your work in your clinical area. However, before you solicit the attention of journalists, be sure that you know some things about the needs, goals, and culture of the world of journalism. You must present a case for why the information on your clinical speciality is timely and interesting. If you are lucky, the newspaper may pick up a press release you sent out about your seasonal workshop on "Shopping and stress during the holidays" and show up at your event to interview you.

You can expect many newspaper interviews to be done over the telephone. Be very cautious if they say that they are on a tight deadline. It is best to never give an interview on the spot. A better plan would be to set up a time to talk after you have composed yourself and succinctly written down your main points. Even if you are fortunate to have an interview, be sure to give them (or fax to them if the interview was over the phone) a copy of the following: (a) your main points, (b) a brief biography, and (c) your brochure.

Giving them a fact sheet with your main points will increase the likelihood that your quotes will be accurate. Be sure the fact sheet has your name and profession spelled the way you want them to write it. Include your address and telephone number. Sometimes an interested reporter will end a story with, "readers who are interested in more information can contact Mary Smith, MFCC at [your phone]." Don't forget to give them a good, professional black-and-white headshot to include in the article. Readers are drawn to a picture in the paper. If they print yours, it will attract more readers while also increasing your credibility and community prominence.

Writing Articles for Newsletters or Newspapers

If you enjoy writing, you can express exactly what you want your readers to know, instead of what a reporter thinks you meant. Large metropolitan newspapers are unlikely to print your story, but small community newspapers or newsletters of professional organizations will often welcome you with appreciation. If you are speaking to a church's singles group, you may want to write an article on "Building rapport, risking your heart, and letting go of fears." The article can be printed the month before your seminar so they will already know something about your work. This piggyback concept will also increase your seminar attendance.

Writing a Book

If you love to write, and you have something to say to the masses, then writing a book may be just right for you. Most national authors start small and write locally as they refine their writing style, concepts, and knowledge of the publishing industry. Many psychotherapists self-publish their first book and after that, large national publishers may begin to look at you. Occasional writing can be fun. Megawriting can create national recognition, but like in all fields, about 1–3% really get to that level. If any of these ideas interest you, look for more in-depth ideas in chapter 4.

Radio Interviews and Talk Shows

For some people, the medium of radio is often easier than television because no one can see what you look like and what you are doing. You can spread out papers with notes, and you will sound impressive without anyone knowing. Others say it is a good place to experiment before attempting to do television interviews, where more seems to be happening at once.

Radio talk shows often require more preparation time so you can fill the airtime comfortably. If you are good with a call-in format, you may reach a popular status in your community. Still, keep in mind that a live show is a *live show*. So you still need to be thoroughly prepared and an expert in what you are speaking about (chapter 4 will tell you more).

TV News Appearances and Talk Shows

TV exposure can be a scary, challenging, exhilarating vehicle. It is also a medium where you can make a significant positive impact on your community. Get training and practice in order to represent you and your profession well. (Chapter 4 will give you some clear how-to training.)

Giving Psychology Away

I think *giving psychology away* is a responsibility that we all share. Our profession can make a profound impact on our individual communities and our world. We need to get out of our offices and share our skills when they are needed on a larger scale, particularly if the issues at hand are related to your area of expertise. Obvious examples are local or national tragedies like the Oklahoma City bombing, massive floods, airplane crashes, and local events with a psychological aspect.

How should people help their children make sense of the stories on the news? What can parents tell their children about a series of teenage murders or President Clinton's "nontechnical lies" and extramarital affairs? We have more knowledge than most professions to provide both perspective and healing. We can find smaller scale examples everywhere, if we are trained to see them. Chapter 4 will outline excellent opportunities as well as the mindset you can adopt so you can spot when your community can benefit from your talents. It also shows examples of how to proceed.

Other endless opportunities to give psychology away include our ability to influence the stereotypes in movies and television shows, helping in local or even international political conflicts, and endless other ideas. Our skills can be generically applied in situations everywhere to make our world a safer, more productive, healthier place.

Assessing Your Current or Old Client Base

Your clients may be your best referral sources because they know the value of psychotherapy and also the value of your work. You can ethically yet effectively keep clients aware of your services when they have a friend or co-worker in need of a good therapist by having brochures in your waiting room, sending them newsletters, and thanking them verbally for their referrals. They will sense your genuine appreciation.

When psychotherapy with a client comes to a close, if appropriate, you can normalize the developmental or life span challenge they went through as one of possibly many times that you can be of service to them. If they entered for premarital counseling, you can mention that down the road, couples counseling can help if conflicts begin to turn into negative patterns. Therapy can also be of help during pregnancy and preparing to have a child, as well as during job stresses and even deaths in the family.

Client satisfaction surveys can be useful tools in both assessing your quality of care and for building a successful practice. The three-part survey that I developed is given, when appropriate, at the beginning of care, at the end of therapy, and 6 months after their treatment is complete.

> The third questionnaire gives the client a chance to reflect on the stability of change that occurred through the therapeutic process. With new habits and life patterns, short-term change may produce episodes of backsliding. If this happens, the survey can help them pinpoint problems that can be helped by further psychotherapy. . . . The final form also asks the client to address any other new symptoms or life challenges that are currently surfacing. This awareness can stop patterns before they are firmly entrenched. . . . The final form will also serve to remind them that you are available and that they can come back and see you intermittently during future life challenges. (Kolt, 1999, p. 318).

WHY MARKETING IS GOOD BUSINESS

In September 1996, Behavioral Healthcare Tomorrow held its annual national convention in San Francisco. The attendance of over 2,000 included managed care executives, health-care purchasers, consultants to the industry, managers from large group practices, and a few small group and solo practitioners.

At the conference, Alan Savitz, President and CEO of Pacificare Behavioral Health, made a very interesting statement. The spiraling down of fees is the fault of,

> providers who see behavioral health, not as a business in which to make a living, but as a calling. . . . There is a surplus of providers and some are willing to take any fee. They don't care as long as they can put bread on the table. (*Psychotherapy Finances*, 1996, p. 9)

Part of what Mr. Savitz said is absolutely true. If we continue to just view psychotherapy as a *calling,* we will no longer be able to sustain a practice that supports ourselves and our families. It is *essential* now to also view private practice as a *business* that must use traditional business skills, tailored to our profession.

Until recently there has been strong resistance from many in our profession to explore any form of marketing. Some therapists have had no exposure to marketing, and intimidation or lack of information can lead to simply not giving it a try. Others are leery of sleazy "come-on" ads with therapists adopting money-hungry attitudes.

Dispelling these concerns can be accomplished most effectively by demonstrating "how-to" concepts and real examples that maintain the integrity of our profession. Then, each therapist can decide for themselves, with real data, how they want to pursue building their livelihood in today's private practice setting.

With such information we can view this paradigm shif not as selling out, or turning into uncaring, money-driven business people. Adopting the appropriate business skills does not require you to sell your soul. Actually, this change in attitude can accomplish several important things.

1. It will help us combat the negative stereotypes that the general public has had for several decades—about how people must be *sick* or *weak* to see a therapist—or that all therapists are pretty weird people, so how can they effectively help others? Programs like the APA's national marketing campaign (APA, 1996) will be much less effective if all practitioners do not join in to educate the public and learn how to be responsive to the needs of more Americans.

2. It will help us reach out into our communities and touch the people who need our services. Sensitive, effective marketing can cause potential clients to say, "Hey, that therapist is talking about my issues. Now I know that I am not going crazy and that there is help. *And* now I know where I can get it."

Developing strong business and marketing skills can be ethical and effective in reaching your target clientele. Without them, practitioners may fall into the desperate trap of survival that Mr. Savitz of Pacificare Behavioral Health may be using to his company's economic advantage. Whether you are for or against managed care is not the only critical issue. By arming yourself with integrity-based marketing and business skills, you will retain the option of keeping your cash practice income fruitful and stable. And as a result, you will not have to cope with drastically slashing your family's economic standards. And you can also retain the pride and enjoyment of viewing your profession as your *calling.*

Do you think your clients want to see a therapist who views him or her as just another paycheck? Or do you think they want to see a skilled practitioner who still manages to find deeper meaning, respect, and enjoyment in their work?

INTEGRATED MARKETING

After being exposed to the multiple options in building a plan, you will get a feel for which ones fit you. If you like talking to people and feel confident in your clinical work, reaching out to new referral sources could be an enjoyable and effective path. If you are more introverted or shy, writing may be a better vehicle. Perhaps you feel a calling or have a passion to help others. Your genuine desire to give psychology away may give you satisfaction as it convinces your community that you are a compassionate, outspoken professional whom they want to associate with. If you are comfortable with risk, you may find media work to be an effective way to "network" in your community and reach huge amounts of people while spending no money.

The following example will show you how you can start with a market niche and weave new layers of marketing, teaching, and public relations into a thorough plan that will make your practice grow. As you read this example, imagine how you could modify the ideas to fit your unique personality, your market niche, and the community demographics.

Penetrating the World of Your Referral Sources

Do you want to set yourself apart from other therapists in the eyes of your referral sources? The example here involves a therapist who specializes in breast cancer patients and their families. It is an example of how to gain a deeper understanding of the world of their natural referral sources. Some good referral sources would include oncologists, OB/GYNs, wig makers, and the American Cancer Society. Some community leaders have also educated beauticians about talking to their women clients about breast exams and breast cancer. Find out if your community is one of them. If not, consider taking the opportunity to "give psychology away" by being in a leadership position to develop one based on a model from an existing town.

Any of the referral source professions listed above could be used to illustrate the following concept. It can also apply to almost any specialty so translate the ideas to your own market niche. Begin first by surveying which professional group you want to start with. It is best to begin with one at a time so you are the most effective. Talking with M.D.s will be different than talking to beauticians. You will gain more insight and reach deeper levels of rapport if you have your mind focused on one "professional culture" at a time until you feel very comfortable there.

By browsing through industry-related "insider information," you will get a new and deeper perspective into their world. You will learn something new with each attempt. Perhaps you will see how their profession is changing as well as what their professional stresses and needs are. Try also to get an idea of how they perceive therapists so you can know how to educate them about the value of your work more effectively.

Use all of this background information to penetrate into the world of your referral source so you can see how you can help them. Consider yourself a human relations specialist, an industrial psychologist, or even a business consultant to their industry. What knowledge do you have as a clinician that can help them deal with job stress? How can you help them improve their relationship and effectiveness with their clients?

For example, what can they do with a tearful or excessively angry client? Can you help them understand what their client is feeling and show them how to help? A medical doctor may have a technical focus on his or her mind. They may be thinking about the latest research or drug treatments for breast cancer. Or perhaps they have just had a fight with their spouse and are considering a separation.

Then imagine that a very scared, angry, or tearful patient is in their treatment room when they walk in with their preoccupied mind. The doctor and the patient may not connect. Either of them may be preoccupied for many reasons. If you develop enough rapport with the doctor, he or she may share this problem situation with you. Some of the issues could include the following: (a) how to center a stressful patient and help her relax and process her feelings; (b) how to explain to her how new drugs bring new options into the picture for her treatment options; (c) how the doctor is feeling about his or her home life; and (d) how they can keep their home stress out of the office.

One goal would be to help them address how they can accomplish their original objectives for that office visit. The closer the two of you are in professional or even person terms, the more you can assist both the patient and the doctor. Since you are a clinician, you probably have plenty of ideas on how to manage many angles of their situation that would never have occurred to them. Can you see how your image as an expert is expanding in their eyes?

Do Your Homework

Even if you are familiar with a medical environment, consider also speaking frankly with an OB/GYN or an oncologist. Perhaps a friend, neighbor, or a relative could clue you in to the nuances of the "culture" so you use correct terminology and really know their perspective. Good rapport building happens best when you can fill in the gaps about their profession on your own. This part of your research can be intellectually stimulating because you are learning about their world from the inside and integrating the information with your clinical expertise. It is somewhat parallel to doing an initial evaluation, where you gather client data and formulate a plan to assist them. Testing out your knowledge and ideas on someone will assure you that you are not saying something naive, outdated, or politically insensitive.

When I was learning these skills years ago, I was to present a talk to a branch of Coldwell Banker real estate brokers. I originally thought that I could tap into the idea that they are helping people to buy their "dream home." By testing my ideas on a broker friend, I quickly found out that my concept was old, and what they were thirsty for was how to attract and keep buyers.

I quickly switched my focus to how to develop strong rapport skills; assist their clients in articulating their housing goals and dreams; and how to lock in long-term relationships for secondary referrals and when they become second-time buyers. I also helped them understand the emotional stresses and life transitions people encounter when they move. This is especially true if their client is moving because of a divorce, marriage, job change, or if they have kids in school.

After my speech and regular mailing, I began to get a steady stream of referrals of new homeowners in transition. I even received a few new clients over the next few years that were brokers with fear of failure or success issues, and a spectrum of neurotic concerns.

Talk in Their Language

Do not make the mistake of using psychological jargon! You may get away with it with medical doctors, but wigmakers and beauticians will most likely get lost in the discussion or begin to stereotype you as one of those "shrink types." It may be appropriate for graduate school, but it will bore most nontherapists. With wigmakers, beauticians, and virtually all new referral source groups, use everyday words and common examples. For all personal contacts, articles, presentations, and talks, be sure to be clear, concise, and understandable *from their point of view.* You want to find a happy medium between explaining psychological dynamics and helping them also see what's in it for them. Keep going back to the question: How is this information going to help them understand and serve their clients better? How will it help them do their job better?

Develop a Multidimensional Plan

A good plan is to start local and small. With each article, speech, presentation, and so on, you will have plenty of feedback and new ideas. Next, we will look at how to create steps to build momentum in a professional community. Perfecting your presentation and widening your exposure is key to getting more and more referrals.

Let's assume that you have already identified your target vehicle to gain your initial visibility. For example, you have contacted the local American Medical Association newsletter editor, and he or she likes the idea of you writing an article on how M.D.'s can handle the emotional aspects of their patients. You know not to use a lot of psychological jargon, and you have outlined a great article that you think they will find educational as well as helpful for their practices.

After you complete it, look at the information that you have accumulated. How else could you use it? Are there speaking engagement opportunities you could pursue to expand upon your article? How else can you expand the frequency of their contact with you? With each article, speech, or presentation, you will have plenty of comments and new ideas. For example, if you spoke to an oncology organization about breast cancer, write a follow-up article for the local association's newsletter. When you get positive feedback on your presentation, don't forget to ask them, "Who else do you know that might be interested in an article, talk, or class on this topic?" If it feels appropriate, ask them for a testimonial letter about how your talk was useful. A list of testimonials can establish impressive examples of your credibility, and it can continue to open doors for you.

Recycle Your Exposure

When you feel confident and ready, begin to branch out into other organizations. Can you create an educational manual for M.D.'s related to the psychology of their clientele? When and where is their state and national association convention—and can you submit a proposal? Don't forget that wigmakers, beauticians, and the local branch of the American Cancer Society can also be contacted with the same general process.

Another way to develop opportunities is to look at the advertising that *you* get at work. You probably receive lots of mail showing how other people want you to come to their seminar, buy their book, or attend their symposium. Many of them bought a mailing list of psychotherapists in your community so they could reach you. Have you seen any seminars targeted to you that are put on by attorneys who want to teach psychotherapists about risk management, divorce mediation, or the legal aspects of family law? They are penetrating into our world in part because they know that we share mutual clients *and* they want your referrals.

For example, in our field, there are licensed professional counselor (LPCs), marriage, family, and child counselors (MFCCs), licensed social workers (LCSWs), clinical social workers (MSWs) psychologists, psychiatrists, and more. Each group has parallel local, state, and national organizations. The attorneys doing seminars had to find out about all of our organizations to advertise to us. We can also find out about their own professional organizations and target their professions. We can even speak at their conventions and conferences.

After you have penetrated into your referral source's world and you understand their needs, you can begin to get to another level. You can go from being a local expert to speaking or writing in their national forums, this will bring you considerable recognition. By penetrating into your own referral source's field to gain widespread exposure, you will find that it can really elevate your expert status.

This is partly because it is a numbers game, and more people will be exposed to your work. The more often people see your name as a writer or speaker, the more likely they will be to attend your engagements and buy your materials. With a little creative effort, it won't take much time to modify your local work for a state or national forum. Can you see how they will view you as an expert?

Doing so has brought one therapist I know, who specializes in stalking, state and national attention, as well as legal referrals from around the country. The therapist now commands one of the highest fees in her town (which is oversaturated with therapists) and has been known to be too busy to keep up with all the work! And when you get state or national exposure, be sure to send a copy of the material to your local referral sources in that field.

This will increase your referral source's knowledge of your skills. You will also be regarded as a respected expert in their industry—*and become the first therapist referral source they think of.* Developing a long-range, thorough plan to penetrate their industry takes time, creativity, and confidence. It will stretch you, but the rewards will bring you an abundant practice, as well as increased income, pride, and career satisfaction.

A SUMMARY ON MARKETING

The acceptance of marketing is undergoing a great change in our profession. What was once viewed skeptically as an unethical tactic is now being seen as a legitimate opportunity to educate or serve the public. Many of us feared that we would seem like the worst stereotypes of money-oriented "ambulance chasers" or used car salesmen. If this was truly the case, our profession would suffer irreparable damage. But now even our own leaders cite studies that say that people don't really know what we do or how to reach us (APA, 1996). And our leaders are starting to say that it now our "responsibility" to market our specialties (Rabasca, 1998).

When viewed from the most humble and ethical perspective, we are not marketing "us." We are reaching out to help people who legitimately need help. Both business planning and marketing provide an opportunity to reach the people who truly need our help. It is also honest to say that your marketing projects are a vehicle to attract new clients to your practice. This gives you the opportunity to take them from being in great pain, feeling frightened, or overwhelmed, and guide them to a place where they can gain the courage and peace to go on. A far cry from selling used cars. By being ready to embrace these ideas, you will have the initial business skills to make your practice enjoyable and also make your practice *thrive.*

Marketing is not

- sales
- sleazy
- necessarily expensive

Marketing is

- a way to get the word out about what you do
- allows people to get help

- educates the consumer
- brings in new patients
- ethically and professionally builds your practice

MARKETING FLOW CHART

The flow chart in Figure 3.9 gives a good perspective on the initial phases of developing and promoting your practice. This chapter covered the marketing flow chart in Figure 3.9. After you choose a specialty, be sure that you are up to date in the field. This will increase both your competence and confidence to develop your specialty to the fullest. The next step is to design your services. This can be done at the same time that you create your brochure because much of the information is similar.

Next, you need to identify your market. Who do you want to reach? Do you want to become known by referral sources, such as doctors, attorneys, school systems, or the businesses in your community? You need to concentrate on what they read, what meetings they attend, where they go, and any other avenues that can reach them. Send a standard introductory letter and a quality brochure to begin a relationship.

It is important to set up regular contact with everyone you establish a relationship with, particularly referral sources. Scheduling quarterly mailings works best, and each mailing can range from a newsletter, an announce-

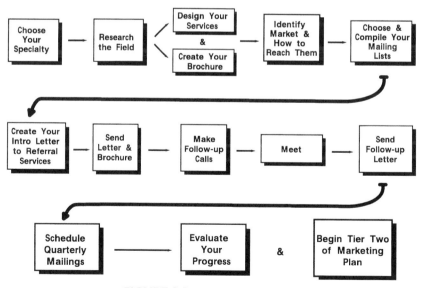

FIGURE 3.9   Marketing flow chart.

ment of a group or a class you are conducting, or something pertinent to their interests.

EXERCISE: BUILDING YOUR ANNUAL MARKETING PLAN

The following worksheets and business forms will help you use the information in this chapter to create the blueprint of your annual marketing plan.

The first business form (Figure 3.10) gives a linear and logical approach to developing your marketing plan. Figure 3.11 is an example of how to use the form. Figure 3.12 will allow your creativity to unfold. Figure 3.13 will provide another example. Use the Project Planner (Figure 3.14) to write down the details of your plan. The more you can break down your projects into small steps, the easier it will be to execute and track them. After you have created your plan, show it to trusted, experienced colleagues to fine-tune it further. Then create separate Project Planner sheets for individual projects, such as writing an article or planning your networking ideas. Be as specific as possible.

Your Annual Marketing Plan Worksheet

Figure 3.10 is the Practice Management Annual Marketing Plan. It will help you develop a marketing plan for your market niche.

In the top section, record the information about your specialty. By studying how the actual (or estimated) figures relate to last year's new client referrals, income, and project expenses, you have a clear picture of what happens with your current promotional efforts. With this information, you can develop new, *realistic* goals for the next year. The accuracy of your growth potential from marketing projects will depend on your market niche, your effectiveness at marketing, and your community demographics. If this is your first year compiling these figures, use whatever estimates you can. After you use the form for a full year, you will be able to create your annual marketing plan with more clarity and accuracy.

After you fill in the specialty information at the top, review all of the possible marketing projects down the right side. Check off the ones that will work well with your unique skills, specialty, and community. The annual marketing plan is divided into annual quarters on the left side. Developing a three-month project series is a small enough time frame to experience progression and keep from feeling burned out. Review your career and family commitments for the next year and schedule in projects that can be realistically completed.

Most business supply stores sell large wall project planners for quarterly periods. Buy one and put it up on the wall to hammer out the timelines

PRACTICE MANAGEMENT ANNUAL MARKETING PLAN

Year/Period ——————— to ———————   Therapist ———————

Specialty ————————————

Last Year – # of Clients: ———————	This Year – # of Clients: ———————
Last Year – Gross Revenue: ———————	This Year – Gross Revenue: ———————
Last Year – Expenses: ———————	This Year – Expenses: ———————

MARKETING PROJECT
OPTIONS:

MARKETING STEPS Per Quarter

		Jan.-Mar. Q1	Apr.-Jun. Q2	Jul.-Sep. Q3	Oct.-Dec. Q4
———	Brochure	———	———	———	———
———	Networking	———	———	———	———
———	Holiday/Seasonal projects	———	———	———	———
———	Workshops/seminars	———	———	———	———
———	Flyers	———	———	———	———
———	Newsletter/mailers	———	———	———	———
———	Open houses	———	———	———	———
———	Advertising	———	———	———	———
———	Press releases	———	———	———	———
———	Conventions	———	———	———	———
———	Offering Continuing Ed. courses	———	———	———	———
———	Key note addresses/formal public speaking	———	———	———	———
———	Health screenings	———	———	———	———
———	Newspaper interviews	———	———	———	———
———	Writing articles or books	———	———	———	———
———	Radio interviews/talk shows	———	———	———	———
———	T.V. news/talk shows	———	———	———	———
———	Giving Psychology away	———	———	———	———
———	Assessing current/old client base	———	———	———	———
———	Other: ———————	———	———	———	———

FIGURE 3.10   Annual marketing plan.

of your projects. As a result, you will find it easier to stay motivated and on course.

Figure 3.11 shows a sample of one way to use the form for a new specialty in cardiac care. Since it is a new specialty for Dr. D, she has no previous statistics with which to compare her goals. If she had a long-standing specialty in this area, she would base her goals on a *realistic* increase in number of clients and revenue from the previous year. In this case, her goals are estimates that are more vague.

FIGURE 3.11   Sample annual marketing plan.

She desires to see 10 cardiac clients per week as one of her several health psychology clinical specialties. Her goal is to have her average fee per hour to be $100. She also wants to take 3 weeks of vacation during the year and she expects one half week of time off being sick or staying home taking care of her children when they are sick and not in school. Therefore, she expects to generate income for 48½ weeks. This will give her projected

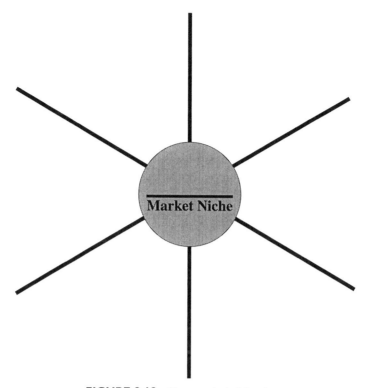

FIGURE 3.12   Your market niche plan.

revenues of $48,500 for the year in her cardiac specialty. She has written her estimated expenses down the left side of the MARKETING STEPS and total an estimated $800.00.

Since she is new to the specialty, her initial quarterly plans include getting current in the clinical specialty, producing a brochure, and beginning her networking with relevant professionals. Valentine's Day is a natural "heart" holiday that can tie into a "health of your heart" type of concept. This is coming a little too soon, but since her initial step will be doing a thorough literature review, she can still write a local article for the public in time. Next year, her Valentine's Day seasonal project will be more creative and large scale. Perhaps she will organize a multidisciplinary community-wide cardiac screening with media coverage for Valentine's Day in the next year or two. With this in the back of her mind, she is collecting ideas and contacts that can help her build her plan.

This year, she expects to develop a series of cardiac seminars on topics such as stress reduction, anger management, and adopting healthy lifestyle changes. These seminars will be designed in quarter two, based on the literature review materials and executed in quarters three and four. Minimal

Your Market Niche Plan

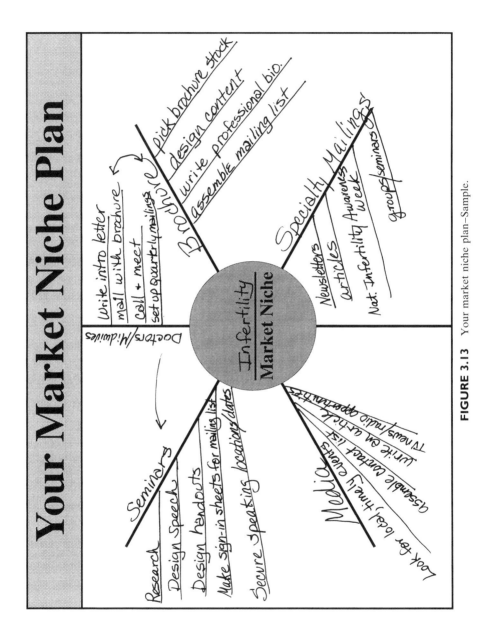

FIGURE 3.13 Your market niche plan–Sample.

PROJECT PLANNER

This form will help you define the steps of your Business & Marketing Plan and other projects. Think and write in terms that are clear, specific and goal-oriented. Use words like, "plan, write, revise, complete mail," etc. By being organized focused and strategic, you will:

◆ GET MORE ACCOMPLISHED ◆ KEEP YOUR MOMENTUM GOING, AND ◆ REACH YOUR PRACTICE GOALS!

Project: _____

Final Deadline: _____

To Do	Target Date	Date Finished		TASK
_____	_____	_____	1)	_____
_____	_____	_____	2)	_____
_____	_____	_____	3)	_____
_____	_____	_____	4)	_____
_____	_____	_____	5)	_____
_____	_____	_____	6)	_____
_____	_____	_____	7)	_____
_____	_____	_____	8)	_____
_____	_____	_____	9)	_____
_____	_____	_____	10)	_____
_____	_____	_____	11)	_____
_____	_____	_____	12)	_____
_____	_____	_____	13)	_____

NOTES: _____

FIGURE 3.14   Project planner.

handout costs are noted. Advertising in the local AMA newsletter forums for referral source exposure as well as in local cardiac patient related organizations will be explored.

She will skip more advanced marketing projects until she (a) understands the culture of cardiac care, (b) has a thorough knowledge base, (c) assesses the opportunities as the year unfolds, and (d) develops her community outreach and marketing progress. Joining professional organizations is another valuable educational and networking avenue that she will pursue early on.

Your Market Niche Plan

Figure 3.12 provides the opportunity to move from practical, left-brain planning to more creative, flowing, and right brain activity. List your market niche on the center line and translate your annual marketing plan (Figure 3.10) onto the form. Play, think, and be creative, and let ideas lead into other ideas. Try to think of ways to develop an integrated plan with several layers throughout the year and several types of promotional projects.

Ask your business-oriented friends and clinical colleagues what they would add or change. Put it away for a few days and revisit your plan later. When you feel it is complete, revise your annual marketing plan to reflect this new information.

Keep in mind that nothing you are creating is set in stone. As you pursue your marketing plan, you will constantly be obtaining feedback and new information. Because you are always learning more about what works for your practice regarding your community, you can refine your plan to make it more effective over time.

Remember that your practice-building plans will become more accurate and precise over time. The most important issue is to get started now. You will be in practice for many years, so you want to get some factual data on your goals and results. Each year your information will teach you more and more about practice development.

Let this continuous process spark your creativity and your analytical mind. The second market niche plan (Figure 3.13) is a sample for an infertility specialty that you can use as a guide (Kolt, 1996a).

The Project Planner (Figure 3.14) is an important tool to capture planning data. Practice building can be a piecemeal endeavor or an overwhelming project if you can not harness your ideas. The project planner will turn your ideas into clear, specific small steps, with target dates to accomplish them. Speed is not the focus in practice building. Thoroughly and effectively completed projects are a key to long term success.

ASSIGNMENT: LAYING THE FOUNDATION AND BUILDING MOMENTUM

After you have chosen your specialty, gather information about your referral sources that are natural referral links.

1. Locate all of the organizations, members, and periodicals in which they are involved. For example, if your specialty is divorce, locate all of

the local branches of the American Bar Association, any psychology and law societies, a mailing list of all family law attorneys (you can get this out of telephone book), law schools, and so on.

2. Then transfer this information into your Practice-Building Binder.
3. Also, use the information to supplement your marketing plan.
4. You will use some of this information in Chapter 4.

REFERRAL SOURCE GROUP #:1 _____

List the major professional organizations to which they belong: (such as their version of the National Association of Social Work, APA, American Counseling Association (ACA) local branch).

NAME OF ORGANIZATION: _____

ADDRESS: _____

PHONE: _____

E-MAIL: _____

NEWSLETTER: _____

EDITOR'S NAME & PHONE: _____

SPEAKER ORGANIZER OR CHAIRS NAME & PHONE: _____

4

HOW TO DO SEMINARS, WORKSHOPS, WRITING, AND LARGE-SCALE PROJECTS

Frequent, communitywide visibility is necessary to build a client base that can sustain your practice. In the last chapter, the initial marketing strategy showed how to help you penetrate your community and interact with referral sources and the public. Despite the fact that many people may need your services, they may not come to therapy right away for many reasons. Most potential clients must see or hear about you several times before they will call. Therefore, you will need to find ways to get in the public eye frequently.

Figure 4.1 summarizes key steps in advanced marketing. It describes a widespread plan to reach the public directly. Your approach here will be quite different from that of networking with referrals. You can reach larger audiences through speaking engagements, radio appearances, and television interviews on your specialty. It is important to set up small steps to be thorough, competent, and effective. Again, an assessment and refinement of your promotional plans should follow each project.

You should be able to determine from the data which projects are best in terms of referrals, income, and increased opportunities. Keep organized, plan thoroughly, set up project timelines, and engage in continual reevaluation so you minimize poor results and wasted time.

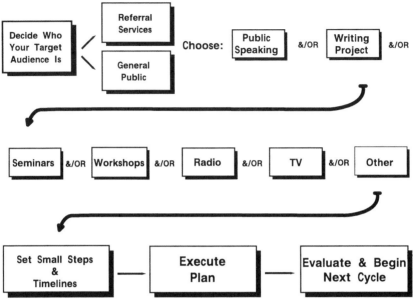

FIGURE 4.1   Advanced marketing flow chart.

When your projects are in place long enough and a predictable flow of new clients is consistently coming in, you will find that your promotional projects have become *fun and creative projects* that you enjoy. Perseverance, patience, and perhaps working with a seasoned consultant or mentor will help you make the jump from a start-up, time-consuming experience to a process that is successful and enjoyable.

WIN-WIN-WIN GOALS

Large-scale projects create opportunities that benefit everyone. Helping the public is not a difficult task if your philosophy of practice development has integrity, creativity, and a strong dose of hard work and commitment. Who can benefit?

Large-Scale Plans to Reach the Public

Molding public opinion by increasing awareness is a key to the longevity of our profession. It is also an incredible tool with which to make our culture more healthy, productive, and fulfilled. Public awareness of the many psychological issues that influence lives can give them more understanding and, ultimately, control over their lives. In a parallel sense, when the public values our work highly, the incentive to see us will rise substantially.

In chapter 3, I reviewed many examples of how to promote your practice and network within your community. This chapter will cover more large-scale methods to reach larger groups, including how to design and implement the following:

1. Seminars and workshops
2. Professional writing
3. Press releases
4. Product sales

SPEAKING ENGAGEMENTS: SEMINARS, WORKSHOPS, AND KEYNOTES

Speaking engagements consist of keynote addresses, seminars, workshops, panel discussions, and other special events where you present information about professional issues. Your audience may be the general public, potential clients, or referral sources. They are an excellent vehicle to reach large numbers of people in your community. Someone who has not been exposed to therapy will then have the opportunity to "hear and feel" new dimensions of issues they may be struggling with. They may be able to take your ideas and develop the insight and courage to work through their challenges.

Why are speaking engagements important in developing your practice? In today's world, you can't expect clients to knock on your door merely because you have been practicing for a long time or because you are a great therapist. Public speaking is an excellent opportunity to get the word out about the value of what you do and invite people to sample your work. Your hope is that some will be touched by your message in a way that moves them through their process enough so they are ready to call you and begin therapy. Your speaking engagement can be a catalyst for some to make great changes that you will never know about. For others, your talk may be the next step in their process so they are ready to begin therapy. Whether you are giving psychology away, gaining name recognition, or building your practice, speaking engagements can be creative and gratifying work. When you become an accomplished speaker, you can get addicted to the electric energy of coordinating all the nuances into such a creative event.

Public speaking in any form can be an excellent win-win-win opportunity for the consumer, your profession, and your own practice. It is also a very lucrative profession in its own right, if you work your way up to a professional level. In fact, seminars, workshops, and classes are estimated to be a $3–4 billion dollar industry!

To be successful, you need to devote time to preparation. To become a powerful communicator, you must take your clinical knowledge and transform it into something that the general public can understand, assimilate, and use.

Benefits

Benefits for the general public:

- It touches people so they know they are not alone.
- They know that someone understands.
- They know where they can go for help.

For your profession:

- Helps the general public understand what therapists are like
- What we do
- How we can help them

For you:

- Helps you develop or refine your clinical concepts and intervention strategies
- Provides you with a forum to express them

For your practice:

- You will become known as a community expert and increase the likelihood of steady community referrals.
- Your hard work developing your concepts and style can pay off even further by repeating the same presentation over and over to different audiences.
- The more people hear about you, the more potential clients you will have. Whether right then, or later on, they know whom they can call when they are ready for psychological care.

By perfecting even one good speaking engagement, you can accomplish all of the following:

- You can get exposure in front of more people than you could through most marketing vehicles (except media work or nationally published books).
- People will have the opportunity to hear your ideas and begin to develop rapport with you.
- Preparing for your talk will help you refine your ideas on the subject so you can develop more precise, as well as creative, offshoots of your topic. Those offshoots can be great for clinical applications, writing, consulting, and other related projects.
- You can stretch beyond your comfort zone, which will help you more eloquently network with other professionals.

Where to Begin

If you have not done extensive public speaking, learning the skills may take time, courage, and practice. But it can be lots of fun. One goal is to select a topic that is flexible so you can give it to multiple groups with small variations in your program. Develop an organized system to manage the many facets of your presentation. Consider it an "evolving organism" that will grow and constantly become more refined, powerful, and eloquent.

Choose a Topic

Your title is the first (and maybe last) thing people will see regarding your speaking engagement, so make sure it's good. Choose a topic that will appeal to people who are busy, stretched by American life, and may want to eliminate pain and stress or ignite their hopes and dreams. You want them to come because your seminar could unlock the key to what they really need in their life. Which one of your specialties is the most timely, marketable, or able to attract an audience?

Research Your Subject and Target Market

Get current in your subject matter so that you feel competent. You can get good information through the internet as well as from traditional sources. For example, if your topic is health related, try AOL's health options or go to a site such as healthgate.com. The local medical library, hospitals, and medical schools can also provide excellent information. Print out all relevant abstracts and review them. Get copies of the key research, articles, and books. Then begin to review them. Summarize the clinical issues on paper.

Understand Your Demographics

Next, you will need to transform your knowledge base into something that is interesting and useful to an audience. Think about the demographic characteristics of your target audience. What characteristics do they have? How many are in your community? Why are they in emotional pain? What are their goals? What behavioral or health habits are increasing their risk? Keep this information in mind as you create your presentation as well as your promotional information.

Finding Organizations

If you want to develop a large speaking schedule, develop an annual speaker's marketing plan. Then start creating mailings to key people, businesses, and organizations. Don't forget to send out promotional information to other therapists in your community and to your professional organizations. If you are a novice at speaking or new to a clinical specialty, you will need to figure out who will want you to speak to their group.

For example, if your specialty is infertility, you will want to contact your local Resolve organization. If you work with breast cancer, a few starting points to pursue would be your local American Medical Association (AMA), oncology-related physicians, and the local chapter of the American Cancer Society. Don't forget to look in the phone book, Chamber of Commerce directories, and professional organizations or trade associations. Computer databases, mailing list brokers, and business as well as personal contacts may also have good leads.

I initially began my own speaking career in the early 1980s as a result of my dissertation. My topic was on women in male-dominated professions and the influence that women's career role models have had on their self-concept and role conflict issues. My initial speaking opportunities were in corporate settings and expanded to over 100 local organizations, including the YWCA career development center for women, The American Association of University Women (AAUW), the Democratic Party, battered women's shelters, several branches of the U.S. government, hospitals, universities, and the list went on.

The goal is to start with one solid topic and find all of the organizations that will benefit from your presentation. When this is going well, you can add new dimensions to your topic to reach wider audiences. For example, if your topic is stepfamilies, you can present a seminar for the general public. You can also present a workshop for caseworkers who could turn into valuable referral sources. Your talk for families could focus on normalizing their anxieties and discomfort with the state of transition in their family, while the presentation for caseworkers could be geared to help them feel empowered to do their job better in working directly with stepfamilies. The presentation for caseworkers could be directed to include the following:

- An opportunity to provide empowerment and purpose in the social worker's job ("Your job is not "Band aid" work.")
- The idea that they may be the first person to really understand the stepfamily
- How to establish credibility with their clients
- Preventing burnout with large, tough caseloads
- Showing them the value of their role as a referral source

Start by determining which groups would be interested in information about your specialty. If you are comfortable speaking to people you don't know, call potential organizations and ask to talk to their speaker chairperson. Explain who you are and your topic ideas. Follow up with your brochure and a summary letter. If you feel more introverted, you can start with an introductory letter as your first contact. When you call, they will already be familiar with your work and ideas. The goals are to (a) assess their needs, (b) suggest relevant topics, and (c) let them know who you are and why you would be a good speaker for their group.

When you find an interested group, be sure that it is a good match for you, too. Interview each new organization before you accept a speaking engagement and begin any work on your presentation. Make sure that their needs are consistent with what you want to talk about. If their philosophy is not in alignment with yours, they are not a good match. When you get proficient at speaking in public and have many engagements under your belt, you may not have time to accept all the opportunities that come your way. Never accept a speaking engagement just because it is offered.

SPEAKING ENGAGEMENT ASSESSMENT

This questionnaire will help evaluate your opportunity to speak to a group:

1. **What is your potential topic and title?**

_____

_____

_____

_____

_____

_____

2. **To whom did you speak? Is he or she an appropriate spokesperson for the organizations?**

_____

_____

_____

_____

_____

_____

3. **How often do they have speakers? Who has spoken recently for them? What topics have they covered? Describe the caliber of speakers and the kinds of topics they have covered.**

_____

_____

_____

_____

_____

_____

4. **Ask them which topics were their biggest draws. How can you make your title and promotional information more likely to draw a large attendance?**

_____

_____

_____

_____

_____

_____

5. **How many people typically attend their presentations? Small numbers will mean a more intimate or interactive presentation. Large audiences may indicate something more formal.**

_____

_____

_____

_____

_____

_____

6. **Overhead transparencies or slides may add to the dynamic nature of your presentation, especially for larger audiences. Incorporate discussions, music, humor, exercises, and other vehicles to maintain interest as well as drive your points home. List the audiovisual equipment you will use in your presentation.**

_____

_____

_____

_____

_____

_____

7. **Ask for a couple of their newsletters and brochures. They will give you information about the group's mission, purpose, goals, and background. Describe their mission. Is this information consistent with your own perspective and objectives?**

_____

_____

_____

_____

_____

_____

Fees

What is the range of money that speakers are paid? It is usually quite large, depending on the type of business or organization that is hiring you, as well as your expertise, notoriety, and speaking history. Speakers regularly work for free (meaning the payoff is exposure or altruism) or receive up to tens of thousands of dollars. Don't ask for a specific fee at first, because if they can't provide it, there is no room to negotiate. As you interview them, look for answers to the following:

- How much preparation will this take?
- What opportunities for clinical work or consulting could this generate?
- Will a good recommendation from this organization help your speaking career?
- Can they provide good leads to other organizations?

All of these factors can add value to your endeavor. If the organization can't pay the fee you want, see if there are other pluses that can help you get closer to your long-term practice and speaking goals.

Set Up Goals and Timelines

I suggest that you use a three-ring binder to hold all of your event information as it evolves. Each tabbed section can capture important information that will continually improve both your delivery and your impact. Here is a list of useful titles:

Tab one: General info: Include key organization and reference papers such as to-do lists, contact people, and final planning information.

Tab two: Marketing: Include pre-event newsletter articles and their contact people. Include your picture. State your postevent plans. Include all relevant deadlines.

Tab three: Speech: Put your speech here. Also add interesting quotes, jokes, analogies, and anything that you may want to integrate into your speech.

Tab four: Site needs: Audiovisual needs, chair arrangements, and so on.

Tab five: Day of the event: Include directions and an extra copy of your introduction in case the person forgets theirs!

Tab six: Handouts: Put ideas here as you create handouts during your speech construction.

Tab seven: Evaluations: Getting feedback from your audience about what they liked or want more information on will help you both refine your presentations and gain new clients. (See pp. 120–123 for a sample.)

Tab eight: Review and follow-up: Make a summary of your evaluations and your own review of the event—what worked what didn't. What changes or updates will you make for future speeches?

Pre-Event Marketing

Your goal here is to get the word out to potential attendees about why they won't want to miss your event. One good vehicle is a feature article on your upcoming event in their newsletter. Find out if they accept articles. If so, submit an article that will get them thinking about the issues you will talk about in your speech. Peaking interest through their newsletter will increase your attendance as well as your credibility. If they sell ad space, think about placing a professional ad about your services in the issue that follows your presentation.

You may also suggest that they include a promotional piece highlighting the talk and what people will gain from attending. And, if you volunteer to write it for them, it will save them time and enable you to present things with the most effective slant.

After the event, consider putting in a classified or display ad. Newsletter ads are generally very inexpensive. After hearing you speak, people will see your name again and remember your talk. For people who were not quite ready to deal with their personal issues, seeing your name again may bring them one step closer to making a call.

Other promotional ideas include having the organization (or you) send a press release to your local media. You can also have "reminder flyers" available at organization meetings prior to the event.

Create a Title That Attracts People

A winning title can make the difference between very few people attending and having large groups of people feeling that they can't miss your presentation. A title like "Goal Setting Workshop" will bring in fewer people than "How High Would You Dream . . . If You Knew You Wouldn't Fail?" "Stress Reduction" sounds like a boring topic, but "What to Do When Life Drives You Crazy" or "Stop Stressing and Start Living!" sound more appealing.

If you work in industrial psychology and business consulting, consider titles such as, "The Only Place Where Success Comes before Work Is in the Dictionary," "How To Avoid Stupid Mistakes While in Business," or "Work Smarter, Not Harder!"

Health topics from cancer to weight management can sound more interesting with a title like, "Making Peace with Your Body." A tag line following the title customizes it to the specific health issue. "Coping with Infertility—Navigating through the Journey to Start Your Family" is one example.

Set a Good Date

The obvious goal is to have your event on a day and time that will attract the most people. By looking at your audience demographics you will get some ideas of what will work. An evening or weekend may fit with people who work. Do not choose a Sunday or a day that conflicts with holidays. Watch out for holidays that you may not observe but which others do, or 3-day weekend holidays. Watch out for April 15th, when people may not feel like spending money after tax time. See a "year-at-a-glance" calendar to view the possibilities.

It is usually best to skip the period from November through January 15th. Thanksgiving, followed by Christmas and Hanukkah, leave many people overbooked with family and religious commitments, so they may not want to add another event to their calendar. They may also be short on cash from buying presents or too tired to go anywhere because they have been traveling.

Create Promotional Material

Potential attendees may know nothing about you or your work. All they will see is your promotional brochure or flyer. Considering all of the time, effort, money, and potential payoff from your event, your presentation materials need to be good. The copy should include the "who, what, when, where, and why" of the event. Here are nine basic ingredients for your mailer:

1. Who should attend
2. What you will cover: include a brief introduction to the topic
3. When it will be held: The date and time should be easy to find on the mailing.
4. Where it will be held. Again, this should be easy to find. Consider including a map and parking suggestions.
5. Why they should come *NOW* and not just think about it.
6. The cost: Consider lower fees for early registration. You will want to know early about room size changes, number of handouts to make, and even whether you will need a microphone. People will often act when an offer is time limited, so discourage procrastination, misplacing your mailer, or finding reasons why not to go.
7. Your biography and picture: Include information about your type of license, qualifications, and anything that will build their trust in you. In your photo, look friendly, open, caring, and competent. Here is an example:

   Dr. Mary Smith has been a psychologist in Manhattan for 19 years and specializes in surviving the loss of a loved one. She is the author of "Letting Go, Healing and Moving On" and teaches therapists in New York about the process of loss.

8. How to register: Be sure to tell them how they can sign up. In small, intimate presentations, you can have a sign-up sheet in the

office or a phone number for them to call. For larger events, your brochure should include the following options to register fast. They can call, fax, e-mail, or mail their registration form to your address. If you accept credit cards, state it clearly in your registration section. Credit card payments can increase your attendance by up to one-third in larger presentations.

Other options include quotes from past participants such as, "Your warmth and compassion really shine through in what you do." "I liked the down-to-earth examples of how to deal with [your topic]," and so on.

PRESENTATION PROMOTIONS WORKSHEET

1. **Tentative title:**

_____

_____

_____

_____

_____

2. **Expected audience size:**

_____

_____

_____

_____

_____

3. **Brochure/flyer:**

_____

_____

_____

_____

_____

4. **Who should attend:**

_____

_____

_____

_____

5. **What you will cover. Be clear and include a brief introduction.**

6. **Date and time:**

7. **Where:**

8. **Why they should come NOW and not just think about it.**

9. **The cost:**

10. **Your biography:**

11. **How to register:**

12. **Quotes from past participants or supporters:**

Choose a Location

In what setting will your presentation take place? The military mess hall, a corporate center, or a college classroom will lend themselves to different types of presentations. The location will also dictate the appropriate clothing and the level of casualness or professionalism you want to project.

A safe, central, and easy-to-get-to location is important. Depending on the number of participants expected, you may want to use your own office or rent a meeting room at a hotel or convention center. Always try to estimate the number of people that will attend and let the structure of your presentation flow from that. Be as intimate with the attendees as the environment will allow. Here are three separate examples.

Your Office

A small, intimate gathering, such as a miscarriage support group, can take place in your group or conference room, your clinical office, or even your reception area at the end of the day. People will feel more comfortable making the jump to enter therapy if they "know more about you" and see and feel your office. It makes it a little easier for someone who may want therapy but is still afraid to begin working on an issue. Name tags (with first names only) can enhance the rapport and communication between people.

Your Referral Source's Office

Presenting your seminar at a referral source's office is another excellent idea. For example, you could suggest to your family law referral sources that you would be happy to present a 1-hour seminar on "coping with divorce" for their clients at their office.

This opportunity presents another win-win-win situation. The attorney gets added value services for his or her clients at no cost, the clients get real help when they are raw with emotion and need, and you have the opportunity to introduce yourself to people who may benefit from therapy. You will be given considerable credibility because you will be linked with the competence and trust that they already have in their attorney.

The door is wide open for good results. You will also eliminate most of the time and costs of marketing your seminar. You don't have to "find" people to attend. A nice flyer on inexpensive four-color, premade stock can produce a quick but professional image. Many varieties of predesigned paper stock can be found at most business supply stores. You may want to bring along some fresh flowers to add beauty and comfort to your presentation.

An Organization's Location

The local AMA, PTA, American Cancer Society, RESOLVE, church or synagogue, support organization, or countless other groups may be interested in having you as a guest speaker. The advantages are plentiful in such an arrangement. Your credibility is linked to the organization's in the members' eyes. They will have a mailing list of members, and they will usually do the mailing themselves at no cost to you. Members already know where the organization is located, and they are a self-selected group of people who have demonstrated an interest in the organization.

Large or Formal Events

For a more formal presentation or for a larger audience, choose a hotel that is near your office or centrally located. Among hotels that appear similar in location and value, rates for meeting rooms vary widely, so don't assume you have found the best deal until you have called several and compared.

When you call, ask for the catering or meeting planning department. They will ask you a series of questions to determine your needs and estimate cost options. They will want to know how many people are expected, your desired seating arrangement, a list of food or refreshments, audiovisual needs, and your tentative date. They will walk you through all the details. If you are giving a seminar that is less than 2 hours long, auditorium seating can handle the most people in the smallest space. This will save you money. Various forms of classroom-style seating are excellent for workshops where people need a surface for writing. The tables hold from three to six people and can be set up in a U formation or with aisles down the middle.

If you have not done your event before or you are new to presentations of this size and cost, consider a few other issues.

First, select a room with removable walls so you can expand or contract the size when you are sure about your turnout. The last thing you want is a huge room with a few people in it. Imagine a band that is playing to a packed house and another band that is playing to a few, scattered people. If you attended both events, you would probably say that the band in the "packed house" played better music and you would have enjoyed yourself more. You may even feel sorry for the band in the empty room. You don't want to be in that position because it will be hard, very hard, to feel comfortable and competent. Always try to make the room appear "full," which translates into, "lots of people want to be there so this must be real good."

Pre-Event Planning

Be sure to ask the meeting planning department to mail you a map and parking permit for the presentation. Nothing can throw you off more than getting lost, not finding a parking place, or arriving right when you are about to go on. You want to arrive early, feel the place out, set up your sign-in sheet and brochures, and test the sound system. You want to be poised and relaxed before you begin.

Introductions

Usually someone from the organization will introduce you before your talk begins. This person may be the president, the organizer of the conference, or the meeting planner. Be sure to find out ahead of time who will be introducing you and get the correct spelling of their name, title, and fax or mailing address. When you are ready to send them your introduction, give them a brief call to tell them it is coming. They will usually be happily surprised because you are being both thoughtful and helpful. The call is also a great opportunity to develop rapport with them before the event. Having them know you in a personal way will help your presentation. During your introduction, they will project more warmth and respect for you than if they knew nothing about you.

Remember that the introduction is a form of marketing for you. So write what you want the members of the organization to know about you. It is a good idea to have long and short versions of an introduction for your presentations. You can pick and choose different professional information to highlight, depending on the particular group to whom you are speaking.

Your introduction should be less than one page and should include your qualifications. Use a larger font than normal because they will often bring it to the presentation and read it at the podium. Include your name, your background, and something interesting about you as well as what you will be covering for the day.

Sample Introductions

Here are two sample introductions:

Mary Johnson is a marriage, family, and child counselor and has been working with [specialty] clients for 8 years. She runs couples groups and works individually with women dealing with [specialty]. She has been in private practice for 12 years. I'm really looking forward to Mary's presentation today, so we can all learn more about [specialty]. Let's give her a warm welcome. . . . Mary Smith.

Sample: Introduction of Dr. Laurie Kolt at the Presentation:

It's NEVER too early to start planning our careers . . . and tonight we will be learning about what we can do NOW, so we can prepare us for that first job after graduation.

We are very fortunate to have with us tonight, an expert who is both a psychologist—who knows about helping people build confidence, motivation, and success . . . and a career counselor—who helps people develop a systematic job-hunting strategy.

She is a frequent guest on TV and radio as well as the author of several articles and magazine columns on personal and career success.

She has been in private practice for 18 years, and her office is on the edge of our campus in La Jolla. Let's give a warm welcome to Dr. Laurie Kolt!

Your Speech

When you construct your speech, start with the ideas you want them to leave with. Then work backwards and create the body of your speech. What do you want them to learn, understand, or do as a result of your talk?

Designing Your Presentation

Start with an outline that covers your main points. Then fill in some succinct details. Next, figure out the transitions between topics. At this point you are likely to see that some topics may flow better when the order is switched. Keep "working your presentation" until it covers your ideas and flows from start to finish. Consider that most people can focus their attention for only a short period of time until they drift off or lose interest.

Tempo and Style

Your next step is to inject timely changes in your tempo and style to keep people involved. Go back through your presentation and "salt and pepper" it with things that create life and interest. Anecdotes are useful. People respond well to stories. Stories can capture people and take them far away to another time or place. They can draw listeners into experiencing something that adds life to your presentation. Try to incorporate two or three case studies, stories, or examples that come to life and illustrate your point poignantly. Your audience will become captivated, absorb your message, and leave with something they will hold on to for a long time. Stories can teach them, challenge them, and keep them involved.

Humor

Humor creates an excellent biochemical lift during a presentation, particularly if people have not had a break. If skillfully used, it is also a unique way to keep people open during an intense topic. Any situation can contain humor. It can lighten people up and open them up. Even the most serious topic can have the spirit of humor sprinkled into it tastefully.

Quotes

Good quotes are rich and succinct truisms that can illustrate your points. They can come from famous people or even anonymous sources. My husband told me about a fortune cookie quote he recently got that said, "The clock of time is wound but once." I chewed on the concept for a few days. It gave me an opportunity to make decisions to alter my life in positive ways.

Start a tabbed section in your binder for quotes, jokes, stories, and other things that you can pull from to personalize and heighten the impact of your future talks. You can also modify quotes that you hear during other talks and create your own.

Props are another creative way to both illustrate your points and keep the pace flowing. I attended a seminar once on letting go of the past. The speaker was introduced and we all expected a snappy professional to approach the podium. Instead, we were interrupted by a strange woman who was wearing a big coat and carried two big suitcases. As she pushed her way through the audience from the back of the room, I thought she was bizarre, to say the least! But she turned out to be the speaker, and she had our attention. She went on to use the visual metaphor of how we carry around "baggage" and how cumbersome it is in our lives. She used the prop as a theme throughout her seminar and had people pushing suitcase against each other when she talked about baggage that couples bring to their relationships and the way it affects how they deal with conflict. She used the metaphor when she spoke about how heavy this makes us, and how free and light we feel when we choose to do what it takes to let our baggage go.

Personalize It to Fit You

I could never do a presentation carrying baggage because it is not *me*. I am more likely to use music to tap into the right side of the brain and anchor a point I want to make. I also like to use graphic, visual words to make a story come to life.

When I start my presentation, I often start at the podium to begin my opening remarks with the security of notes in front of me. Since I am 5'2", many podiums can make me feel small and hidden. So when I get in the flow of the presentation, I like to step away from the podium and get up close to the audience. I use facial expressions and my arms to illustrate my points. I like to look right in the eyes of the people there. When I feel a connection between us, I am really enjoying the moment.

Other people are naturals with planned humor or spontaneous comedy about their subject. The goal is to find your own way to be the best presenter that you can be. One way to do this is to become a connoisseur of presentations. Each presentation you attend is an opportunity to see what others are doing that you like and modify it for your subject matter. If you have been going to continuing education workshops, use them to build your own presentations. You can learn new little touches all the time. Each presenter brings new ideas on how to present, set the room up, illustrate examples, and keep people involved. They can also provide fresh examples of how you can construct your promotional materials and handouts. Examples of new and better ways of public speaking are everywhere. So be curious and keep looking.

Discussion Questions

Getting a discussion going can add depth and real-life examples to your presentation. You will learn a lot about the needs of the audience, and you can instantly customize your presentation with information geared to their focus. A good question-and-answer period can also let other people help, which adds a new level of value to your presentation. It can also give you a break while several members engage in dialogue. The break can let you glance at your notes, take a mental pause, or check the timing of your presentation. No one will know you are experiencing "down time" because they will be involved in what other people are saying.

Here are a few basic things you can say to get a discussion going:

1. I'd really like your input here . . .
2. What about . . .
3. Suppose we . . .
4. Does anyone have any suggestions here?
5. That's really interesting . . . Does everyone agree?

Outstanding Openings

After the majority of your presentation is written, you will have a good perspective on the speech as a whole. This is a great time to work on the beginning. How you begin your presentation sets the stage for the success of your talk. You can say something personal or even something funny. The idea is to use this opportunity to attract your audience's attention while they are open and judging how interesting your presentation will be. The content may be less important than how your presentation pulls them in. Build in ice breakers, rapport builders, images of sound and sight, humor, and anything that will capture their hearts or their attention.

Excellent Endings

Your ending needs to have impact. How can you open them up, teach them how to do something important, and then leave them on an impactful, emotional note? Create a presentation that provides them with substance, emotion, and a commitment to improving their lives. Your ending is the culmination of your presentation. It is your opportunity to truly give psychology away and have them remember your points for a long time.

Perhaps you can include an exercise that commits them to action. If they can begin to make changes on the day of the event, you may be helping them set new, healthy, and effective behaviors in motion. For example, in a stop-smoking seminar, you can end your presentation on an emotional note of hope and pride. You can set the stage by having them write a private letter to themselves about how proud they are to beat the odds and finally quit. How grateful their family is that they will have their loved one healthy and alive. While they are writing, you can play an emotional song in the background to open them up even further.

Another idea is to use music that taps into their emotional side to cement your points. In a parenting workshop, you can have them close their eyes and listen to Bette Midler's "Wind Beneath My Wings" to get them to connect with how their children look up to them and cherish their special relationship and loving guidance. Then you can talk about both the joys and responsibilities of good parenting; that it takes a commitment for them to change and be the best they can be.

In a goal-setting seminar, I like to play Gloria Estefan's "Don't Want to Lose You Now" as a lead-in to a guided visualization that gets them in touch with their dreams. It brings up emotions and taps into how precious it would be to reach their goals and realize their dreams.

In any case, your ending can be motivational, but it must stand on a foundation of solid information and skill building—not fluff.

Add a tabbed section to your binder, called IMPACT, to collect and create the many ideas that will make your presentations powerful and distinctive.

Sharpening Your Presentation

When you feel that you have your presentation well developed, tape-record it to hear how you sound. After your next set of revisions, tape-record a good, final version and listen to it in your car or while getting ready for work. It will help you view it from a distance and develop more thought and overall perspective on what you want to convey. This will also make it significantly easier to memorize your order and your concepts. When you are actually giving your presentation, you may want to glance at an outline from time to time. With this type of preparation, you won't feel tied to your notes or an outline. You never want to resort to reading it, or you will sound stiff and uninteresting.

Put your presentation away for a couple of days, and return to it when you are fresh. Then listen to it again so you can evaluate it from a removed perspective that can improve your refinement process.

You Are What You Eat

Treat your presentation as you would an important sports event. Get enough sleep the night before. Take vitamins and eat lightly on the day of the event. If you are speaking right after breakfast or lunch, eat filling but light, nutritious food that will give you energy but won't weigh you down. Don't eat garlic or other odor-producing spices that can put off a person who wants to converse with you after your presentation. You want to leave them with the memory of how great your presentation was, not the foul odor of your breath. Also, if you think you may be excited or anxious, don't drink caffeine or eat sugar. The last thing you want is to feel scattered or tired when you are speaking in front of your audience.

Looks Count

Wear clothes that make you feel comfortable, confident, and competent. Bright colors that enhance your skin tone will help you look alive. Look professional yet approachable. Be sure that your clothes are cleaned and pressed days before your event. You don't need lots of last-minute details to create stress.

Sign-in Sheets

Professional sign-in sheets should accompany every speaking event so you can retain a mailing list of people who are familiar with your work. You will also be able find out what proportion of gender and locations your are drawing from.

Handouts

Handouts can consist of a few pages that serve many purposes. A cover sheet can have the title, your name, address, and phone number at the bottom. You can create an exercise page for them to complete during the presentation. This is a good vehicle to mix up the tempo. Also, if they have written down personal information, they are more likely to save your handouts after they leave. Be sure to number your pages to eliminate any disorganization that could occur if people are ruffling through pages trying to find the exercise. You don't want anything to slow down your presentation, unless it is something you plan.

Other good handouts include summary sheets, references, reading lists, and your group flyers. If you used overheads or slides, you can consolidate them on one or two sheets. Microsoft PowerPoint will do this in one click of your mouse. These make very useful and impressive handouts.

Lasting Impact

It always amazes me when I get a call for a therapy appointment from a person who heard me speak at a workshop or seminar over a year ago. I ask them why they decided to call now and they often mention the following: During the presentation, I said something that touched them, but they were not ready to deal with it yet. They saved my handouts because they found them informative. They found them again later and it reminded them about the talk. Because my name, address, and phone number were on them, they just picked up the phone and called right then. As a result, when I design a presentation I take extra time to (a) build in things that I think will touch the audience, (b) make my handouts attractive and interesting, and (c) always make sure my name, address, and phone are on the front page.

Evaluations Forms

Seminar evaluation forms are useful in capturing new names for your mailing list, as well as letting you know what the audience thought about your work. Many speakers are harder on themselves than the attendees, so you may feel uplifted when you read their comments. The following two-sided speaker evaluation form provides a useful format. This is an excellent way to understand what they liked, what they got out of it, and how you can improve your presentation the next time.

SEMINAR FEEDBACK FORM

Name of event and date: _____

Name of organization _____

Speaker: _____

It is our intent to provide high-quality programs that are both interesting and useful. Please complete this questionnaire so we may continue to improve the services we provide. Your honest feedback is greatly appreciated.

1. How would you rate this presentation? (circle one)

POOR   FAIR   OK   GOOD   EXCELLENT

2. How would you rate the presenter in terms of being interesting, clear, and effective?

POOR   FAIR   OK   GOOD   EXCELLENT

3. What did you like most about this seminar?

_____

_____

_____

_____

_____

4. What could we have done to improve the seminar?

_____

_____

_____

_____

5. Please use the following scale to rate how *useful* the following seminar segments were:

1_____2_____3_____4_____5

NOT AT ALL   OK   SIGNIFICANTLY

_____ List a major topic here   _____ List an exercise here

_____ List another major topic here   _____ List anything else you want
                                                    feedback on here

6. **Please place a (√) by each item you would like to have more in-depth information on, through our newsletter, advanced seminars, groups, classes, or individual consultations:**

List various topics you covered here

_____

_____

_____

_____

_____

_____

List services here (individual, couples, family, and group services, etc.)

_____

_____

_____

_____

_____

_____

_____Other: _____

7. **Any additional comments?**

_____

_____

_____

_____

_____

8. **May we quote you?** _____ **Yes** _____ **No**

OPTIONAL: Please put me on your mailing list for other seminars and information:

Name: _____

Address _____

_____

_____

E-Mail _____ Fax (_____)_____

Phone: (_____)_____ Best time to call: _____

Please contact me now about your services (check your response):

_____ **Yes** _____ **No**

Transforming Anxiety

Many people find the idea of public speaking very scary. They have images of forgetting what they are talking about, making fools of themselves, or being challenged by an angry audience member, wanting to create trouble. Others find that public speaking can give them an exhilarating rush. With the right training and mindset, you can transform your attitudes towards public speaking into an experience that you enjoy and profit from. See chapter 8 on how to deal with anxiety around public speaking.

CHECKLIST—WHAT TO BRING TO YOUR SEMINAR OR WORKSHOP

___ 1. Videotapes (label now), video camera, battery, cord, tripod

___ 2. Audiotapes, tape recorder, batteries (label tapes now)

___ 3. Press release packets (if you are speaking at a big event)

___ 4. Handouts (with promotional information in the the back)

___ 5. Your appointment book to schedule any new clients, etc.

___ 6. Extra brochures and business cards

___ 7. Extra copy of the introduction in case your introducer forgets theirs

___ 8. Overheads or slides

___ 9. Credit card slips and machine if people can pay at the door or purchase books or tapes

___ 10. Cash box, money, and order forms

___ 11. Price list—you can also offer a seminar "special" price

___ 12. Calculator(s)

___ 13. Bring speech!!!

___ 14. Set up a 4-hour block of time after the event to analyze the seminar, process new contacts and opportunities, as well as to make revisions in your speech, overheads, handouts, promotional materials, etc.

The Day of the Event

Now that you have done your homework, you know all about the group you are speaking to, what their needs are, and what they want to hear. Your advertising is in place and you may have an article appearing in their newsletter. Your handouts look great and your speech is complete. When you reach the day of the event, take the time to stay relaxed, balanced, and in a positive mindset.

Remember to keep focusing on your most positive outcome and that people are coming because they really want to hear what you have to tell them. There are people coming who will be open to your message and there are lives that you will touch. Imagine that it will be fun, flowing, and effortless. When the time comes, let go, trust, and have fun.

As an athlete in training, you want to "train" and prepare for the event. Here are some last-minute things to address:

- Your food intake and the timing of when you eat
- Get enough sleep the night before
- Pack everything up early
- Have your clothes cleaned and pressed
- Get your handouts done
- Bring audio/videotapes ready to play
- Know where you are going and arrive early
- Check the room set-up and the sound system
- Set up your sign-in sheet, brochures, and business cards

Analyzing Your Results

After it is over, give yourself a big *congratulations* for successfully completing such a creative, complex, and multifaceted task. Hopefully, you are feeling exhilarated and are planning to do something special to celebrate. But, before going into a celebration mode, there is one more important thing you need to do before the presentation is complete.

As soon as possible, sit down and write out some notes on how it went. Include things that worked well and challenges that developed. Go through your speech and make any revisions that come to mind. Alter any handouts if necessary. Then gather all of your evaluation sheets and make notes on things that the audience liked and changes they suggested.

At another time you can tally up the responses on the speaker evaluation forms. Create a "Speech revision" file to put all of your feedback in. Add to it after each presentation for the rest of your speaking career. It will help you continually improve on what you do.

At a later time, the financial analysis can begin. Create a column for all of your costs. Include photocopies, graphic design, ads, and anything else that costs money. Create another list of the clients that you gained and track how much money they paid you in fees for a full 6-month period.

Silent Successes

Some clients may wait over 6 months or even a year before they call you. They may call and remark on how something in your presentation really spoke to them. They may even quote you—to your amazement. This points to the reality that there are often many *silent successes,* where you have no idea that someone has "engaged" with you because they have not called yet. Your message struck a cord in them, and they were waiting until they were ready to go into therapy and make the life changes that they need.

In this tabbed section keep the notes you make after all presentations. Before you leave the site, write down some speech, motivation, audience comments, and other suggestions to make it even better. Listen to your tape of the event and record things to remember such as whether you said "um" a lot or "you know." Body language pointers are also important. The volume of your voice, speed of talking, comfort with microphones, and hand gestures are other key issues to get feedback on and work to perfection. Think stance, gestures, and eye contact.

How to Raise Attendance

1. Be sure that no other related event (like a similar topic or one that would appeal to the same audience) competes with the attendee's schedules.

2. Be sure that bad days are not scheduled, such as typical holidays or busy seasons of the year.

3. Your brochure is often the only thing people have to go on when deciding if there is enough reason to make room in their busy schedules for "any extra event." To be impactful and effective, your brochure should ideally, have at least two colors. If your budget is tight, you can use one color in two contrasting shades to save the cost of two-color printing. Make sure that all of the content is good and none of it "just lays there." The graphics need to imply quality and value and a "must-do" event.

4. You can also send special mailings to your relevant database of clients and referral sources.

5. List the seminar in key listservs.

6. Build in an "urgency factor" or a "passion factor." For example, if your seminar is on career development issues you could use the following in your promotions: "How much longer will you wait until you get your career soaring?" or "Can you afford to keep your career moving in the direction it is going?" This line can be adapted to many topics, "How high would you dream if you knew you wouldn't fail?" "This seminar can pull your [subject of the workshop] dreams down to earth and turn them into clear and specific reachable goals."

Comfort with Community Exposure

With time, you will find yourself not just enjoying public speaking but feeling exhilarated by it. Your referrals will become steady, and you will expand your speaking topics and the groups you speak to. By this time, you will probably also be making money. You will not view it as a free opportunity to promote your practice but as an income-producing venue in its own right. And it will also add clients to your practice.

Summary Presentation Timelines

1. Discuss the topic with potential organizations—or decide on self-producing your own seminar.

2. Secure an agreement with an organization and establish a topic, date, time, fee, approximate audience size, location, possible audiovisual needs, and contact person.

3. Plot out key timelines following in your appointment calendar so you have plenty of lead time to both enjoy your project and prepare thoroughly.

4. Begin your presentation research and design the talk.

5. Prepare sign-in sheets, handouts, overheads or slides, and evaluation forms.

Two weeks prior to the event do the following:

- Check attendance figures.
- Give your introduction to the introducer.
- Audiotape your presentation and listen to it.
- Fax your diagram of the desired room set up.
- Confirm audiovisual needs.
- Mentally prepare to have a successful and interesting presentation.

Other tips to break into speaking:

1. Join Toastmasters or the local chapter of the National Speakers Association. (See the resource section in the back for contact information.)
2. Volunteer, volunteer, and volunteer to speak in your community.
3. Subscribe to trade journals and magazines in the group or industry that you want to speak for on a regular basis.
4. Learn from more experienced speakers. Their hard work and experience is very useful. If you can find a coach or mentor, you can grow phenomenally faster than going it alone.

As you grow, consider working through a speaker's bureau. They will handle your bookings, fee negotiations, and increase your visibility as a professional.

PROFESSIONAL WRITING

The Sacred World of Writing

If you are a writer at heart, you already know it. Writers love to write. They get immersed in it and experience it as an art form. For those of you that are of this breed, you have been born with the love of an excellent vehicle for your ideas. Imagine the fulfillment of combining your unique knowledge as a therapist with your skills as a writer. Imagine that you can reach many more people this way and also earn money.

Not everyone can relate to this sacred club of writers, but all therapists can learn to write effectively. Writing is a great way to reach the public with your message, increase your visibility, and build your practice.

The best experts in any clinical specialty still have the challenge of synthesizing their information into a style and format that is interesting, understandable, and powerful for the public. Dr. Daniel Goleman, an award-winning *New York Times* writer and author of *Emotional Intelligence* (1997) is a great example. One key to his prominence and success is his ability to make complex psychological concepts accessible and interesting to the public. He has a wonderful ability to put the best research into practical news stories. He is an excellent role model of how we can use the vehicle of writing to enhance social and emotional health.

All clinicians need to find their own way to recognize human opportunities and problems and help our culture evolve. This opens up the dual opportunity to be repaid for our good work with more clients who read our ideas and thus seek therapy to take them further.

Newsletter Articles

Many organizations publish newsletters. They are directed to a narrow target audience of people interested in a particular topic. If your specialty lies within that topic, this can be an excellent opportunity to reach the people who could benefit from your work. Here is a procedure that can help:

1. Read a copy of the newsletter to get an idea of their slant, needs, and interests. Do they have guest expert writers? Do they have a column? What psychological issues do they deal with? Call the editor and approach them with your ideas.

2. Write the article and be sure to have a biographical section that says who you are and how readers can reach you.

3. You can also follow up with a classified ad for the next several months. Newsletter ads are generally much more affordable that other ads, and they reach your targeted population. These readers will have already heard about you and your work, too.

4. Consider calling the organization's speaker chair and begin a conversation on doing a speaking engagement for their organization, too.

Writing a Book

A successful national book may be a dream for many therapists, but few actually make it to a level where they are widely read. "Self-help" and "how-to" books, such as Dr. John Gray's, *Men Are from Mars, Women Are from Venus* (Gray, 1992), is a natural category of book for therapists to write. Gail Sheehy's (1984) *Passages,* and *New Passages* (1995), are another type of "developmental/sociological" book that clinicians can produce effectively.

An idea that has value may also be influenced by things beyond the merit of the idea. For example, Carol Gilligan's landmark book, *In a Different Voice* (1982) was a great addition to thought about the differences between men and women. Yet many of the feminists of the time were not ready to hear that men and women were different. Gilligan, a Harvard professor, also wrote in a scholarly style that appealed to a more educated or intellectual population.

Interestingly, John Gray wrote his pop psychology book decades later when the public was ready to embrace the notion that there were vast differences between the needs and communications styles of men and women. This in no way implies that more scholarly contributions have less value. But it does point to two important variables in book sales. The timing of a concept must stand up to the current cultural context. Second, to reach the public at large, the style of writing and the examples used must be easily understandable and fit in with what the culture is comfortable hearing.

Like in any high-profile profession, best-seller authors comprise an incredibly small percentage of the national writer population. But it can be done by people who are willing to learn how to proceed correctly. If this is your calling or your dream, here are some ways to increase your chances of success:

1. Learn all you can about good writing. You can take a college or Learning Annex course on professional writing. You can also read essential books on writing style such as *The Elements of Style* (Strunk & White, 1979). Many communities have a local writer's club, and they can provide you with both mentoring and practical how-to advice about the profession. For about $100, you can join the Writer's Guild, an organization based in New York City that represents writer's needs and rights. They can provide legal help in negotiating a book contract and lots of insider information you may never have considered.

2. Complete a string of local or self-published articles or books. It will show an agent or a publisher that you know something about the field of writing and will give them a sample of your writing style.

3. Understand the procedures and business side of the publishing world. Your goal may be to reach an agent who will contract to work with you. They may want you to change several things before they accept you as a client. They will need to convince a publisher that your book will be a good economic choice for them. Your publisher will probably also want you to make changes that will improve the salability of work. They are focused on the costs and benefits of your work. You may have a more personal and idealistic perspective. When you find the right mix, you will feel excited, and have clear, ethical guidance on how to get your message out to the public effectively.

4. The next step is to put your book ideas together into an organized and complete proposal. Your proposal will get you into the arena where an agent will take you seriously.

5. *Do not write a complete book* if you are directing your book to the public! You will have your best chance of securing an agent first.

6. If you are writing a professional book, you can often approach an industry publisher, such as Academic Press, John Wiley & Sons, or Professional Resource Press directly.

7. Your proposal should consist of the following:

* Generate a winning title (identify a problem, offer hope, etc.).
* Turn main themes into minor theme chapter headings.
* Create an outline that flows from point to point.
* Look for missing elements.
* Keep it specific.
* Self-help—Help people overcome personal problems or achieve certain goals.
* How-to—Teach people specific skills.
* Develop a style that draws readers in.
* Look for spin-off ideas from the original book. For example, *Men are from Mars* (Gray, 1992) went to *Mars and Venus in the Bedroom* (1997) and later to *Mars and Venus Starting over* (1998) and even a game.

Things to Include in Your Proposal

* Table of contents
* A brief description of the book
* General overview of the main objectives
* Target audience
* Why the book is needed
* How it is unique
* A comparison and contrast to related books
* Timelines for completion

- Total estimated pages
- Information about the author
- Samples of your published work

Tentative Table of Contents

Introduction
Chapter 1: Your First Topic Here
 Problems, challenges, and solutions
 How and why _____ happens
 Qualities of good _____ versus qualities of _____
 Possible questionnaires or exercises
Chapter 2: Your Second Topic Here
Your chapter subtitles here
Chapter 3
Chapter 4
Chapter 5
Chapter 6
References
Index
About the author
About your practice and other services

Brief Description of the Book

- The history of the problem or issue
- How things are today
- Why this topic needs to be addressed now
- How this book is timely
- How each reader will be guided through the process from point A to point B
- Use of any other possible learning formats included, such as examples, case stories, worksheets, forms, flow charts, paper-and-pen exercises, and/or assignments
- Mention that the book offers an opportunity for the readers to _____. It is directed to a wide audience and will be essential reading for people who want to _____.

General Overview of Main Objectives

- Address the problem or challenge the book addresses.
- Mention if the concerns are widespread or universal.
- Describe the forces that have contributed to this problem.
- Readers will be assisted in overcoming _____.
- The main objective of this book is to _____.

Here are four key issues that will be discussed in detail:

- characteristics of _____
- stage of _____
- motivational blocks to _____
- completing the process of [grief, doing an effective job search, etc.]

Target Audience for the Book

- Describe the demographics of the majority of the readers.
- This comprehensive book is designed for all people wanting to _____.
- Most people _____.
- They also want _____.
- They will respond to a prescription for _____.

Why This Book Is Needed

- People across the country (or across the world) are searching for solutions to _____.
- They are looking for a way to _____.
- People with no training now have a valuable book that will help them.
- Today people need _____.
- This book will help them overcome major roadblocks, such as _____.
- This book is designed to inspire them to _____.
- This book outlines many practical ways to _____.
- This book will receive widespread interest because _____.

How This Book Is Unique

- This is the first book that powerfully and effectively demonstrates a model that _____.
- It approaches the subject matter from a position that will _____.
- It incorporates several learning formats that ensure understanding, skill development, and success. The practical, how-to format is filled with examples, illustrations, forms, and exercises.

Comparison and Contrast to Other Books

- List reference information for other books on related topics.
- State how or why your book is different and better, such as, it may have more contemporary concepts, relates to a different audience, have a different purpose, goes further in exploring certain areas, is grounded in research or other assumptions, and so on.

Timeline of Completion

- Unless you have written a full book before, you should overestimate the time it will take to complete it. Don't forget that other work commitments, family time, and unexpected crises can alter your expected timelines.

Total Pages

- Estimate a range of pages that you think the book will be.

About the Author

- List the experience and credentials that make you an authority on the topic.
- List your published works in this and other areas.
- If you have done speaking engagements or media appearances on the topic, mention this as well.

Related Published Works

- Provide samples of your writing.
- Include any publication specifically on the topic.

MARKETING THERAPY-RELATED SERVICES AND PRODUCTS

Unique Services

Once you have a clinical following, you know that your message is effective. Expanding your line of services beyond the traditional gives new people the opportunity to use your message in a more comprehensive or deeper way. It will also give you a chance for nontraditional income streams or even passive income. Opportunities to generate income while bypassing the constraints of managed care are worth putting some creative thought into. Here are some ideas:

1. Create a retreat: A mountain retreat provides a welcomed opportunity for people to get away from the hustle and bustle of life and connect with themselves at a more meaningful level. Workshops and seminars can be an excellent choice for a retreat. You may do it alone or bring in other related professionals.

2. Perhaps a day on "growing through divorce for women" can include a clinical person easing members through the process of loss; legal professionals helping them see what their options are; accountants giving them factual information on how to economically start over; family experts sharing tips to help their kids cope with divorce; and career counselors guiding their work interests and suggesting potential career paths that can help them design careers that meet the needs of single parenthood.

Therapy-Related Products

1. The Ungame (Western Psychological Services, 1997) is one example of a product that helps people process issues and communicate. It can

be purchased by therapists and given out as an assignment, or the public can purchase it. The original creator, Rhea Zakich, developed an excellent product that has been used widely.

2. Make and sell audiotapes of your workshops.

3. A calendar such as Ann Wilson Schaefs "Women Who do too Much" or Mark Victor Hansen and Jack Canfield's Chicken Soup series are excellent examples. People learn to develop new cognitive habits with daily repetition. Focusing on a structured meditation or concept that promotes positive self-esteem, awareness of goals, or other spiritual or personal objectives is a useful practice for many people. These resources are also less expensive than therapy and may be easier to engage in than getting up the courage to call a therapist.

You will notice that many nonclinicians put out simple self-help or "feel good" products. The reality is that they will be made. Trained clinicians should do them, or else someone else will fill this consumer need.

Similar to "giving psychology away" concepts, these types of product can expose people who would never consider entering treatment to good therapeutic ideas. There are dozens of ideas. Look at your specialties and see which types of products you could create.

EXERCISE: PUBLIC SPEAKING—FINDING YOUR PURPOSE AND MESSAGE

1. **Find the message that is uniquely yours: Write down why you want to be a speaker. What subject are you competent in, passionate about, and would like to speak on?**

_____

_____

_____

_____

_____

_____

2. **List five reasons why someone should invite you to speak for their organization.**
(e.g., your enthusiasm, you're knowledgable in the subject, dynamic in front of a group, energized by a group presentation, organized, have good rapport skills, caring, and so on.)

_____

_____

_____

_____

_____

_____

3. **List five reasons why their organization will benefit from inviting you.**

_____

_____

_____

_____

_____

_____

4. **List five reasons why participants will benefit from coming to your presentation.**

_____

_____

_____

_____

_____

_____

_____

5. **What would you like to gain from public speaking?**

_____

_____

_____

_____

_____

_____

6. **How do you want the organization to perceive you?**
(Are you going to perform a service, be an expert, help them in a certain way, provide information, and so on?)

_____

_____

_____

_____

_____

_____

7. **In what context will your talk take place?**
(What will happen right before and after you talk? Will there be a tense announcement of company cutbacks or an award ceremony for their peak performers? Will the mood prior to or following your presentation be tense, humorous, boring?)

_____

_____

8. **How can you flow best with this?**

9. **What can the audience "discover" as a result of your presentation?**

10. **How can you feel connected to the audience and have them feel connected to you?**

EXERCISE: EXPLORING THE WRITER WITHIN YOU

1. List three topics that you could write about that are timely, interesting, and related to your clinical specialty.

_____

_____

_____

_____

_____

_____

2. **Which newspapers, newsletters, or other community resources may be interested in your article?**

_____

_____

_____

_____

_____

3. **Sketch an outline of your article.**

_____

_____

_____

_____

_____

4. **After testing your ideas and reader responses in a shorter form, would you like to develop your topic into a book? List your title, audience, general proposal content and tentative date to begin developing your project.**

_____

_____

ASSIGNMENT: PREPARING TO REACH THE PUBLIC

1. **Decide to pursue either a speaking engagement or a writing project. If you are new to this, be sure to start with something small and doable. State your initial goals.**

_____

_____

_____

_____

_____

2. **Find the name and phone number (or E-mail address) of the best contact person for this project. Express your interest and present your idea.**

_____

_____

_____

_____

_____

3. **Set up a three-ring binder to organize your project.**

_____

_____

_____

_____

_____

4. **Set a realistic start date. Also write down tentative timelines all the way through to completion. Be sure that your timelines are realistic, given your other personal, relationship, and career priorities.**

5

GIVING PSYCHOLOGY AWAY

There are universal truths about how to navigate the journey of mourning or loss as well as how to go after one's dreams and goals. Erik Erickson and others point to the relatively consistent path we all take through life's developmental milestones (Erickson, 1975, 1982). This knowledge is not ours because we studied it in graduate school; it belongs to everyone. I believe the real purpose for developing your practice is to make the world a gentler and more fulfilling place. When you become a seasoned professional, you will have the opportunity *and the responsibility* to give psychology away.

This chapter will cover several avenues to reach out into your community, your nation, and the world at large. It will outline opportunities for you to shape and heal communities with your clinical expertise. The avenues you choose will depend upon timing, luck, your clinical specialties, and your comfort zone. We will cover how to work with radio, newspapers, and television. We will also cover how to participate in health screenings such as National Depression Awareness Day.

WORKING WITH THE MEDIA: TELEVISION, NEWSPAPERS, AND RADIO

When you decide to work with the media, you are taking the opportunity to affect the lives of literally thousands and, sometimes, millions of people. In the 1970s and 1980s, psychology began to venture into media work. Initial exposure was often in the form of call-in shows. Dr. Joyce Brothers was one of our first nationally recognized media pioneers. In 1985, the American Psychological Association (APA) began Division 46, which is the Media Division of the APA. Membership in the division will give you insight, training, and contacts to go further.

Entering this new arena requires some initial training. You will need to consolidate your information into a style that the public will understand and find interesting. Typical media work will present information at the eighth- to tenth-grade level of comprehension. Television interviews differ from radio or print media. You will need to understand the different interests of your audience, as well as those of the media source that wants you to speak.

Working with the media is *not* for everyone. Several important conditions must exist before you can determine if this is where you can make a contribution.

1. You need to be extremely knowledgeable in the area for which you will be interviewed.

2. You need to understand the nuances of the medium so your message is clearly communicated and then reported accurately *in the context that you intended.*

3. You need to know how to evaluate an opportunity and know when to accept or reject it.

4. You need to have the personality type to be comfortable with the possible stresses of last minute stories, live interviews, and the impact of what you say.

When to Turn Down an Interview

It is important to choose wisely when soliciting or accepting an interview. Here are some examples of questionable circumstances:

1. If you sense that interviewer has a hidden agenda or you feel that your professionalism or message may be compromised

2. An interview that is not within your area of expertise

3. An interview that exploits people who are psychologically vulnerable: Some appearances by therapists on popular sensationalistic talk shows can be construed as unethical attempts to exploit personal pain for ego gratification or voyeuristic pleasure. Be sure that you know who you are

dealing with and what their angle is. Studying past shows will also give you an idea of what you may be stepping into.

The Business Side of the Media

Despite our altruistic or even innocent ideals, remember that the media is composed of money-making businesses. You may want to help people, but you need to remember that they want to fill space and sell something. They may view your knowledge as a commodity and want you to give the information or slant that they are looking for.

In defense of their journalistic needs, they are in a fast-paced profession and look quickly for the most articulate, knowledgeable, dependable, and media-savvy experts they can find. To report quickly, accurately, and in a captivating fashion on every breaking story is a coveted goal, and the competition is fierce.

Your job is to evaluate each opportunity and then decide if you want to participate. Each interview will be different. Through continued media work, you will grow significantly in your sophistication and effectiveness. To be good, you must practice, evaluate your interview, and practice some more.

Conducting a Preinterview

Always have a preinterview discussion. Ask the reporter what the story is about and what they would like you to discuss. Offer some preliminary approaches on the subject and see if they are receptive or if they have a preestablished agenda. If you are called to do an interview immediately, turn it down if they will not allow you to do a preinterview.

With quality journalists you have learned to trust, the preinterview process will be more focused on understanding what they are looking for and less on whether they can be trusted to use your information accurately. It can be especially gratifying when you develop a good working relationship with a journalist; they already trust your expertise and knowledge of how to package good information into sound bites. Your interviews can flow with a common mission or goal of "giving psychology away." The journalist may also be open to your educating them about the issues so they understand the essence of the psychological components. If you can teach, enlighten, and even inspire them, your message can be conveyed powerfully and have a strong impact. A great idea is to make good friends with sharp, ethical journalists who appreciate psychology. This type of partnership can produce the ultimate impact in giving psychology away.

But even with your most trusted journalist relationships, I don't recommend doing an interview on the spot. Tell them you will call them back (perhaps within the hour if they have a tight deadline) so you can sit back, evaluate, prepare talking points, and get yourself centered.

A good idea is to fax or give them a brief one-page summary of your topic and your talking points. Be sure to let them know how you want to be identified. If you want to be identified as Dr. _____, write that on your information sheet, too.

When you have your worksheet completed, you can prepare for your media interactions. The following two examples are true stories that serve as good examples of giving psychology away.

Baby Sara

The first example is pertinent if your specialty is pregnancy issues or dealing with death. In 1996, Children's Hospital in San Diego County had received some bad press and was looking for a way to improve community relations. A poignant story emerged within the hospital at the right time for them to display their excellent team of doctors as well as their sense of goodwill.

In a nutshell, the story is as follows: a Mexican couple came across the border to give birth. When the mother gave birth to Siamese twins joined at the chest, special infant surgical teams tried to save them. When the story hit the news, the two little girls were in critical condition. The story quickly garnered international media attention. Helicopters flew above the hospital with news crews searching for footage of the family or the doctors throughout the day. For the San Diego community, the story came out of nowhere and quickly reached highly visible proportions.

It unfolded as a story about innocent children in a life-and-death situation with their parents caught in a waiting game between tremendous hope and grief. After a very high-risk, delicate surgery, one of the twins died. The community's heart was instantly captured. Therapists with specialities ranging from pregnancy issued and infant deaths to grieving and loss had an excellent opportunity to educate the public. When a *Union-Tribune* article covered the community outpouring of gifts and toys for Sara (after her sister's death), it included a quote from Alicia Acosta, a clinical social worker who was helping the twin's parents cope with the situation. Acosta said that although the parents were grateful, it was best if people stopped sending things until they knew that Sara was going to live (Clark, 1996).

What issues could you offer to discuss with the media?

- Why an infant death or a miscarriage is uniquely devastating
- What a parent goes through when they are grieving the loss of a child
- The emotional trauma when someone you love is fighting for their life
- Grieving and loss in general

- How people in the community may find their own emotional wounds revived by these losses
- How to help friends and family members going through similar trials

A Living Organism

When a dramatic or emotional issue strikes, the community becomes like an organism. The citizens feel and react. Who is better qualified than we are to provide sound, practical advice on such emotional issues for our own community? Getting out in the media and sharing your skills will certainly touch many more lives than you will even know. And what better way to get massive, public exposure, at no cost to you? Media exposure will also build your confidence and pride by showing that you can risk getting in front of the public—when they are primed to listen—and doing something to educate, to help them understand, and even help some of them heal.

Some community events spark the interest of therapists with completely diverse specialties. The clinical issues relevant in the following example provide useful information to the community. If your specialty is children, or even mediation, the following example may serve you well.

The Teachers' Strike

In 1996 the San Diego Unified School District's teachers went on strike. (A strike voted, 1996). This unprecedented event raised many issues that provided an excellent opportunity for a psychologist to assist the community. Young children were scared to see their teachers angry on the news and out on a picket line. Older children were happy to escape the normal school workload. Children at all grade levels were seeing their role models acting out of character.

The community launched a desperate search for substitute teachers to keep the schools running. Inappropriate substitute teachers ranged from a high school student disguised as a teacher (who got hired!), to a woman who flashed her breasts in front of a news camera. The sudden and unprecedented demonstrations and disagreements between the teachers and the school board were reported to have been especially upsetting for young children.

This was an unexpected yet timely opportunity for therapists who specialized in young children, teens, and mediation. By calling the local TV news directors and newspaper editors, a therapist would have certainly found someone receptive to ideas presented as timely and important to the circumstances. What could you talk about in response to such an event?

- How to help kids make sense of things
- Teach parents how to use this example to teach kids about anger, social chaos, compromise, and negotiation.

When a Story Is Timely

The stories are endless. And so are the ideas. Catastrophic events like the Oklahoma City and Olympic bombings, and the massive floods caused by El Niño, touched the lives of millions of Americans. If a timely story breaks that touches your community *and* is within your area of expertise, you will have a brief window of time to decide if you want to act. You must weigh the benefits and the risks. Could you help people cope or heal? Or would you be contributing to copycat violence by keeping the media limelight churning? How would your intervention affect your career? The following questionnaire is designed to help you to decide whether to move forward with a media opportunity.

MEDIA INTERVIEW QUESTIONNAIRE

Use this form whenever you are preparing for a media interview.

1. **Why is your angle or perspective on the story newsworthy?**

_____

_____

_____

_____

_____

_____

2. **Describe your angle and perspective.**

_____

_____

_____

_____

_____

_____

3. **What segment of the audience will be interested in this information? How will you convey this to the people who will decide if they want to interview you?**

_____

_____

_____

_____

_____

_____

4. **List your conclusions from your research or knowledge base of the subject.**

_____

_____

_____

_____

_____

_____

5. Write a summary in 25 words or less:

_____

_____

_____

_____

_____

_____

6. List (and memorize) 3–4 clear, succinct sound bites:

a. _____

b. _____

c. _____

d. _____

7. Write a brief opening statement for an interview that sets the tone you want to convey.

_____

_____

_____

_____

_____

8. Write a closing statement with a strong finish.

_____

_____

_____

_____

_____

_____

9. **What news programs, shows, or publications do you want to approach?**

_____

_____

_____

_____

_____

10. **Date and time of the interview:**

_____

11. **Who will be interviewing you? What is their angle or approach to the story?**

_____

_____

_____

_____

_____

13. **Location and directions to the site:**

_____

_____

_____

_____

14. **Date the segment will be aired or published (if known):**

15. **Comments:**

TELEVISION INTERVIEWS

Television interviews are perhaps the most difficult, because you have to watch what you wear, how you carry yourself, and what you say. You will need to be comfortable in front of the camera, exude confidence in yourself and knowledge of the topic, and *stay grounded*. Because of all this, TV interviews can also be exhilarating and fun. Here are some pointers to help you develop a good camera presence:

- Imagine that you are educating your community through the eyes and heart of the interviewer. That is how you are making an impact. Trust that your audience will be open to your message. Imagine that you are talking through the "vehicle" of the interviewer to reach all of the people in your community that can benefit from your words.
- Let your expertise shine through your succinct talking points. Don't expect the interviewer to ask the right questions. Plan to integrate the sound bites into the first questions he or she asks. Then you will be sure to have time to set the right impression and express your most important points.
- Keep your back erect, yet natural. Lean forward slightly in your chair to demonstrate involvement. Don't swivel your chair or fidget with your hands. Try to rest your hands in your lap or in a stable, natural position.
- Always assume that the microphone is on, even when they move to a video segment during your interview or when you think that they have cut to a commercial.
- Remember that in essence you are educating your community through the eyes and heart of the interviewer. That is how you are making an impact. Trust that your audience will be open to your message.
- Look in the mirror right before you go on.
- Be prepared to do a "voice check" so they can set the microphone level before you go on. You can repeat your name and your topic a few times until they have things set just right.
- Don't look at the camera. Get lost in a comfortable conversation with the interviewer.
- Don't get distracted by any people walking around in the background.
- Television journalists often have pressing dealines. If you want to work with them, be prepared to work at inconvenient times; you may have to rearrange other commitments to comment on a breaking story.
- Maintain eye contact with the reporter. Practice your talking points in a mirror so you can refine your voice and mannerisms.

- Keep in mind that they have a limited amount of airtime. They will try to edit the whole interview down to the time frame available. End your comments definitively so the interviewer will know when to start speaking. If you ramble on and on, they will have a tough time reducing the 5 minutes you were interviewed into the one and a half-minute time frame that the story is allotted. They may end up cutting valuable information.
- Be sure that you don't cut the reporter off. It will not sound good on camera. End your comments in an obvious way so an editor can go in, splice your discussion, and keep the best parts.
- Be aware that you may be on camera before you think the interview starts, while the reporter is making a long point, and even after the interview appears to be over.
- Do not pay attention to the studio monitor if you are in the studio or it can easily make you lose your concentration.
- Don't drink anything with caffeine or alcohol before your interview. A sip of water can help you clear your throat.
- Don't eat a large meal right before your interview; you want your thinking to be sharp and your energy high.

What to Wear

Very bright colors can appear to vibrate on camera and will detract from your message. Loud patterns, checks, or stripes can also look odd or unflattering. You will probably be seen only from the chest up or even just at your collar line. Study on-air reporters and anchors to see examples that work best.

Dealing with Interview Anxiety

Some degree of nervousness before an interview, especially a live one, is natural. Work on your anxiety using your clinical skills for a couple of days before an interview. Memorize your sound bites so you will be able to glide into them with minimal effort. The real goal is to relax and use your natural interest or passion for the issue to reach through the camera and into the hearts of your audience. Be yourself and *trust yourself* to do well.

Practice in the mirror so you can observe your natural hand gestures and facial expressions. Then start playing with them. If your gestures seem tight, exaggerate them so you are almost clown-like. When you return to a more normal demeanor, you will feel more comfortable being physically expressive. Remember that effective expressions and gestures make you appear more natural and convincing.

PRINT INTERVIEWS

Print interviews are often done over the phone or after a workshop, seminar, or conference. Don't expect to be provided with questions in advance. If they ask you a question you can't answer, simply say so. It is not a sign that you are uninformed. Your honesty will keep you out of trouble.

To be prepared, have a page of talking points for your own use and also give it to the reporter. Giving them a fact sheet of pertinent information will increase the chances that you will be quoted accurately. Keep a record of the name of the interviewer, his or her affiliation, the subject on which you were interviewed, and how your interviewer can be reached in the future. Now that you have met them, it will be easier to call them directly if you have an idea for a breaking story or feature.

Always request that they send you a copy of the article for your records (unless the article will be readily available to you). Your name in print can make a good quarterly mailing to your referral sources or be used for other promotional opportunities. Keep a file that has the originals of all of your articles for future use. It will be an excellent investment in your career.

WORKING IN RADIO

Radio news interviews are easier than television because you can spread papers around your work space, and no one will know you are using notes while you talk. Often, you don't even have to be at the studio, and the entire interview can be done live, over the telephone. If you are doing a call-in show, you might find it hard to discuss people's questions without being able to see them. Fortunately, you will usually have *someone* to look at, whether it be your host or the engineer. Looking into the eyes of a person will make your voice and tone sound more natural.

Some Radio Tips

- Prepare an initial opening sentence or paragraph. Tell the listeners what you are going to talk about. Invite them in and make them want to stay tuned. Don't *read* your opening but be sure that it has a good, solid impact.
- Try to make your points succinctly. You often won't need to produce short sound bites (as with television), but don't let yourself ramble on while making a point.
- Be sure that you don't say, "um" or "ya know." Your words are your only tools to convey your message.

- Look at your cohost when you are conversing with him or her. It will help your voice flow with theirs and keep you from unintentionally cutting each other off.
- Tape-record a test run so you can hear yourself. You want to have animation, good intonation, and in some cases, a sense of humor.
- Prepare an ending monologue so you can drive your main points home. Memorize it and then paraphrase it eloquently on the air.

Radio Talk Shows

From Dr. Joyce Brothers to Dr. Joy Brown, call-in psychology shows have always been popular. You can use your regular forum to make people think and to teach them how to handle relationships, life decisions, and virtually any topic you want to pursue.

If you can get one in your own hometown, you might fill your practice to the brim. Some of the people who listen may find themselves building a relationship with you. That regular communication can build a public perception of trust and support. But clients who find you through the radio may idolize you or think that you are someone that you aren't. Be thorough in your initial screening with new clients from talk show audiences. There are times when they will get more effective care if you refer them to another therapist who can get down to work without the transference concerns that can sidetrack them.

There are also many controversial radio talk shows. The airwaves are shared with "shock jocks" like Howard Stern, as well as people in the radical right and left political extremes. As with television, be sure that you don't accept an interview or talk show guest spot unless you have listened to the show and have a good understanding of the format and type of callers attracted to the show. Make sure that you don't walk into a situation where a hidden agenda becomes evident and you feel compromised.

One practice-building client of mine told me how he was thrilled to get a national radio interview in his specialty. He felt able and ready to do it and prepared very thoroughly. However, he quickly discovered, "live on the air," that the talk show host was against his point of view and turned the interview into a debate. He could not get his information across and he felt he was made to look like a fool. The therapist was a pawn for the host to extol his point of view.

Public Radio

The Public Broadcasting System (PBS) will often provide an excellent forum for therapy topics. If your community has a local PBS station, follow the programs and find one or two that could be a good match. They may be interested in your professional opinion regarding social trends, psychological issues, managed care controversies, and the kinds of issues on which you can state your position. They also have fewer sound bites and longer stories that go into more depth than most other media formats. Demographically, the listeners will often be the most highly educated in your area. They are also very connected, loyal listeners, as they not only tune into but actually support their public stations. They often make excellent clients for your practice as well as good people to get involved with in community projects.

The Ideal Radio Talk Show

As a cohost on a national radio talk show, I have experimented in combining the best of psychology with perspectives and solutions to life's daily challenges. Here are some thoughts I have developed to take my show further. Come along as my *new* cohost and join me. Perhaps you will want to do something similar in your own town.

I think the ideal radio show is a forum to analyze ideas, make the complex coherent, and teach people how to live better lives. A good talk show is a forum to help Americans *hear* one another more vividly and understand issues more deeply. The goal is to engage listeners so much that they want to stay in their cars after their drive home so they can keep listening to the program. They should be riveted to the conversation because it provokes thought as well as understanding in them.

The ideal radio show creates vivid pictures and immerses people in the telling of a story with long-lasting images and impressions. One of my favorite visions is to have one segment of the show start with the hosts watching the sunset on the beach, describing the smell of the sea salt and the colors, and the feelings it inspires. I'd get listeners to "*be there*" and slow down and relax. Then I'd proceed and do a show on "information overload," discussing the way we Americans stretch and exhaust ourselves with today's pace of life. Then I would segue into an examination of how we got this way, and how it affects our culture, families, industries, and so on.

The ideal show would use the radio (sound) to create an experience rich in depth and dimension to awaken people, challenging and encouraging them to think and take the show's ideas into their day and into their lives.

I would obviously present a good part of the psychological and human interest point of view. I see it as an opportunity to educate the public about the value of our work and also to normalize the life issues people experience. Call-in guests can add more questions, perspectives, and stimulating, nourishing food for thought.

My ideal radio show would be called *Perspectives*. Here are some initial topics I think would be interesting:

1. Health Habits in America: Why some people change and others don't (for example, unhealthy diets, overeating, smoking, addictive behaviors, etc.).

2. Why Americans Don't Plan for Retirement: Psychological issues including fear, inability to visualize retirement, coming to terms with aging, the challenge of delaying gratification, etc.

3. Choosing a Life Partner in an Era of High Divorce: What our role models teach us about love; the anatomy of a dysfunctional relationship; letting go of the past; how to embrace healthy intimacy; how premarital counseling can help, etc.

4. Dying in America: Coping with life-threatening illnesses; how our culture handles death; examining assisted suicide; how families with an ill loved one can learn to cope; saying good-bye and letting go, etc.

5. The New Radical Men: Dad's rights and responsibilities movements emerging in America, why fathers are so important to their children's academic and life success (according to 1998 White House research findings), fathers and divorce, etc.

6. Divorce issues: I was once a guest on a radio talk show on divorce. The talk show host began with a powerful quote out of a chapter called "War of the Roses" from attorney Louis Nizer's book, *My Life in Court* (1961). He talked about how it gets intense when former lovers divorce. In the court room, they can cut each other's hearts out. We began with what that image brought to mind. We talked about the searing pain and disappointment associated with the shattering of a dream—that of a partner for life.

Then we talked about how astounding it is that a couple can become so vengeful, when they were once so intensely in love. The show centered on the intensely painful feelings people experience when letting go of love. We explored the gamut of emotions from the vibrance of fresh love, to the despair of unfulfilled dreams, to the anger and pain of betrayal. The show was full of feeling and the callers were honest—some with their pain and others with their desires to somehow make things work. We spent a good deal of time talking about holding on to hope long enough to get help. Then I described what couples counseling really is. It was a great opportunity to educate the public about the value of our work.

AFTER YOUR MEDIA INTERVIEW OR SHOW

After any radio, television, or newspaper appearance, you will have the opportunity to evaluate how it went. Allow each interview to be a learning process. You will always notice areas for growth, but be sure to also note the good things. The important things to ask yourself are, Did you state your main points clearly and effectively? Did you come across competently and comfortably? Did you reach in and touch people's lives? Did you successfully give psychology away?

Organize Local Media Trainings

There is a tremendous opportunity for us to help each other get more media-savvy. The more therapists become trained to speak in front of the media, the more we can educate the public. That will help the public as well as our profession. We are not in competition with each other when it comes to developing our media skills because each of us has a unique set of specialties, as well as interests, in selecting media projects. There is plenty to go around, for everyone that is willing and able.

Start with a small core of your local therapy association members to create a media committee if you don't already have one. Ask your national organization or a therapy media expert to help you get started. Invite local news producers and journalists from all of your major local media outlets to participate on a panel discussion. Provide them with some questions to discuss. Have your media coordinator or chairperson moderate the discussion. Here are some sample questions they can prepare responses to:

- What do you think is our greatest asset to the media?
- What are some dos and don'ts in doing media work?
- How can we spot timely stories?
- Who would we contact in your organization and how?
- What makes you want to use a story? How can we sell it to you successfully?
- What are your stereotypes about our profession?
- What do the most effective, media savvy therapists do, on and off the air, that you like or respect?
- Discuss some local stories that benefited from a using a therapist's perspective.
- What are some other stories that could have benefited, had a therapist been available?

Usually new media therapists need to start small and safe before they allow themselves to discover the exhilaration and benefits of media work. You can give your members some basic skills in an article in your association newsletter that also promotes the initial first training. Your first training should be playful and create an environment that allows people to take risks in front of their peers. Perhaps you can start with a *Jeopardy*-style format and ask people, in teams, how they would convince the media to cover a therapist's perspective on specific topics. You could move into small sound bite exercises on silly topics. Then move up to longer interviews on real community events and real clinical specialty topics. Participants can bring their own video- and audiotapes to record and take home for their own self-evaluations. Further workshops could cover the nuts and bolts of planning a ready-response task force in your community to mobilize when a timely story hits.

NATIONAL MEDIA EXPOSURE

Some therapists are confident, experienced, and comfortable with national exposure. Most therapists are not. At some point in your career, the opportunity may seem right for you. For other therapists, it will never be an interest. Yet the opportunity to do national work is an opportunity to educate the larger public about the value of your work and your ideas. Imagine the millions of people you can touch.

If the opportunity scares you, don't pursue it unless media training makes you feel more comfortable. If the opportunity brings out grandiose visions, you may be walking into danger. Being quoted in *The National Enquirer* or being a guest therapist on a sleazy national TV talk show will not help your professional reputation. Even if it does bring in some clients, they may not be the kind that you want to see, because they are likely to have a mythical relationship with you in their minds.

Keep in mind that few people are ever paid for sharing their expertise with reporters. Media work, especially *live* media work, is a difficult task. Conversing in front of a camera shooting live footage while you try to sound interesting, articulate, and succinct is comparable to being an elite gymnast doing back handsprings on the balance beam during a critical meet. How well can you handle that kind of pressure?

Thrill seeking is an inappropriate reason to do media work. But it can be OK if you find that you temper the rush with a sense of humility. If you can maintain your composure, vision, and focus, entering this arena can often give you instant name recognition. Americans are addicted to experts, and this massive exposure in a legitimate news forum can work wonders to fill your practice. It can often present other opportunities to use your expertise, which can be fun and rewarding.

Advantages of National Media Coverage

Advantages for You

You have an opportunity to get your message across. If you have just released a book, you may be an articulate guest to educate the public. It is also an excellent opportunity to increase your book sales. Good publishers who see that you can present your ideas with a good style can book you on a multitude of radio shows and local television talk shows in a vast sweep across the country. In a 2-week period you can be whisked around, "telling your message" in a whirlwind blitz. A publisher who believes your *product* (how *they* see your book) can make good profits can use their connections to get you on the national talk show circuit.

Few therapists achieve the coveted guest spot on *Oprah*, where millions of viewers embrace the books that Oprah supports. Larry King has been known to tell his guests to "keep it short, keep it simple, and keep it funny." So if you can flow with his kind of style and directness, this could be a plus for your career.

Advantages For Your Community or the Nation

Some psychologists such as Dr. Sonia Johnston, Dr. Ellen McGrath, and Dr. Noemi Balinth have become regular guests on network news shows to deliver important psychological slants. During the Atlanta Olympic bombing, Dr. McGrath was interviewed live on CNN and talked very eloquently on ways parents can help their kids feel safe and make sense out of the scary event. Her on-air presentation was so superb that the American Psychological Association now uses this footage to teach other psychologists how to use the media to help and heal the public.

There will always be painful or frightening issues that strike a community. The violent death of a high-profile person, such as Princess Diana and the Oklahoma City bombing, natural disasters, such as the 1989 Bay area Earthquake or the 1998 floods in the Midwest, all undoubtedly affected the hearts and minds of people everywhere. Trained professionals can help communities across America make sense of these events, teach them coping skills, and guide them through the healing process.

If you would like to be one of these professionals, start by studying the opportunities, building some talking points, and then observe how the media covers them. Do not rush into the act until you have studied the opportunity enough to have confidence in your ability to make an intelligent, positive impact. For example, at the writing of this book, today's headlines around the world are about President Clinton's admission of sexual involvement with White House intern, Monica Lewinsky. Last night on live national television, his four-minute confession sent out shock waves. Throughout the endless bantering and debating, few comments were about the following:

- This issue may have ripped open old wounds for people who have lived through the pain of their spouse or a parent having an affair.
- What might *they* be feeling right now? Do they know that their painful reactions are normal?
- Do they know that they are not weak or going a little crazy?
- Do they know that talking to a therapist can help?
- What do people tell their children about the importance of telling the truth, the sacred trust in a successful marriage, and the damage that an affair can create?

- How can people going though something similar right now find a way to cope?
- Does the fact that it is not just their parent or spouse, but our President, somehow *make it OK*?

Advantages for the Profession

Unfortunately, there is a lot of trashy psychology promoted in the media. Academics generally don't look and sound good in the media, so research-based psychological facts rarely get out to the masses. Researchers and academicians tend to talk on and on, qualify what they are saying, and have difficulty synthesizing their information into people terms. Their difficulty with sound bites often stems from the reality that science is inherently ambiguous. Yet the media wants to report things in black-and-white terms.

If competent clinicians don't step in, others less knowledgeable or professional will. The real challenge is to give the public useful information in a context that works in a media setting. Done well, the public benefits and the various psychological professions benefit by showing the public who we are and what we do.

Some Thoughts on Media Ethics

Again, media work is not right for all therapists, or appropriate at all times in your career. You are not a better or worse therapist if you dabble in communicating through the media. If you feel that you would be indulging in ego gratification, *don't do it.* If you feel that you would be capitalizing on someone else's pain or tragedy, *don't do it.*

It is only when your clinical expertise, your heart, and your integrity are all in alignment, and you can see that you can make a positive contribution, that media work is worth pursuing. You need to be ready to take a risk that could develop into an uncomfortable situation that you did not expect.

Media Nightmares

Media work puts you on the line. Even competent and experienced people can get lost in a media frenzy. When a national story reaches hysterical proportions, stay out of the arena, unless you are ready to get broadsided. Here is one example.

During the O. J. Simpson trial in California, psychologist and developer of the "the battered women's syndrome," Dr. Lenore Walker, found herself in the eye of a hurricane. When the veteran Denver forensic psychologist was placed on the witness list for Simpson's attorneys, the media jumped on what they billed as a change in the political position of this "once-feminist" leader.

The media attention quickly turned into a shark attack for Dr. Walker. Reporters barged into her office, snapped pictures, and demanded interviews. Headlines from Australia to Europe included, "Champion of Abused May Testify for O. J.," and "O. J. Unlikely to Kill, Denver Expert Will Testify" (Walker, 1998). In her own hometown, the front-page headline in the *Denver Post* was, "Walker Triggers Shock Wave: Battered Women's Champ Is Now O. J. Defender" (1995).

The spin was both inaccurate and unfair. Dr. Walker was a well-respected professional who had made significant contributions to her profession for decades. The media appeared to not want to stop to hear the truth. Even credible news sources including *Time* magazine reported the story inaccurately, when they wrote that she was going to testify the very next day. Not only was this news to her, but she ran across the story while on vacation in Paris. With all the frenzy, it was ironic that Dr. Walker never made it to the witness stand in the criminal trial.

For a less confident psychologist, it could have been a career-destroying experience that they may not have recovered from. The worst attack was a political cartoon that implied that Dr. Walker had sold her soul for big money. But Dr. Walker had enough experience in the public eye to do two strategic things. She chose not to alienate the media by banning all interviews or refusing to disseminate any information. She knew that getting the reporters mad and blocking their stories would create an additional backlash. So she chose to give several reporters small, succinct pieces of information. She also made the move to hire a public relations firm.

This second move began to create a balance with a new emphasis on stories about Dr. Walker's involvement in the trial. New stories described this as an opportunity for her to educate the public about the battered women's syndrome. The trashy and inaccurate headlines began to be replaced by others like, "O. J. Trial Troubles Women's 'Hero.'" Dr. Walker began to feel that she was able to control the media to some extent.

The final positive result was that Dr. Walker's expertise became known in wider circles, and it brought much more forensic work to her practice. In retrospect, she said, "It was impossible to really eliminate the distortions and attacks, but I tried to use the forum to educate people about the Battered Women's Syndrome" (Walker, 1998). Evidently, if you can live through the controversy, you can come out pretty good—a variation on the old truth, "that which doesn't kill you makes you stronger."

Newspapers

Although large, metropolitan papers are unlikely to accept an article you wrote (or want to write), they can be good sources of interview opportunities. For example, when the "big quake" of 1989 hit Northern California cities, it was certainly an emotional issue for residents. In San Diego, many residents had friends or family in the Bay area. Although San Diego has never had a major quake, it is possible, according to seismologists, so the Bay area earthquake tapped into an underlying fear among San Diegans. A psychologist could have called the local writer or editor covering the San Francisco quake for the San Diego *Union-Tribune,* and enlightened them on some of the special psychological issues facing the local community.

The Oklahoma City and the World Trade Center bombings and the string of 1997–99 teen killings in schools are other examples of catastrophes that stretched beyond the community immediately affected. How safe are we? How do we come to terms with the realization that we are ultimately not in control? What can we say to our children who are frightened? What causes kids to turn so violent? The existential questions are endless.

If you feel that commenting on this type of community pain is exploitation, don't do it. If you see an opportunity to move forward with caring, compassion, and a knowledge base that only a licensed clinician could bring, consider it your responsibility to "give psychology away."

MOBILIZING OUR PROFESSION

The leadership in our profession has seen the value of these opportunities and has begun to develop cohesive national projects. According to Dr. Dorothy Cantor, past President of the APA, "The Executive Board of Division 42 authorized a 3-month trial public education/rapid response media campaign" (Cantor, 1998, p. 1). Press releases on key national topics with psychological components were targeted to educate the public about the value of seeing an independent practitioner of psychology.

The pilot project was tied to the division's Brochure Project, which was started in 1997. As a joint divisional project, Division 42 (Independent Practice) and 29 (Psychotherapy) developed several specialty professional brochures that psychologists could purchase to project a professional and established image. Initial topic areas included breast cancer, separation and divorce, difficult behavior in children, aging, serious illness, and heart disease.

The ready-response pilot project looked for current events related to the topics of the Brochure Project. For example, the project targeted a Mother's Day story on parenting difficult children. Clinicians across the country were able to provide education to the public about the issue and also gave them a phone number they could call for further information.

Public Education Idea #1—Making Psychology Appeal to the Masses

An obvious goal in giving psychology away is to help people improve the quality of life of others. The more we share our expertise in our clinical offices, classrooms, and communities, the greater our impact. An initial goal is to get people to listen to us and value our expertise. Perhaps by looking at the following parallel example, we can see a fresh perspective on new approaches to achieve this goal.

In the *Parade* section of the Sunday edition of the San Diego *Union Tribune* ("Bike Helmet," 1998), an interesting article appeared about bike helmet safety for kids. When I read it, I saw some creative avenues that I could use to promote the profession of psychology to the consumer. The title lead-in on the front cover mentioned how "children's lives are saved with bike helmet use."

In Seattle, where bike helmets for kids are not mandatory, a doctor realized how important they were for children's safety in an accident. He cited some pretty impressive and convincing statistics as to how and why they help. According to the article, bike helmets produce a 65 to 80% reduction in head injuries caused by accidents. If you replace the words, "bike helmet safety" in the article with "the services of therapists," you can see some new ideas in how to educate the public about the value of our services.

Although only 2% of Seattle bicyclists wore helmets a decade ago; about 70% do today. The article went on to describe how it takes time and a lot of hard work to develop community support for a bike helmet campaign. But they did it astoundingly! For example, they (a) established a coalition of interested groups such as health-care providers, PTAs, civic groups, and so on. (We need to consider the demographics of who cares about people using our services.) (b) they got an underwriter to offset costs; (c) they developed materials, handouts, and tip sheets on how to use bike helmets; (d) they used local celebrities to wear a helmet and talk about the benefits of bike helmets.

We can play with some parallel ideas about how to reach the consumer with the value of what our services do for people. As a practice development trainer, I always enjoy looking at other industries' attempts to increase their market, or support their perspective. The "Got Milk" campaign instantly springs to mind (effective, indeed!).

Imagine what could happen if we gained the visibility that caught the public's eye like the bike helmet or milk campaign. Can you imagine how many people would learn about when and why they should see a therapist at certain challenging times in their lives? When we are successful at raising the awareness of this need in the public's eye, private practices will be flourishing everywhere.

Public Education Idea #2—Shaping Policy so Large Groups Use Our Services

Most consumers don't see psychology in the same league as bike helmets or milk. But, some of us can promote a concept with a personal twist, and that can create real progress!

So how *can* we make psychology appealing and accessible to the masses? In California there is some talk about requiring people who want to get married to have a set of mandatory premarital counseling sessions. The goal is to reduce divorce and keep families intact.

We could push to endorse this policy and share with the public (a) how and why divorce has risen so high in America, and (b) how kids are affected by divorce in emotional and economic ways. We could also set up a structure to make premarital counseling sessions easily available. If they are required, people will see that normal and healthy people see a therapist for really good reasons—they are in love, and, of course, they want to stay married. This will also erode the stereotype that one has to be "sick, crazy, mentally ill, etc." to see a therapist. We can meet these clients in a brief premarital counseling environment and also let them know that we are available throughout their relationship to address life challenges before they get out of hand.

The public may accept the value of premarital counseling if they have some succinct examples of how it can help. It would expose thousands of people who never would have sought out a psychologist to the reality of the value of what we do.

How many times have you had a client come to a first session with negative stereotypes about therapists or therapy and leave feeling glad they came? Once they see a positive direction for their problem, the value of therapy becomes obvious. This "exposure" alone could create better marriages, good role models for healthy relationship strategies, and more business. From the initial contact and intermittently, over their life span, therapy can do wonders.

The concept could be duplicated for key life transitions. For example, prenatal and childbirth classes are offered by most hospitals and even midwives. But they could include a psychotherapeutic component on being new parents, how a baby effects a marriage, infant emotional needs, and so on.

We could provide nationwide community services on divorce, death of a spouse, and other life markers. The initial workshop or session would be an opportunity to create mass public awareness of the value of our work.

Public Education Idea #3—Impacting Movies and Television Story Lines

In the summer of 1998, there were rumors in psychological circles that Tom Cruise and Nicole Kidman were going to do a movie about a couple who were both psychologists. Any clinician with connections with the movie/entertainment industry could be a valuable lead person in making an impact on this or any other Hollywood story. With the right contacts, one of us can get involved in script development to represent the "psychologist couple" in a light that portrays the integrity and value of the profession. We could contribute to client plot scenarios so the public could see therapy clients as normal, healthy people dealing with tough life stresses that many of the audience can face. They could also see some realistic scenarios of how people were benefiting from Tom and Nicole's care.

I attended the APA national convention in Los Angeles about two decades ago when Ed Asner spoke. He mentioned how we can be of service to the entertainment industry by helping them portray human emotions and human needs with more accurate depth than they can. He suggested that we do this in movies and television.

We should explore possibilities like the Cruise–Kidman movie because the best case payoff would be fantastic. Do you or someone you know have any movie or television contacts? Newer possibilities include our input in Oxygen, the new cable channel that will compete with Lifetime. With Oprah Winfrey as a developer of the concept, you can be sure there is room for our input.

Public Education Idea #4—Helping Corporations Be Responsible

Clinicians can also be of tremendous service when they link up with companies that have a moral or legal responsibility to convey an important message to the public. Anheuser-Busch, Inc., is one company that published the kind of national magazine ads that we can help develop. One full-page ad has a picture of a sweet-looking grade school girl near the top and a teenaged girl near the bottom (Anheuser-Busch, Inc., 1997). The copy was written on an old-fashioned typewriter to capture attention:

> This is the perfect age to talk to her about drinking.

The remainder of the ad said

> Whether your child is 8 or 18, there's one topic that's always timely to discuss: underage drinking. And talking about it can make a difference. According to kids themselves, their parents play the most influential role when it comes to making decisions about drinking.

> That's why Anheuser-Busch offers a free guide for parents called, "Family Talk about Drinking." Developed by authorities on child development and family counseling, this guide covers topics like peer pressure, self-esteem, and drinking and driving.

> So start the conversation now. Call 1-800-359-TALK. Your timing is perfect. (pp.)

Can you think of other companies and industries that also have this type of obligation? Is one related to your area of expertise? In November 1998, the U.S. government and the major tobacco companies reached an historic agreement. This unprecedented event will lead to a huge change in how tobacco companies can promote themselves to the American public. Billions of new dollars are targeted to health injuries caused by smoking and campaigns to curb teenage smoking. The opportunities of this massive and timely court decision are vast and perfect for our involvement. Working locally to develop programs is one way. By linking our state and national organizations, we can create a response to this new mandate by doing the following:

- teaching critical habit-cessation skills to people who are addicted and advocating the emotional benefits of quitting
- helping a major American industry retool its thinking and goals
- helping our youth let go of industry and peer pressure related to smoking
- working with people with serious smoking-related illnesses
- literally saving lives
- adding new clients to our practices
- adding one more opportunity to revitalize our profession.

Public Education Idea #5—Helping Companies Help People

Sometimes what will benefit a large company can also benefit us. Here is an example that New York psychologist, Dr. Noemi Balinth, is currently pursuing. Jergens Lotion is interested in reaching the middle-aged woman with a new skin product. They have hired her has a consultant to be a spokesperson on women and aging gracefully. As a sharp and ethical psychologist, Dr. Balinth, who is also the President of the New York State Psychological Association for the year 2000, reviewed her ethical guidelines and consulted with leaders in the APA as well as in her state to be sure of her boundaries.

She assisted Jergens in developing a national test poll that was sent to a thousand people. The information revealed what men and women say about self-esteem and attitudes about aging. At the time of this writing, the poll was being statistically analyzed. Dr. Balinth prepared to schedule a series of interviews with magazine editors, television appearances, and even professional conventions to discuss some of the interesting results. The topic of healthy aging is an area in which she feels that she has both experience and competency. She continues to review the literature and develop information to share with the public as a part of the Jergens funded project.

Public Education Idea #6—Screenings

Health screenings are excellent vehicles to spot people who need help while also giving psychology away. What kind of screenings can you do? Think of natural links to your profession. If you specialize in breast cancer, you may want to plan a countywide screening during October's National Breast Cancer Awareness Month. If you are the one who develops the screening, it will give you lots of community visibility and networking contacts. From contacting hospitals and doctors to participate, to coordinating press releases and securing media coverage, your event can have an excellent public service role and also save lives. Since the public education event takes place in October (during the third quarter of the year), start planning a series of seminars, workshops, and articles during the second quarter so you have plenty of lead time. You can also send out press releases to the media whenever you do *anything* related to breast cancer for the public.

Health Screening

The following events can help you plan your screening. You may need to call for exact dates.

February

National Eating Disorders Screening Day
Eating Disorders Awareness Week
Wise Health Consumer Month
American Heart Month
National Girls and Women in Sports Day

March

National Nutrition Month
Children and Healthcare Week

April

National Child Abuse Prevention Month
National Cancer Control Month
National Public Health Week
National Alcohol Screening Day

May

National Mental Health Awareness Month
National Anxiety Disorders Screening Day
National Suicide Awareness Week
National Running and Fitness Week
National Employee Health and Fitness Day
National Senior Health and Fitness Day
Older Americans Month

September

Prostate Cancer Awareness Month
National Cholesterol Education Month

EXERCISE: CONTACTING THE MEDIA

1. What public education or health screening ideas sound interesting to you? Write out a brief plan.

_____

_____

_____

_____

_____

_____

2. As with all practice development, get organized and do your homework before you reach out to the media. Start by creating a computer file or three-ring binder for your media work. Subdivide it into type of media, such as TV, radio, and newspaper. Then subdivide those into each station, such as your local ABC, CBS, and NBC news affiliates, your local newspapers (city, community, etc), and radio stations (name, news show, talk shows, etc). This will create a good visual picture of the amount of possible avenues to impact your community. Begin to study various media, formats, interviewers (reporters or hosts), and their slants or interviewing styles. Complete the following worksheets before you solicit any media interactions. They will help you plan your strategy and act quickly when a timely story presents itself.

The odds are that one media outlet may be interested at one time, and another story in the future may interest another outlet later. By compiling a database of all of your possible media contact options, you will be in a good position to choose who to contact at any particular time. Keep your up-to-date list in your practice binder.

TYPE OF MEDIA _____

NAME OF OUTLET _____

Name: _____

Address: _____

Phone: _____

Anchors/hosts/reporter = _____

   Their style & slant = _____

Producers = _____

   Name: _____

   Phone & Fax: _____

   E-mail: _____

   Their style & slant= _____

People you know or have access to through work, family, & friends: ____

_____

News shows = _____

   Contact Person(s): _____   _____

   Phone & Fax: _____

   E-Mail: _____

Talk Shows = _____

   Contact Person(s): _____   _____

   Phone & Fax: _____

   E-Mail: _____

Relevant Feature reporters _____

   (health, family, education, business, etc.) = _____

Stories they cover & their style & slant = _____

_____

   Contact Person(s): _____   _____

   Phone: _____

   Fax: _____

   E-Mail: _____

Comments:

_____

_____

_____

_____

_____

_____

_____

_____

_____

_____

_____

ASSIGNMENT: START GIVING PSYCHOLOGY AWAY

You do not have to actually contact the media to complete this assignment successfully. The purpose of the assignment is to take you through a dry run so you can understand the procedures and be familiar with them when the time to act is appropriate.

1. For three days this week, take your daily and national newspapers and cut out all of the articles that have relevance to psychology. Be sure to include your Sunday edition of the paper. Even if some of the stories are not within your scope of expertise, the assignment will stretch *you* to see opportunities for you to *give psychology away.*

2. Select the articles that have direct relevance to your clinical expertise. Put them in your media binder under a new "Current Ideas" tabbed section. Next, develop the information you would need to contact the media and explain your angle on the event. Create your background information and sound bites. Complete an information sheet to give to the media that summarizes your professional information as well as your name, credentials, specialty information, and how they can contact you.

3. Write a letter to the editor of your paper explaining a psychological angle on a relevant local or national story. Give psychology away and be sure that you mention in it that you are a licensed clinician in the community.

6

ANATOMY OF A SMALL BUSINESS

No two therapists, clinical specialties, or communities are the same. Blending the unique variables that describe *you* and your ideal practice is an evolving process that you will refine throughout your career. Glance at the following list of components to see some of the elements of practice development. Remember that all of them can be transformed into creative and enjoyable ideas that will put a unique stamp on your practice.

1. Your characteristics as a therapist
2. Stage of practice development (newly licensed, seasoned, just moved, etc.)
3. The changing therapy profession and its effects in your community
4. Your short- and long-range goals
5. Service and product research related to your targeted demographic region (what services will people pay money for?)
6. A competitive analysis (who else is doing it?) How are they unique, timely, or better?
7. A marketing strategy (developing an initial 1-year plan)
8. Administrative and organizational needs

9. Financial data and projections
10. Time frame for specific milestones
11. Goal-setting steps that are clear, specific, measurable, and realistic
12. Tracking progress and assessing results
13. Adjusting the plan for unexpected results, new information, or timely opportunities
14. Motivational blocks to success

WHY WRITE A BUSINESS PLAN?

A business plan is an opportunity to organize and refine your practice. The following information will give you a working knowledge of business planning. If you have never completed a business plan, it does not have to be a long or intimidating process.

There are several different reasons why you may want to develop a business plan. You may

1. Be fresh out of graduate school and wanting to start your first private practice
2. Be a seasoned therapist in a paid position but ready to begin your own practice
3. Be relocating to a new community or state
4. Be applying for a business or family loan to
    a. start your practice
    b. expand your practice
5. Want to review your current practice and set new goals
6. Be transitioning between being a solo practitioner and a group practice
7. Be selling or buying a practice

A New Graduate Starting Your First Practice

Welcome to the wonderful world of private practice! Although you are "book smart" and full of energy to begin your career, a business plan will help ground your goals in a well thought-out structure. For a new practitioner, your business plan will increase your chances for achieving business success. An advantage you have over someone with years of experience in the field is that you will not be retooling your existing practice and expectations. You can build a practice without the "resistance to change" that seasoned practitioners are more likely to face.

A Seasoned Therapist Beginning Your Own Practice

Unlike a newly licensed practitioner, you are confident and experienced in your clinical skills, mature in your understanding of networking, and clearer about your goals. Some of you may run into frustrations about how your "calling to help others" has been chopped down by the bottom-line business demands of managed care. A business plan gives you an intelligent head start to regain control of your career.

Relocating to a New Community or State

Even if you have had a thriving practice in another area, a new community is a new culture. It will have different patient needs, attitudes about psychotherapy, and a different business climate. Your business plan will help you sort through all of the details so you can begin your new practice with efficiency and effectiveness.

Applying for a Business or Family Loan

Will you need to apply for a business loan? If so, for how much and from whom? If you want a lender to give you money, your business plan can demonstrate to them that you are organized, goal oriented, and positioned for economic success. A financial institution will base their decision, in part, on your demonstration, that you have a thought-out plan that you can follow through. If your lender is a family member, it is even a stronger reason to ensure that the practice will flourish. Lending money to a family member or a friend can create an embarrassing or difficult strain on your relationship. A business plan makes practical sense.

Reviewing the State of Your Current Practice

The profession is changing, the times are changing, and so are you. A business plan can help you assimilate these changes into a plan that will keep your practice flourishing and keep you satisfied with the direction your career is taking. You may want to review your business plan periodically, similar to the times you review your practice-building binder.

Making the Transition from Sole Practitioner to Group Practice

Have you ever heard the joke that getting a group of therapists to agree on how to join together and build a practice is like herding cats? A business plan is an excellent vehicle for all principle parties to provide business input and consolidate ideas into comprehensive goals. It is an essential planning and management tool. A group practice has more complexities than most sole proprietorships. Be sure to know the business background and practice-building success of the main group partners. If you can't make it through the business plan, you are working with the wrong people. Remember that your success in a group depends on more than *your* individual clinical talent or business and marketing skills.

Selling or Buying a Practice

Your business plan can impress a potential buyer with the assets, value, and earning potential that you have built into your practice. It will increase their incentive to purchase it. The buyer is taking a risk in purchasing a practice that is based on another's professional reputation, referral sources, and past productivity. A business plan will show them all the things you have in place that they can walk right into. It adds comfort, reduces risk, and will show them exactly what they are paying for.

WHAT IS A BUSINESS PLAN?

When you write a business plan, the perspective is about profit and loss. Practitioners who are successful in building practices realize that a practice is not only about serving others; it is about achieving financial goals and dreams. It is about creating an effective vehicle that will pay your mortage, put food on the table for your family, put your kids though college, pay for travels, support you in retirement, and more. You owe it to yourself to create a business plan.

Throughout the plan, your primary goal should focus on *what people need and what makes them buy,* not on the services you provide or what you sell. You may have spent years in graduate school and have been trained to focus on intricate psychological issues. Practitioners are introspective people, but are rarely trained in business. Your business plan will help you focus your attention on clear, specific, and measurable goals.

HOW TO WRITE A BUSINESS PLAN

Here are some categories that can comprise your business plan. Complete the worksheet portion of this section to begin your business plan. Once started, you will begin to see its value.

Executive Summary

This section includes your goals and is tailored to the source who will read your business plan. If you are applying for a business loan, gear the content to the bank or lending institution. A good executive summary will encourage a bank to read on. If the plan is for your own benefit, your executive summary will help you gain a deeper yet succinct perspective on your practice, goals, and timelines. It will also help you spot gaps in your thinking. The summary is the real foundation of the plan. Keep it succinct and simple. The best time to complete the summary is *after* the rest of the plan is complete.

My Executive Summary

_____

_____

_____

_____

_____

_____

_____

Keys to Success

Different kinds of businesses have different keys to success. If you are starting a restaurant, location, atmosphere, and great-tasting food will often be the key. In psychotherapy or consulting, professional competence, recognition as an expert in the community, and creating comfort and rapport with clients are often keys to success.

My Keys to Success

_____

_____

_____

_____

_____

_____

_____

Objectives

List your goals here. Make them clear, specific, measurable, and realistic. Your goals must be tangible and trackable. Otherwise you will not be able to create a clear plan to build them and know when you have reached them. It is best to cover only three or four goals at a time, or you may find yourself getting scattered. You can break them down into subsets though. Here are some potential categories.

Clinical Specialties and Market Niches

For example, forensic evaluations, divorce counseling and executive coaching. (See pages 25 and 26 for a sample listing of the Top 125 Practice Specialties.) My practice specialties include:

_____

_____

_____

_____

_____

_____

_____

Client Statistics

How many clients do you want to see each month? How many "new" clients do you want to see? See Chapter 8 for further details.

Achieve Expert Status in The Community

You may think this objective is less tangible, but it can also be turned into measurable information. Perhaps another goal is to gain community visibility and expert status. You can track this by measuring the media exposure, speaking engagements, and locally published articles that you produce within the specified period of time.

Client Satisfaction

If you have a goal that encompasses client satisfaction, then you can use client satisfaction surveys as part of your assessment.

Operating Expenses

You can compile this information from software, such as Quicken, or by reviewing your business checkbook. Typical expenses are listed below. Write down your expenses per month for all relevant categories.

My Current or Projected Expenses

Cost	Item
$ _____	Business cards and stationery
$ _____	Professional library

Cost	Item
$ _____	Office rent
$ _____	Fax machine
$ _____	Internet/E-mail company
$ _____	Pager and voice mail or answering services
$ _____	Insurance (malpractice, disability, income protection, life, medical)
$ _____	Telephone—local and long distance
$ _____	Billing software or a billing company
$ _____	Photocopier
$ _____	Typewriter
$ _____	Office supplies
$ _____	Psychology supplies (testing materials, play therapy toys, etc.)
$ _____	Association dues
$ _____	Advertising
$ _____	Brochures
$ _____	_____
$ _____	_____
$ _____	_____

Break-Even Analysis

If your monthly operating expenses are $1000, your personal draw is $3,000, then you must bring in $4,000 a month to cover all expenses. Your yearly revenues must exceed $48,000. This is what you need to break even.

Now, let's look at the other side of the equation. If your goal is to see six clients per day at an average fee of $80 per hour, this $480 will generate $2,400 per week. This equals $115,299 per year, with a 48-week work year (1-month total vacation time). By subtracting the $48,000, your net income is estimated to be $67,000.

You can keep playing with the figures and adjusting them until the equation is balanced in what appears to be a "realistic" projection. List the figures that are desired and realistic for your practice.

Market Analysis

Focus initially on what the consumer needs rather than the services you have to sell. Look at your current clients. Demographic information such as breakdowns of age, gender, work and home zip codes, length of care, average fee per hour, and so on can be reviewed. Be sure to spend time looking at *who* you want to attract. This is particularly good to include in a business plan for a bank loan.

My Business Market Analysis

_____

_____

_____

_____

_____

_____

_____

Promotional Literature

Simply put, promotional literature gives people information about your services. From business cards to lengthy pamphlets about your programs, they provide substance and credibility to your practice. They are a practical way to describe what you do and also give people a sense of who you are and your philosophy of therapy (or testing, consulting, coaching, etc.) so that they can imagine working with you. This last mental step begins to build rapport, which gets them closer to calling you.

Promotional Literature I Plan to Develop

Ownership

Historically, the majority of clinical practices have been sole proprietorships. In more recent years, group practices, partnerships, or corporations have become more common. These hybrids of ownership affect the legal, accounting, tax, and liability status of your practice. If you are new to private practice and you are starting alone, you will probably call it a sole proprietorship. Contact an attorney or the small business administration in your community for more personal assistance. Be sure that you understand the compliance laws in your area as well as the opportunities that each "version" of running a business offers.

What type of business structure do you want to operate and why? What other professionals may be helpful in understanding the advantages and drawbacks of this choice for your particular business?

Office and Location

Describe the office location, square footage, and use of each room (receptionist area, waiting room, kitchen, your office, etc.). If the business plan is for the sale of your practice or a business loan, more detail here is needed. Location will be more important to some clinical specialties than others. Health psychology specialists may want to be near a hospital campus. People focusing on a cash practice may want to locate their office in a prestigious area of town.

Services

In this section, you will write how you are positioned in the market. Write a comparison of your services and those of other therapists providing similar services in your community. Include a comparative analysis, education, experience, fees, community visibility, expert status, and anything else that seems relevant. Include the relationship you have with key referral source groups and individuals. This information should describe why people would come to you rather than your competitors.

_____

_____

_____

_____

Future Services

Include plans for growth such as new office locations, associates, and services. These may be related to a specialty already in existence. For example, if you work in infertility psychotherapy and currently provide individuals and couples work, you may plan to learn the Harvard Mind/Body Medicine group intervention model that applies to infertility. Perhaps you want to learn a new therapy technique that you can use across several populations. You might decide to take a continuing education class in EMDR. Or you might start doing executive coaching, which keeps you away from managed care and can keep you working with high-functioning clientele.

Describe your long-term strategy, including timing and how it relates to each new service. A haphazard approach will most likely cost you time and money. A plan that is well thought out will allow you to build momentum that has a strong base to grow from.

My Future Services Include

_____

_____

_____

_____

_____

_____

List the things that are changing or may change with your specialties. For example, managed care has hit many clinical specialties hard but not others. If you work with character disorders and chronic patients, the insurance industry has probably hit your practice hard. However, if you specialize in infertility or executive coaching, you can concentrate on building a high percentage cash practice.

Also consider *the major industries* in your community and how they can be affected by the economy. If your practice resides in a tourist destination in Florida, hurricane damage or terrorist scares can affect vacationer's travel. This may not appear to affect you, but they may affect your clientele and their families. Although some problems can cause your client base to feel that they cannot afford therapy, other events can bring in more clients that are in psychological stress.

Also consider what the general population trends are in your community. Are people moving out or moving in? Is it full of young families or aging baby boomers? Is it a time of growth and prosperity or decline and economic recession? How long is the current economic cycle likely to continue? If you live in an aging community, perhaps a specialty in baby boomers or the life transition into older adulthood may be timely and even fun.

The goal is to look at your community's trends and anticipate what is needed. Then set up your specialty and get there before they do. With this strategy, you will become a leader in your community regarding your specialty. You will be a visible and well-seasoned professional before others join in. Your brochures, speaking engagements, and articles will pave the way for your community to understand the psychological issues involved and see the solutions in the perspective that *you* present.

What are the market trends in your community that relate to your clinical specialties? What other sources of this information can you review to refine your understanding?

_____

_____

_____

_____

_____

_____

_____

Buying Patterns and Competition

In this section explain how you think clients choose one therapist over another in your community. For some specialties referral sources may be key. For others, location and even parking can be a variable. Word of mouth and past clients referring their friends and family is an ideal ultimate goal because it takes less time and money to fill your caseload.

The secret may be visibility, perceived value, fees, reputation, image, or outcomes.

List Your Three Main Competitors

Describe the strengths and weaknesses of their practices. What is their business and marketing strategy? If you don't know, what are some ways to find out? What threats and opportunities do they present to your own practice? What collaborative projects can you pursue with them to reach more people?

Therapist or organization #1: _____

_____

_____

_____

_____

_____

Therapist or organization #2: _____

_____

_____

_____

_____

_____

Therapist or organization #3: _____

_____

_____

_____

_____

_____

Value-Added Comparisons

Another dimension of both perceived value and client choices in therapist can be affected by value-added dimensions. Convenience, parking, back door private exits, an initial complementary phone consultation, payment plans, use of credit cards, phone consultation when they are traveling, extended hours, and weekend work adds value to your practice. The issue of accessibility and convenience is important in today's fast-paced world. Once you establish what your value-added benefits are, find a good way to communicate them to clients and potential clients. Brochures can be a good place to mention this information. For example, the convenience or location, hours, and use of credit cards can be stated on your practice brochure.

What value-added components will you (or have you) developed for your practice?

_____

_____

_____

_____

_____

_____

_____

Promotions Strategy

This can be condensed to, How do you communicate to the public about the existence and value of your services? How do you communicate to your potential clients that you are out there? There are many ways to spread the word. Your strategy may include brochures, speaking engagements, working with the media, professional writing, newsletters, open houses, and other forms of marketing that are covered in chapters 4 and 5. Take another look at your community demographics, economic trends, and personal preferences. Check to see that what it takes to build a flourishing practice is truly reflected in your marketing plans. Your marketing plans must be thorough and fit _you_ in order to be effective.

What are your promotional plans for the coming year?

_____

_____

_____

_____

_____

_____

_____

Referral Sources

List the professions and specific people who can send you clients. If you do personal injury work, obvious professions would include attorneys and doctors. In this case, you would list the personal injury attorneys and medical personnel with whom you have (or will have) established referral relationships.

_____

_____

_____

_____

_____

_____

Strategic Alliances

This section includes collaborative projects with other people, groups, or organizations. For example, you may do a seminar on stress reduction at the local hospital or at a doctor's office. Have these alliances served you well? Has the hospital picked up your marketing costs by including your seminar in their mass mailing to the community? Perhaps they are letting you use a hospital group room for your 10-week class on stress reduction without charging you for the space.

It is often profitable to align yourself with an organization that is well known in your community. But make sure that your alliances are competent and ethical. The bad reputation and bad press that they can cultivate may rub off on your professional reputation.

List your current or projected strategic alliances. Assess the current and potential value and risks of each one.

_____

_____

_____

_____

_____

_____

_____

Your Competitive Edge

What makes you stand out? How is your practice different from others? Is it your great one-on-one rapport skills or your comfort with the media? How about your special gift in being able to reach into people's hearts and touch them through your writing or workshop exercises?

_____

_____

_____

_____

_____

_____

Specific Marketing Strategies for Each Specialty

Reaching rape survivors is very different from reaching people wanting a career change. Each specialty should have its own plan that takes into account _why_ a person needs your services and _how_ you can reach them. From fee structures to promotions, each specialty deserves a separate focus and strategy. The initial plan will be the most time consuming. Then developing the others will flow from the template that you create.

What are your specific marketing strategies for your clinical specialty? This will be a short version of your marketing plan designed in chapters 4 and 5.

_____

_____

_____

_____

_____

_____

Employees and Contract Service Professionals

In this section, list all the people behind the scenes that make your practice run and grow. Draw an organizational chart for a good visual impression of who does what. This will also help you spot gaps.

Perhaps you don't think you need other employees if your practice is new or small. The most successful business owners surround themselves with others to fill the gaps in their knowledge. Obviously, no therapist can know all of the legal, accounting, finance, and marketing aspects of practice development. You simply don't have the time or knowledge to do it all! Although it makes sense to keep your practice lean and mean, remember that you should not do all the tasks all of the time.

The psychotherapy industry as well as governmental and regulatory bodies often change the rules of doing business. Be sure that you note any national or state-related changes so you can incorporate them into your plan. Again, the assistance of other professionals can give you good, fast information so you don't have to feel overwhelmed in a sea of nebulous regulations.

From a business perspective, your goal is to use your time generating income (seeing clients or public speaking) or making money through other avenues that do not take your time (such as associate-generated income, book royalties, or therapy product sales). If you are not making money or generating income with your ideas, you are taking up valuable time. Perhaps a staff person can do your mass mailings, phone calls, or test scoring for you.

Create a chart of all the people that can assist your practice. Remember that you will not want to add all of these members to your team until each of them can directly or indirectly add strength, value, or revenue. Include people such as an accountant, secretarial person, practice-building consultant, marketing assistant, graphic designer, intern or psychological assistant, attorney, project manager, and so on.

Key Financial Indicators

Operating expenses and revenues (and subsets such as cash income and aging reports on your accounts receivable) are critical indicators of the health of your business. Each variable can change independently. Percentage changes over time provide useful information about the state of your practice and indicate problems as well as accomplishments. For example, growing revenues from $45,000 to $75,000 is a great sign. So is a 14% reduction in your operating costs. But a 35% increase in the time you wait for your money can spell trouble, despite the other two indicators.

List the status of your key financial indicators:

Last quarter	Year-to date	
$ _____	$ _____	Revenues
$ _____	$ _____	Operating expenses
_____	_____	Number of cash or credit card clients
_____	_____	Number of insurance clients

Aging Receivables—breakdown by number of months without payment

1 mo:$ _____ 2 mos.$ _____ 3 mos. $ _____ 6 mos.$ _____

Milestones

This is where a business becomes a real plan. In this section you will add the real results of your labor of love. Ideally, you should utilize business forms or software that allow you to assess your budget, actual expenses, projected revenues, net profit, and other relevant variables. Chapter 8 will provide further information.

_____

_____

_____

_____

_____

_____

_____

EXERCISE: DESIGN YOUR BUSINESS PLAN

Review the business plan components in this exercise and complete each section, except the final piece, the executive summary. Include as much information as you can. Don't get discouraged if it takes time to dig out the information to complete each section. Do as much as you can and know that you can continue to build in accurate information over time.

ASSIGNMENT: COMPLETE YOUR EXECUTIVE SUMMARY

After creating your business plan from the model presented in this chapter, write your executive summary. Be sure to tailor it the purpose of your plan: for your own use to assess and grow your practice, for a business plan, or for the sale of your practice.

7

STARTING A NEW OFFICE
OR RELOCATING

This chapter will cover special needs for the following:

- graduate students wanting to prepare for private practice
- newly licensed professionals
- established clinicians relocating or expanding to a new community

Welcome to private practice!

If you are about to embark on starting your first practice, congratulations! For those who have dabbled in private practice, now is a strategic time to develop sound plans so you can go into the 21st century poised for a successful and rewarding journey. If you are relocating your practice, you can take advantage of combining your existing experience with the need to organize and retool your new one to reflect the new ingredients needed in a practice today.

In any case, you are about to embark on an incredible adventure where you learn new levels of being your own boss, setting your own pace, and determining your lifestyle and economic destiny. If you like to sleep late and miss the morning rush hour traffic, you can create a schedule that will allow you to do so. If you enjoy a particular clinical specialty, you can dive in and work in the areas that stimulate you. You are about to shape your destiny, and it is an exciting time.

The American dream is all about going after your passion and working hard to build a fulfilling lifestyle that makes you proud. Like all small business owners, private practitioners are a special breed. Even if your new practice choice is employment in a group setting, much of the information here will be of use to you.

Many details and responsibilities will need attention. At times they can be intimidating or confusing if you are new to private practice. This chapter will provide information that can dispel some of your anxiety and fortify you with useful ideas to develop a solid beginning.

DIFFERENT WAYS TO BEGIN

• An apprentice—Depending on your state and type of license, being a psychological assistant or marriage, family, and child counselor (MFCC) intern can give you a practice model to observe, an opportunity to work with a mentor, an introduction into your community's referral network, and some initial income that can get you started.

• Going lean and mean—Subleasing in an existing therapist's office on an hourly or half-day plan is especially practical for therapists who are balancing student loan payments and start-up expenses when little capital is available.

• Employment in a group practice—A group practice offers an existing business structure. Many group practices have marketing plans in place and plenty of supervisory and collegial interactions. Some group practices are geared towards working with managed care clients. Find out about the clients the practice targets and be sure that you want this particular mix of payor source.

• Small business loans—Later in this chapter, you will learn how to write a sound business plan to secure financing.

• Second mortgages—If you own a home with extra equity, a second mortgage may give you start-up money or sustain you through the initial lean times.

• Teaching or working part-time in another setting—A steady paycheck is a must for many practitioners who have children or other responsibilities. A teaching position in a local college or working in a community mental health organization provides community contacts and the opportunity to transition into your new practice more easily.

A PRIMER FOR GRADUATE STUDENTS

How Will *You* Pay off Your Student Loans?

Graduate school has traditionally been a time of appreciation for the intellectual intricacies and artistic nature of psychotherapy. However, this perspective alone will fall short in paying off your loans. Student loans today can reach $100,000, making many students leery of entering private practice. With the reduced income and caseloads, you may fear that you will never make it in private practice. With no formal business training taught in graduate school until now, these concerns are common but not necessarily realistic (Kolt, 1997).

Extinction or Expansion?

The possibility exists that with such strong barriers to entry, the field of independent private practice may begin to die. There is no other vehicle for performing psychotherapy that allows the highest level of autonomy, confidentiality, and case control than independent practice. It would be a shame if you were to enter the field only to feel that your only career opportunities were limited to being employed by someone else for the majority of your career.

Today, it is essential that you receive adequate exposure to business concepts *before* you graduate, or you may simply not give private practice a try (Kolt, 1997). New, young blood is a critical ingredient for the health and stability of the profession of private practice. Here are some avenues that can help:

- Before you choose an internship or field placement setting, consider how it will help your training to enter private practice (Kolt, 1996a). Some settings will not provide exposure or transferable skills, but others will help you learn skills to conduct effective outreach, which you will need in your future private setting.
- Consider choosing a thesis or dissertation topic that will assist your private practice. My dissertation was on women and careers and it led to over 100 speaking engagements, business consulting opportunities, professional writing assignments in my community, television interviews, and a large private practice even before I was fully licensed. Pick a dissertation topic that you love and that is also timely and needed in your community. Your research will help you understand the literature and feel up-to-date and competent in your future specialty. This will give you more confidence and sense of purpose than most newly licensed professionals.
- Choose your clinical supervisors wisely. Some will be very knowledgeable and supportive in teaching you the ropes of private practice (Kolt, 1996b).
- Several consultants do national practice development workshops that provide excellent training. Work with your school to bring one in to do, at minimum, an all-day workshop. With this training,

you can start early to absorb information and set some goals to build your own practice.

- Supervised assistantships and internships can provide additional "hands-on" experiences. In this role you can grasp business concepts and observe the cycle of practice development in action. However, be sure to work under a licensed professional that has a thriving practice and can mentor you well.
- Join your professional association to learn more about life as a licensed professional. Many professional organizations have special interest groups that focus on your needs. The American Psychological Association of Graduate Student (APAGS) is a branch of the APA that provides an excellent knowledge base for graduate students. Division 42 of the APA is geared exclusively to independent practice issues.

If you are still in graduate school, this is a perfect time to get stimulated, educated, and inspired about the possibilities that private practice has to offer. By gaining a good perspective *now*, you can start to build a path that will help you get a practice started when you graduate.

Issues for the Newly Licensed

The newly licensed practitioner must keep the following issues in mind:

> Malpractice insurance
> Finding an office
> Combining steady pay and private practice
> Transitioning into private practice

RELOCATING AN EXISTING OFFICE

Remember that you have the advantages of being a seasoned professional. Here are some steps to making your move more efficient and strategic and less stressful.

Prior to Your Move

Prior to your move, do the following:

> Join the local psychotherapy professional associations and find a mentor or sponsor.
> Have community demographic information sent to you.
> Read the community's newspaper. Learn about their culture and their psychological needs.

Review the phone book for referral sources and ideas.

Send change-of-address cards to your malpractice insurance company, clients, insurance companies, and all professional mailings

Select your first choice specialty to develop and start building your plan. Remember that you do not need to physically *be there* to get yourself ready to open your doors.

Set your goal to have all of your marketing and business plans in place before you move.

Locate local or state internet professional groups that can assist you.

Moving Your Existing Practice

Some of your clients, particularly those with character disorders or those that are lower functioning, may be traumatized by a move from a familiar and safe office to an entirely new setting. There are other costs in relocating, such as getting new stationery, business cards, envelopes, brochures, and possibly a new phone number. It will take a lot of time to send change-of-address cards to all past clients, referral sources, and psychotherapy organizations with which you correspond. Consider the effects of losing touch with the following critical organization: the board that renews your license, your malpractice insurance company, provider panels, old clients who want to see you, referral sources, and so on. When you choose an office location, try to choose it for the long run so you can spend your time focusing on your practice.

BUILD IN PRACTICE SUCCESS FROM THE BEGINNING

There will be a lot of things to decide, do, and coordinate. The best approach is to *stay organized.* By this I mean *be clear about your goals.* Visualize your ideal practice and try to create it. Here are some initial tips:

1. Choose the best geographic location that fits with the clients you want to attract.

2. Choose an office setting in which you enjoy working and that your clients are likely to find pleasant.

3. Make sure you have adequate malpractice insurance before you see your first client.

4. Have a billing system or patient accounting system in place before you get busy.

5. Plan for the long run. Buy or rent good quality furniture and have an ample quantity of office supplies.

6. Decide on a secretary, an answering service, voice mail, or paging system to handle your new clients and other incoming calls.

7. Have basic practice management goals and plans in place so you know what you are building and can monitor your progress. (See chapter 8 for more details).

8. Take time for yourself so you are a refreshed and healthy person who can stay balanced and enjoy your work during this building phase.

9. Find a space with other mental health professionals if you enjoy collegial relationships and company.

10. Know that you may not have all the answers and that everything may not go exactly as you have planned. This is also the nature of business. But if you are committed to your goals over time, you will find yourself immersed in a fulfilling practice.

Where to Begin

Go over your ideal practice visualization in chapter 2. Now is the time to put life into those goals. The building blocks of your dreams can begin now. When you have clarity in your direction, you are ready to begin.

Finding the Right Office Space

Choosing an office setting in which to work is an important step. You will spend a lot of time there, so you'll want to feel comfortable. In some cases you may want to be close to your key referral sources. You will want to select an environment that your clients will find comfortable.

A practice that specializes in health-related issues like breast cancer or cardiac care would do well in a medical complex on the campus of a hospital. If you work with kids, check the demographics of your county and find an office in an area saturated with kids. If you provide executive coaching or career development services, a high-tech business setting with access to a conference room might be just right. If you are a "down-to-earth type," a wood building surrounded by beautiful trees could make you feel right at home. If you are outgoing and like a lot of stimulation, a large city environment or a group practice setting that has social opportunities may be right for you.

Your office space is really an extension of your identity. As they say in real estate sales, a critical issue is "location, location, location." Your personality and the demographics of your specialty will indicate where you should place your practice. Decide what fits both *you* and your practice profile. Go out and explore until you find it. What fits *you*?

Combine Your Specialty, Location, and Practice Strategies

Health Psychology

Locating your office on the campus of a major hospital is a good option. People seeing their doctor will find your office convenient, and it will have a "medical" impression so they may see working with you as an extension of their health care. You will also have closer contact with many health-care professionals that can lead to further referrals. This is particularly true if you enjoy educating the public (which includes medical people) about the value of psychotherapy. A hospital campus is a natural location for developing a newsletter for medical offices that covers stress questionnaires, changing bad habits like smoking, promoting healthy eating styles, and reducing stress.

Business Consulting and Career Development Clients

An executive suite is usually an entire floor or a wing of an office building that caters to multiple types of small businesses. Your "neighbors" on the floor may be software developers, attorneys, insurance salesmen, investment planners, and various breeds of entrepreneurs. This gives you access to a small business culture and not just a psychotherapy perspective. You may even find your business neighbors coming to you for goal-setting or stress-reduction sessions. Their clientele may also end up being your clients once they know how you help people. There is often a general secretarial staff that may answer your phone, do word processing for you, and send your mass mailings.

You often only pay for the services as you need them, so this environment can be a good way to start small and build at your own pace. Also, if you have a major workshop in the planning stages, the built-in business resources can provide the benefits of a support staff without your having to take the time and effort to advertise, hire, and train a person to work for you. You will probably have access to basic office equipment such as a copier and a fax machine, which is convenient, particularly if you do not have the capital to purchase such equipment now. Each service will be billed to you, so be careful that the convenience does not outweigh the expense. An executive suite is also an excellent option for a clinician who sees "nonpsychology" clients, because the clients will not feel as though they have to be dealing with emotional problems to be there. It will help your nonpsychology clientele to understand that they don't have a "problem" if they are coming in for career or coaching-related services.

Family Counseling and Child Therapy

With a specialty in family therapy, locating your office in a "family part of town" makes sense. Look at newer, developing communities that are not saturated with therapists and get involved in the schools. You can also offer in-service training for teachers on related topics, such as identifying and working with attention deficit hyperactivity disorder (ADHD), helping kids coping with divorce, and drugs and violence in schools.

Your waiting room should be "kid friendly" and have interactive toys for kids to occupy themselves with if they arrive early, or if you are seeing their parents during a session.

A Managed-Care-Free Practice

A direct-pay practice would fare best in an exclusive part of town. In part, of course, because you want to cater to the wealthy, but also because many people will assume that if you can afford the rent there, and you have the confidence to have an office there, you must be good. They will expect to pay more for your services. If you work with executives, high-profile, or successful people, they are likely to gravitate to these areas of town.

Bright, successful people can make great clients. They are articulate and motivated. They have the potential to make a large impact on their community or even the world. You have an opportunity to guide them in refining their life goals and realizing the full potential of their talents. But they can have problems like everyone else. They have marital challenges, family deaths, and job stresses; they deserve psychotherapy as much as anyone else. The demographics of some clinical specialties and clientele fit well into this environment. This list includes high-level business executives, entrepreneurs, couples coping with infertility, university professors, people with inherited wealth, local political leaders, sports figures, community media personalities, and members of the entertainment industry.

HOW TO FIND AN OFFICE

After you have narrowed down the location, you need to hit the pavement. Although you can look in your professional organization's classifieds, you may find many more office opportunities by looking in the phone book in the location you want and simply calling every mental health professional listed. Let them know the number of days you want and ask about parking, mix of clientele, and so on. Your goal can also be accomplished by driving or walking down the street to see and feel what the different office buildings are like. When you see a nice one that has a therapist, jot down the name and number and give them a call. The key is to compare different options so you begin to develop a feel for what things cost and what items are a high priority.

Other Office Selection Tips

1. Bring your spouse or close friend to see the final choices. They will know if it fits you and notice things that you may not have considered. You may have fallen in love with an office that is really not a good fit.

2. Sleep on it! Don't make a decision unless you have had time to get over your initial (good or bad) impression.

3. Read your lease carefully because it is a serious legal document. Consider all clauses as well as the length of the lease. Here are some issues to consider:

- Does it have adequate options to renew?
- Stated cost of living increases?
- Free parking for you and your clients?
- Include electricity and water?
- Adequate janitorial services?
- First right of refusal for additional office space?
- Give you the option to sublease to other therapists to share the rent?

4. Consider the economic and community climate. Is it currently a "landlord's market," where few spaces are available and rents are high? Is it a "tenant's market," where many vacancies exist so that you can negotiate for lower rent and more perks?

5. Go to the office at different times of the day and night. Is traffic noise or flow a problem during your work hours? Is the parking adequate during all office hours?

6. Ask other tenants on the floor if they are happy there.

7. Have the other tenants been there a long time, or does the building have a high turnover rate? This could indicate an unpleasant landlord or hidden, not immediately obvious problems. A professional practice should be in a setting with high professionalism and low tenant turnover.

8. Find out if the landlord is considering selling the building. A change of ownership could create problems or, at the very least, introduce an unknown variable in your business equation.

After You Have an Office

Getting your office is a big step. You will probably feel both proud and tired after you have finally moved in. The next step is to start building the foundation of your practice. This will be an opportunity to execute procedures that fulfill the mission and business plan you have in mind. If you stay organized and take one step at a time, you can build a professional practice image, good relationships with referral sources, and you will be headed towards your practice goals. Remember that the initial setup phase is a long-term and evolving process. Look at your role models and consolidate the best of what you see with your unique professional goals.

OFFICE MANAGEMENT

Running an efficient, ethical, and successful office is a simple yet complex task. It is simple because all of the steps can be learned fairly easily. It is complex because there are many different dimensions of running a practice. The following information will cover possible office management issues. Remember that you can modify many things to fit your unique personality and needs.

Hiring Staff

Some practitioners have no office support staff, whereas others have several. If you have a large practice or a managed care-based practice, you may need help to process your paperwork so you can concentrate more on doing income-producing work. Many therapists who bypass managed care and see, primarily, people who pay their fee at each visit, find that little support is needed.

At times, however, many marketing projects will run more efficiently with intermittent help. Examples include assembling a mailing list database, distributing a mailer, or doing a large-scale speaking engagement.

Support staff can be hired by placing a classified ad in the newspaper or your professional association newsletter. Excellent, inexpensive help with special projects can often be found by talking to your local graduate school and having them post your job information for psychology students. Graduate students make hard-working and reliable assistants because they are interested in the running of a practice and will work hard yet inexpensively.

Writing Their Job Description

Training is important to building a good working relationship and running an efficient practice. A thoroughly written job description for your employee will serve to clarify their role and responsibilities. It can also be their responsibility to update the description on a regular basis as your practice and the position evolves. If you ever need to hire someone new, all of the updates will reduce your training time considerably. Here are some points to cover in the written description:

Pay and raises
Marketing projects
Billing and record keeping
Specialty projects
Monitoring contracts
Work schedule
Holiday and sick pay policies

Confidentiality
Updating their job description
Procedures for termination or resignation

Office Policies

When you establish a practice, you want to create a working environment that projects professionalism, caring, and comfort. Each practitioner needs to decide what policies they want to create that reflect their unique personality and needs and also fit in with the culture of their community. Here are some points to consider:

1. *Office hours and days*—The more flexibility you offer, the more clients you will attract.

2. *Using voice mail, answering services, and pagers*—Voice mail lets you hear the time and exact message of your callers. A service can screen your calls and find you. A pager is an inexpensive way to be reachable in emergencies.

3. *Billing procedures*—You must be comfortable with psychology billing software to use it effectively. If you have support staff, and they leave suddenly, you must be able to follow the current stage of billing cycle and continue the process. This unexpected burden adds to your workload until you can find and train new help. However, software gives you the most efficient, flexible, thorough informational system for the financial aspect of your practice. Your other option is to have a billing company or in-house person handle your work.

4. *Methods of payment*—You can choose to wait for insurance payments or have clients pay you the fee at each visit, as long as you are not working with managed care companies that won't let you do this. The best options are to accept checks or credit card payment on the day of service to keep your cash flow simple and up-to-date.

5. *Malpractice insurance*—The amount and type of coverage may depend on the degree of pathology in your typical caseload. Managed care companies require more coverage. Group practices will require you to have coverage in case your whole clinic is sued.

6. *Extra or emergency cash on hand*—As with any small business, you need to have reserves for slow periods and the possibility of being out of work due to an illness or family crisis. Usually six months' worth is a safe amount to have readily available.

7. *Disability and income protection*—This insurance is necessary. More people will become disabled at some point during their career than they expect. If you can't work, you will still have your same practice and personal bills.

8. *Purchasing versus building a new practice*—When you purchase a practice, you are buying an existing caseload, as well as the goodwill and

assets that the practice has already generated (*Psychotherapy Finances,* page 4, Vol. 14, No. 5 1987). Take the time to research what to look for, making certain to examine carefully the risks and rewards of stepping into an established practice. Building your own practice takes more time, but it will reflect your unique personality, preferences, and clinical interests.

THE AGE OF INFOMATICS

Twenty years ago, many private practitioners had an office, an answering service, and sometimes a secretary. Today, we have computers, printers, fax machines, voice mail, cell phones, e-mail, and the list goes on. In this age of fast information transmittal, you will want to get up to speed on at least some of these resources. Some will make you look more professional, which can enhance your credibility. Others will simply save time and money. For some therapists, certain resources feel fad-like and unnecessary. I suggest that you start slow, purchase what you can afford, and master what you can *without* compromising the timelines of your other practice goals.

Computers

If you are not computer literate, start learning now! Computers will save you time and make many things you do more efficient and professional. Getting familiar with *a word-processing program* like Word or WordPerfect is the best place to begin. If you want to send out many letters to potential referral sources, a word processor can do it quickly. If you want to create handouts for your seminar and modify them a year from now, your changes will take little time. A word processor is a must if you plan to write a book. In fact, new technology is now available that actually writes while you speak.

Billing software can save time and increase your practice management capabilities. It is often more expensive because it's industry specific and cannot take advantage of cost reductions in large consumer scale sales. *Database software* such as Microsoft's Excel or Access can help you analyze your financial picture and marketing projects so you can see the real results of your efforts and plans. With this information, you can refine your practice goals and navigate more clearly towards success. *Presentation software,* such as the popular and easy-to-use PowerPoint, can help you create impressive overheads or slides for your seminars and workshops.

Apple is generally easier to use, but IBM-compatible software has more business applications. The main point, though, is to start now and get comfortable with these tools over time. Then you will see the vast advantages to your use of time, ability to stay organized, and ability to project a professional image in your work. If four-year-olds can use computers, so can you!

The Internet

The internet provides access to a vast array of information without your having to leave your home or office. You can tap into medical libraries for the latest research in your specialty. You can find groups of people interested in virtually any topic. Listservs are great groups to join if you want to "talk" to others with similar interests. For example, APA members who join Division 42 (Independent Practice) can join the Division 42 listserv and just "listen" quietly or participate in intense or pivotal conversations on many issues. A sampling for spring of 1998 included the following topics: our responsibility to educate the public about how to handle the epidemic of teen murders across the country; and President Clinton and sexual addiction; key health-care reform that affects psychology. Other emerging uses of the internet include taking continuing education classes for relicensure. Check your state regulative body to see if this option is available to you.

E-mail is a subset of what the internet has to offer. With an E-mail address, you can communicate with people on the other side of the country (or the world) instantly. Instead of spending the money on a phone call or waiting until people in another time zone are awake, you can plan national convention seminars you are jointly conducting and discuss professional articles that you coauthor. It is a valuable and practical tool for busy people.

Beware, however, of the addictive quality that the internet can have for some people. Track the amount of time spent talking or surfing the net so you don't shortchange your personal or career priorities. If you do experience a bit of overuse on the internet, you will appreciate the legitimate value of internet addiction counseling. Look at the literature already available. It can make an interesting clinical specialty.

Some therapists are pioneering telehealth *therapy* which may take place over the telephone or the internet. At the point of this writing, it is not established as a valid and ethical domain. The quality of the practitioner-patient relationship in telehealth practice when compared to face-to-face consultation is not well researched or understood (Maheu, 1999). It is sighted as good for rural or isolated communities, or people who are housebound or travel frequently. Be careful, though. An initial evaluation requires a face-to-face meeting with any client. A therapeutic relationship demands that you hear and see how your client is doing in many nonverbal ways. Still, there have been several internet therapists popping up, including one that was featured on the front page of America Online.

According to APA President-Elect, Patrick DeLeon, telehealth will forge forward, with or without us (1999). Ethical therapists are now adding video sessions to help compensate for the lack of face-to-face contact. With the field in its infancy, it is important to proceed with caution.

Telehealth

Here are some issues to consider before venturing into this virtually untapped practice domain:

• Because the internet spans states and even countries, be sure to obtain a professional license to cover all the states in which you practice telehealth therapy.

• Obtain malpractice insurance for the specific duties that you will be doing and discuss the issue with your malpractice company.

• The internet can tend to rush a therapeutic relationship along. Be sure to gather a thorough history on your client as well as information regarding precipitating events to therapy, symptoms, diagnostic indicators, sociocultural contexts, information on previous treatment, diagnosis, treatment planning, and any supervision on consultation services you have sought on the case.

• Confidentiality is unique in telehealth because using a computer or telephone can present several possible breaches that you may not anticipate. Computer storage and retrieval breaches may occur on either end of the therapeutic relationship. Perhaps family members may find sensitive information or an e-mail is sent to the wrong address. Hard copies of e-mail or a video session may fall into the wrong hands. Special policy statements should be signed and returned to assist the potential client in understanding the unique nature of disclosing information to telehealth therapists.

• Correspond with your local, state and national professional organizations to get a clearer understanding of the ethics, validity of care and risk management issues as the field continues to evolve.

Confidentiality

The best rule of thumb is never to assume that anything you type into a computer is 100% confidential. Guard your computer carefully. Does anyone else use your computer? Could you lose a disk with client information on it? Your E-mail may also not be completely private. If someone really wants to get into your files, the likelihood is that they can. Even though few hackers or eavesdroppers may exist, the ethical and legal responsibility of security and safety issues lies with you.

Backing up Your Computer

The flexibility, efficiency, and storage of data by computers is unmatched. Because of this, we tend to rely on them. But what would you do if your hard drive crashed and you lost all of your data? If you really think about what that could mean, it clearly spells trouble.

Buying a backup system is a must for any business computer. Look into the latest technology before you make a purchase. Your options are getting more efficient as well as less expensive over time.

Viruses

A computer virus can enter your system, your friend's floppy disk, when downloading something off the internet, or even through your E-mail. Gone undetected, viruses can destroy both your valuable documents or even damage your operating system. You may not even know that you have a virus for a long time. However, they can do silent or very obvious damage. Virus protection software is a necessity in today's world. Every day, new computer viruses are created and spread. Check out *PC Magazine's* latest editor's choice before you buy. McAfee's VirusScan is a current favorite. The manufacturer suggests that you should not only purchase the software, but go to their website and download their new versions every month.

EXERCISE: PREPARING FOR PRIVATE PRACTICE WHILE YOU ARE IN GRADUATE SCHOOL

This is an excellent time to take a clear look at what your *ideal career* is and what you can be doing *now* to get there. This can set the stage for building a consistent direction in your decision making about everything from your dissertation topic to your postdoctoral internship. Remember to integrate your interests with (a) the new realities of the health-care industry and (b) the population you want to work with.

Sit down for a few minutes; take a piece of paper and take some time to reflect. Close your eyes and imagine that you have graduated and you received your license 10 years ago. You enjoy your private practice. Here are some questions to address:

1. How did your (a) internships, (b) supervisors, (c) thesis or dissertation increase your knowledge and expertise to develop a successful private practice?

2. What clinical population to do enjoy working with most?

3. Where did you receive your practice-building training? How did it help you?

4. Who were your mentors in school and as a newly licensed professional? How did you find them? What are the best things they taught you about psychotherapy and private practice?

5. How can managed care affect your career?

6. What opportunities exist for you to take on leadership roles in shaping the profession of private practice?

EXERCISE: RELOCATING YOUR EXISTING PRACTICE

Check below when completed.

___ 1. Get subscriptions to the local newspaper in your new town.

___ 2. Complete membership applications for your new, local professional organization.

___ 3. Call the president of this organization and find someone to mentor you into the community.

___ 4. List three new specialties that interest you that are timely and needed in your new community.

___ 5. Establish a tentative moving date.

___ 6. Write a brief description of your tentative business and marketing plan, including estimated timelines.

ASSIGNMENT: CHOOSING YOUR IDEAL OFFICE LOCATION

Choosing an office is also a very important business decision. There are legal, financial, and strategic decisions you will need to make to secure the right place that can affect your practice. Here is a worksheet to help you weigh your choices.

Rate the importance of the following using the scale below:

1 = Very important
2 = You would like it
3 = Nice but not really necessary

___ The building's aesthetic is pleasing to you.

___ It has a nice-looking and feeling waiting room

___ Quiet—no outside traffic or inside noise heard while in your office or waiting room

___ Dual entrance—if you are late you can rush in without your clients knowing it. If you have a high-profile client, they can come and go without concern.

___ Neat, clean, and well-kept building

___ Your office has a window

___ Your waiting room has a window

___ There is enough space in your office for a desk, sofa, chairs, file cabinet, and/or other essentials you will use.

___ The waiting room furnishings, if provided, are attractive, comfortable, and fit your style.

___ There is enough storage space for terminated files, testing equipment, business management files, fax or copy machines, your computer, etc.

___ The lease gives you security that you will not have to be uprooted, but it does not lock you in for a period longer than you can afford.

___ It is near convenient places such as your bank, copy place, business supply stores, your home, etc.

___ There are friendly, enjoyable colleagues in your suite or nearby.

___ It is a safe location for clients to get to and for you to be alone in at night.

___ There is ample parking for you and your clients at little or no cost.

___ The building or suite has signage with your name and occupation on it.

___ If it is not on the first floor, there is an elevator beside a stairwell to reach your office.

___ There is a reflective place for clients to go to (a roof view of the city, a park bench and a tree, etc.) before or after their session to relax and process the session.

___ Ease to get to from most parts of town—either near freeway interchanges, trains, buses, etc.

___ A commonly known location such as in a recognizable building, or on a well-known street.

___ The cost is under $ _____

___ It has a kitchen.

___ It has a bathroom inside the suite.

___ It is conveniently located for your current client base and the new clients that you want to attract.

Summarize the most important variables in selecting your new office:

_____

_____

_____

_____

_____

_____

PRACTICE MANAGEMENT TRACKING AND STATISTICS

THE VALUE OF MEASURING THE PROGRESS TOWARD YOUR GOALS

For many therapists, their practice is more than their livelihood; it's an opportunity to pursue their calling and their dream. But you can no longer expect to be exclusively idealistic and stay in business. Today, you must integrate that valid purpose with the ability to feed your family and pay your mortgage. If you are serious about private practice, you must adopt new business tools and strategies to analyze and build your practice.

Many therapists find practice management forms and tracking practice statistics to be foreign at the least, and intimidating or distasteful at worst. These concepts are not taught in graduate school (unless your degree was an MBA). But they give you the opportunity to stay in the field the way you want to—with a thriving practice of which you are in control. They will help you see what is working, what is not, and why. You can also increase your cash practice referrals with the knowledge these forms give you. If you choose, you will have the power and control to navigate your practice away from managed care and towards the increased autonomy, income, and career satisfaction that a direct-pay practice can bring. You can also use the data to make your managed care practice larger.

If you feel that the time and effort to create forms to track your practice figures will take too much time, spend the money to purchase them. They will more than pay for themselves, so why try to reinvent the wheel?

Most importantly:

- You will have the tools and technology that can turn your practice goals and dreams into factual data. You will know when you are on the right track to achieve them!
- This will give you a feeling of exhilaration, as well as a sense of control over your life and your practice.

Key Variables: New Clients, Income, Expenses, Draws, and Marketing

Adopt a simple system that makes it easy to record new data and see your trends. Organized, accessible, and cumulative records are important in effective practice management. A three-ring binder system will allow you to accumulate, track, and review your key practice variables. The month-end and year-end analysis will give you invaluable information.

Here is a sample of tab titles for each section:

1. To-do information
2. New client referrals
3. Monthly practice summaries, including:

   - Weekly client summaries
   - Profit and loss statement (easily done with Quicken software)
   - Sample information from any marketing endeavors

4. Your business plan
5. Yearly practice summary (previous year)
6. Next year's goals

NEW CLIENT REFERRAL FORM

This is an important form to track essential information about all new clients that enter your practice (Kolt, 1996). Always have copies of the following form with you at your office, home, and anywhere you may be. You never know when a call will come in and a new client will want to see you.

Fill out the form during your first contact over the telephone with your potential new client. Even if they are just therapist shopping or if they are a "no-show," it is useful to keep their information. A small percentage of scheduled new clients will never come. If your statistics are high, you had better find out why.

Date of Referral

The date at the top will help you track when a large flux of new business comes in and when you hit dry spells. When you get many referrals, you can determine what precedes them and increase your efforts in those areas. Perhaps you have been meeting with a series of referral sources, or an article you wrote was recently published.

You may find that your practice has a slow period in the summer or during the December holiday season. Understanding, predicting, and even developing corrective action prior to slow cycles can bring your statistics back up the following year.

Type of Care

Here is an opportunity to see if you are getting referrals for your targeted specialties as well as your marketing. Again, this will help guide and refine your plans for growth and success. The more you understand what the public and referral sources respond to, the more you can tailor your plans.

Referred by

Two types of referrals are useful to track: people and events.

A Person

Do you know who your best referral sources are? They may be the ones who refer the most clients to you each month or the ones who refer clients that pay the full fee at each session. Perhaps they are sources who simply refer the people you enjoy working with most. By comparing the referral source information with the fee information, you will get a good picture of which referral sources, ads, workshops, or other marketing efforts bring in the most income. Be sure to call your referral source or send a thank-you note after each referral.

An Event

Keep in mind that some of your marketing projects may not bring people in right away. Your new client referral form (Figure 8.1) is designed to capture this key data so over time, you will be able to determine the value of each event. Perhaps you have just presented a seminar in your community, mailed a newsletter to referral sources, or given a television news interview. You will be able to track how long it takes for your referrals to come in terms of quantity and source of marketing.

NEW CLIENT REFERRAL FORM

Date _____

1.   Name(s) _____   Phone(H) _____

       _____

       Address _____

       _____

2.   Type of Care

                ☐ individual   ☐ couples

                ☐ family   ☐ group

                ☐ workshop/seminar   ☐ other

3.   Referred By _____

       Address _____

       _____

       _____

       ☐ Contacted By Phone Or Letter On _____

4.   Insurance Company _____ Phone No. _____

       Type of Insurance _____

       Insurance Payment $_____ + Cash $_____ = Total Fee $_____

5.   First Appointment/Status _____

6.   Important Dates and Information _____

7.   Clinical Issues _____

       _____

       _____

       _____

FIGURE 8.1   New client referral form.

Perhaps your work was featured in a local newspaper and you get an incredibly high number of calls. You can contact the reporter and let him or her know that you received many responses and the articles touched a chord in their readers. You could offer to do a follow-up article to address the specific areas of reader interest.

Insurance Information

This will be a key variable before you finalize any fee negotiations. It is best to know if their deductible is met, what the cash portion is, and the details of allowable treatment. After obtaining the information, you can set your fee with your client.

I suggest that you (or your assistant) call all insurance companies directly prior to the first visit for this information. You know the insurance industry and its ever-changing nuances better then your potential client. Handling this can help build trust and rapport. You have gone the extra mile. The benefit for you is accurate information before you set their fee.

First Appointment/Status

If an appointment is made within three days from the initial telephone contact, the no-show rate goes down. This section will help you track your success in this important area. If they did not schedule an appointment or if they call you after they return from a business trip, you will have a reminder of their status as a potential new client.

Important Dates

Since you will use this form during your initial telephone contact, these two sections will help you document pertinent information. Important dates may include court dates, divorce filing dates, a psychological evaluation deadline, or other timely information that you may need to act upon.

Clinical Issues

This section will provide rich information when you sit down and review your new clients statistics each month. Use the back of the form if you need to write more information.

WEEKLY PRACTICE SUMMARY

This is an excellent form to compile your detailed business statistics. On the appropriate day of the week, you can enter the client initials or name, and the fee that you expect to earn, in each cell. The form is set up to accommodate up to nine client hours per day.

You can also track other key information, such as the number of new clients per day and per week. "Nonclient" work time is particularly important because it is valuable time that is not spent generating income, being with your family, or enjoying other worthwhile pursuits. This time typically includes making phone calls, report writing, marketing project time, seminar preparation, ad design, and all of the large and small tasks that don't directly bring income into your practice.

Your projected revenue figures are the total fees that you've generated and expect to receive. This takes into account any discounted fees for sliding-scale clients or managed care contracts, as well as your full-fee cash clientele. The figures do not represent the money that you've received that day, but the money you are expecting to receive.

The comment section will record any unusual events that explain your statistics. If you are out on vacation or are on call for a referral service, your statistics will probably be affected.

Weekly Totals

The weekly practice summary (Figure 8.2) allows you to do a quick assessment at the end of each week of how your practice is doing. Your weekly totals will also be compiled and used to create information for your monthly practice management statistics.

Figure 8.3 shows an example of a therapist with a goal to make $150,000 a year in revenues. This breaks down to subgoals of $3,000 revenue a week with a 50-week work year. With $600 in revenue earned per day, their average fee for each six-client day is $100 per hour. You can see by the Monday and Tuesday figures, the fee per hour may vary, but the average fee remains $100 to maintain progress towards the yearly goal.

MONTHLY PRACTICE SUMMARY

This two-page form (Figure 8.4) will provide an excellent recap of how your practice is doing. The new client form and the weekly practice summary lead up to this form. These figures will help you evaluate an unlimited number of dimensions of how you are achieving your practice goals. It will also uncover reasons for less successful periods and projects. As a result, you will gain knowledge about your practice and how to grow it more efficiently and effectively.

By dividing your projected revenue by your total client hours, the monthly practice summary will also tell you what your average fee per hour is. This will tell you how hard you are working to earn your money. Your collection figures can be compared to your expenses to produce your net income figures. Business draws and business savings are also included because they are both important monthly expenditures your business must be able to produce to keep you going, and especially to keep you thriving.

Weekly Practice Summary

Week/Month _____

	Monday	Tuesday	Wednesday	Thursday	Friday	Saturday	Sunday	Weekly Totals
1.								
2.								
3.								
4.								
5.								
6.								
7.								
8.								
9.								
New Clients								
Total Client Hours								
Total Nonclient Hours								
Projected Revenue								

Comments: _____

FIGURE 8.2 Weekly practice summary.

Cardiac Sample

Weekly Practice Summary

Week/Month **August 1**

Notes:
1) Goal = $150,000/yr.
2) $3,000/wk @ 50 wks.
3) = $600/day
4) = $100 Average fee per client in a 6 hour workday

	Monday	Tuesday	Wednesday	Thursday	Friday	Saturday	Sunday	Weekly Totals
1.	LB $100	SG $125	→					
2.	BM $100	HP $100	→					
3.	SP $100	RB $75	→					
4.	DB $100	JH $125	→					
5.	HK $100	MS $75	→					
6.	WL $100	LT $100	→					
7.								
8.								
9.								
New Clients		1						1
Total Client Hours	6	6	6	6	6			30
Total Non Client Hours								
Projected Revenue	$600	$600	$600	$600	$600			$3,000.00

Comments:

FIGURE 8.3 Sample Weekly practice summary.

MONTHLY PRACTICE SUMMARY

MONTH _____

_____ NEW CLIENTS	$_____ COLLECTIONS	
_____ TOTAL CLIENT HOURS	$_____ EXPENSES	
_____ TOTAL NON-CLIENT HOURS WORKED	$_____ NET INCOME	
$_____ PROJECTED REVENUE	$_____ DRAW	
$_____ AVERAGE FEE/HOUR	$_____ BUSINESS SAVINGS	

LIST OF REFERRALS, REFERRAL SOURCES & FOLLOW-UP:

_____

_____

_____

_____

_____

_____

_____

_____

_____

ACCOMPLISHMENTS & FOLLOW-UP IDEAS:

_____

_____

_____

_____

_____

_____

_____

_____

FIGURE 8.4   Monthly practice summary.

The monthly practice summary lets you sit back and reflect on what has happened in the last month. Important referral information and key follow-up ideas will not be lost if you use the form. Your creativity and motivation will remain high when you list your accomplishments and capitalize on how to expand them while they are still fresh in your mind.

List challenges and solutions so you can address any conflicts or roadblocks that may have occurred during the month. You can also include

PROJECTS, MARKETING & ETC.:

_____
_____
_____
_____
_____
_____
_____
_____
_____
_____

CHALLENGES & SOLUTIONS:

_____
_____
_____
_____
_____
_____
_____
_____
_____
_____

OTHER COMMENTS:

_____
_____
_____
_____
_____
_____
_____
_____
_____
_____

FIGURE 8.4   (*Continued*)

information that will explain low statistics, such as a 2-week vacation or a sudden bout of the flu.

YEARLY PRACTICE SUMMARY

When you accumulate the 12 months of monthly practice summaries, you can then summarize the information on a yearly tracking form (Figure 8.5).

This will give you a snapshot of the last year at a glance. You will have enough data to see clear trends and clear results. In short, you will know how close you are to reaching the practice goals that you have set. Take the yearly summary on a retreat when you are alone, relaxed, and in a reflective state of mind. Look at each variable and analyze what has happened and why. Integrate this data into your practice development goals for the next year.

YEARLY PRACTICE SUMMARY

YEAR _____

_____ NEW CLIENTS	$_____ COLLECTIONS
_____ TOTAL CLIENT HOURS	$_____ EXPENSES
_____ TOTAL NON-CLIENT HOURS WORKED	$_____ NET INCOME
$_____ PROJECTED REVENUE	$_____ DRAW
$_____ AVERAGE FEE/HOUR	$_____ BUSINESS SAVINGS
_____	_____

LIST OF REFERRALS, REFERRAL SOURCES & FOLLOW-UP:

_____
_____
_____
_____
_____
_____
_____
_____
_____
_____
_____

ACCOMPLISHMENTS & FOLLOW-UP IDEAS:

_____
_____
_____
_____
_____
_____
_____
_____
_____
_____

FIGURE 8.5 Yearly practice summary.

PROJECTS, MARKETING & ETC.:

_____

_____

_____

_____

_____

_____

_____

CHALLENGES & SOLUTIONS:

_____

_____

_____

_____

_____

_____

_____

GOALS FOR THE NEXT YEAR:

_____

_____

_____

_____

_____

_____

_____

OTHER COMMENTS:

_____

_____

_____

_____

_____

_____

FIGURE 8.5 (*Continued*)

THE YEAR IN PERSPECTIVE

In the composite analysis of your year-in-review, write a narrative summary. Then revisit your annual business plan and compare your goals with your actual results. Before you complete your summary analysis, look at other information that could have helped or hindered your plans. For example, examine the following:

The Trends in Your Community

- Has the economy gotten better or worse?
- Has the population increased or are people leaving?
- Have new and robust businesses come in or have major employers undergone massive layoffs?
- Have economic issues or natural disasters (like a hurricane or an earthquake) hit your community?
- Have any events created a community crisis that resulted in excessive emotional pain (such as teen murders or suicides)?

Demographic trends that touched your practice:

- Are there more young people moving into the region, or are baby boomers a growing population?
- Are there new opportunities for your current specialties, or are other opportunities opening up that sound interesting to you?

Evaluate state of your profession:

- How is managed care affecting your community and your practice?
- Have your fees gone up or down?
- Has your nonincome-producing time increased or decreased? This can be due to a strong drive to market a new specialty, which is fine. It can also be due to more reports and paperwork in general.

How have you and your career needs or goals changed over the year?

- Are you more experienced and established in your career?
- Are you nearing retirement?
- Do you have extra resources from an unexpected source to invest in growing your practice (such as book royalties or an inheritance)?
- Do you have new financial responsibilities (such as the purchase of a new home or college tuition for a child)?

YOUR FINAL PERSPECTIVE

Incorporate all of the above information into a final written summary for the year.[1] Put your summary page at the front of your binder where

---

[1] All practice management forms were originally published in Kolt (1996b) the *Business and marketing training manual,* (3rd ed.). They can be purchased in a 25-form package called, *25 Essential Forms for an Efficient, Professional, and Ethical Practice.* Contact Kolt Consulting at 858-456-2005.

it will be accessible to you when you are ready to begin your plan for the next year.

EXERCISE: MAKING GOALS CLEAR AND MEASURABLE

Complete a sample *ideal* weekly practice summary (Figure 8.3). This will help you understand how to use the form and it will help you refine your practice goals.

ASSIGNMENT: UNDERSTANDING YOUR PRACTICE AT A GLANCE

Complete a monthly practice summary form (Figure 8.4). This will help you understand how to use the form. It will also help you refine your practice goals as well as understand and anticipate the many challenges and successes that can occur as you grow your practice.

9

MOTIVATIONAL BLOCKS TO PRACTICE SUCCESS

You gain strength, courage and confidence by every experience in which you stop to look fear in the face. . . . You must do the thing you think you cannot do.

—*Eleanor Roosevelt*

HOW HIGH WOULD YOU DREAM . . . IF YOU KNEW YOU WOULDN'T FAIL?

The Courage to Create

Growing your practice takes courage. Some people feel it costs too much in terms of time, effort and money. But the two biggest expenses in building your practice are the commitment to grow personally and the ability to find creative ways to serve more people. When you are committed to practice growth, you allow your creativity to thrive. You combine your unique personality and specialty, and build a plan to make your mark in your community or even the world.

For many people, it is safer to dabble than to create. Creativity is too risky. This may be true for many unsuccessful practice builders. I believe that in order to reach your full practice potential, you must journey to the center of the self. You must trust yourself. But without courage, trusting yourself is very hard. Your challenge is to trust that your courage and commitment to your livelihood will lead you to exactly where you are supposed to be.

What Is Holding You Back?

- Old habits
- Excuses
- Fear
- Poor self-confidence
- Lack of vision
- Lack of time

Like the deer standing frozen in the middle of the road, the paralysis you may experience from burdens of managed care, lack of time, and the need to step out of your comfort zone can stop your practice dead in its tracks. You must begin a new level of practicing what you tell your clients to do during their own life crises and transitions. You must begin to walk your talk at a new level (Kolt, 1996).

Get mobilized and armed with the necessary ingredients to take your practice to the next level. Reawaken goals and dreams about why you chose to be a therapist. Let go of mental blocks or feelings of being overwhelmed. Accept that there is a way to build a thriving practice without compromising your ethics, your integrity, or your love of your work. If you believe this, things will begin to change.

WHO ARE WE?

In a sea of tens of thousands of therapists, these rocky times can make us feel as though we are in a life raft with a huge storm approaching. We come in all ages, sizes, cultural backgrounds, licenses, specializations and practice dreams.

We are 300,00 strong. In 1998, *Psychotherapy Finances*[1] published the following statistics:

Psychologists, 65,525
Social workers, 106,428
Marriage, Family, & Child Counselors, 46,924
Licensed Professional Counselors, 31,756
Pastoral Counselors, 2,400
Sex therapists, 1,800
Additional unspecified therapists, 60,419

But many times, we can feel alone, discouraged, angry, and even afraid. Being immobilized is a state of mind. Of course, we need to listen to ourselves when we teach our clients to breathe and get centered though a

---

[1] Statistics available from http://www.psyfin.com/lists or call 1/800-518-4492.

crisis. Our profession's crisis does not have to be ours. If other people in large and small towns can build thriving practices today, so can you. And it can be done with integrity and a commitment to service. It can also give you a livelihood that can support you for a lifetime. And it can give us a feeling of accomplishment and success. It is up to you if you want to make it happen.

PRACTICES ACROSS THE COUNTRY ARE HURTING

Across the country, you will hear the same concerns. Whether therapists work in a small town or large metropolitan area, new and even experienced therapists are deeply concerned about the state of their livelihoods. Therapists are consistently making less money, putting in more time, loosing patient control, and feeling less autonomous. Either directly or indirectly, managed care and other forces have contributed to this problem. Some feel that they may need to sell out by adapting to managed care tactics that seem to compromise quality of care and patient control.

There is no question about it. Private practice has changed considerably in the last several years. People used to be drawn to the field because they cared about helping others, and it felt gratifying to help them. It was interesting work that provided therapists with a peephole into the hearts and lives of so many people from so many walks of life. Therapists could see the world through others' eyes—and gain the wisdom and perspective that the profession provided. It was also a profession with a lot of autonomy, satisfaction, income, and flexibility.

Today, therapists can still reap these rewards. They can still enjoy their profession. Coupled with sound business and marketing skills, clinicians can maintain the benefits that many now only dream of.

REAL-LIFE EXAMPLES

What stops therapists from building their practices? Here are some scenarios from my practice-building client base:

1. "I was working at a community agency for almost no money and I was trying to make the transition to private practice. The whole world of it intimidated me. *Own a business . . . me?* I wanted to make more money and have more autonomy. But I wasn't sure that the sacrifice to stretch so far would be worth it, or even possible."

2. "The classic signs of depression were there. I felt depressed, saw most of my colleagues feeling dismal about managed care, and the future seemed to be filled with only more managed care rules, fee cutbacks, and fewer referrals."

3. "I am just too busy to get a marketing plan going. Raising a family and working is too exhausting to put even more time in. All I can do is see my few clients, hope to get more, and just tread water until something else happens."

4. "I have a pattern of being scattered. I will start one marketing project and then see another opportunity. Then I will go off and pursue that one. Before long, I feel like I have been working hard and nothing really has been developed. No new clients have transpired. So I get discouraged."

5. "I thought it would be easy to build my practice because my dad is a prominent physician and I thought that I had an "in" in the medical community. It turned out that I got a lot of people saying 'good luck' and 'I'll keep my eye open for referrals to send your way' comments, but no referrals materialized. It sure didn't amount to enough to even pay my expenses, not to mention to make any money for myself to keep."

6. "I dreaded the idea of networking. I didn't really know what it meant, and as a shy person, I expected that I had to just grin and bear it because it was a necessary evil."

7. "It was a surprise to me that I felt incompetent because I had always viewed myself as a competent psychotherapist. The practice I built in my old city developed over a long time. Now that I have moved to a new community and I am starting over, I feel lost and intimidated by the process of turning my practice into a business."

8. "I'm admitting it now. My practice was going down and I was scared. I could hardly make the mortgage payment anymore. Not having enough money to pay for my kids' college tuition was a big, depressing blow. I was beginning to feel like a failure. I could see my self-esteem falling. All of a sudden, I felt too much like my clients, and I began to question whether I could really keep working in this field. I was becoming immobilized."

9. "Being just out of school, I wasn't too confident about my clinical skills yet. So to have to, all of a sudden, use the business skills of an MBA was just too much for me to imagine doing. Therefore, I took the easy way out and got a job with a paycheck, a large caseload, and someone else to tell me what I could do. In the back of my mind, I knew that someday I would have to figure out a way to build a private practice or I would begin to feel like am imposter."

10. "I was hostile and angry about managed care. They took the integrity out of the spirit work that I felt so honored to do. Out of necessity, I began to accept managed care clients and work by their rules, but it made me feel guilty. I was a good therapist, so why was I selling out? I knew I had to build a fee-for-service practice somehow."

11. "I love cognitive work and I have few problems with managed care. Short-term work makes sense to me. However, I still want to have more say in my cases. I feel like a kid having to ask for something I should

not have, when I corresponded with managed care companies. At times, I felt like I have a conflict of interest because how I wrote my report would determine if I made more or less money. I began to think about the strategy of communicating with managed care companies."

OVERCOMING RESISTANCE TO CHANGE

All industries change over time. When we see that we are not alone, we can begin to get past denying or complaining about the inevitable progress in our profession. Accountability is not a bad thing when it is done accurately and fairly. When our leaders use political clout and savvy to explain the case for psychotherapy, the true value can become understood. Our role, and it is a crucial one, is to believe in our profession and to tell people about the value of our craft. We see the profound results of therapy. We need to remain optimistic and confident that people will want to pay for our services *because they work.* Our own positive energy and belief in our profession can pull us forward into a flow or progression and not the stagnation of resistance, anger, or fear.

HOW HARD DO YOU TRY?

Mental toughness is not inherited, it is learned. With clear goals, focus, consistency, and self-discipline, you can build your practice bigger than you ever have before. Don't fall into the trap of going all out and expecting big results fast. You will quickly become discouraged. Approach practice building like you would prepare for a marathon instead of a sprint. Getting through graduate school took many years and hard work. So give your practice the necessary time and effort to really flourish. Today, business and clinical practice are not mutually exclusive. Make the shift in your mind and develop a new strategy, a new mindset, and mobilize yourself into action. Then enjoy the process and rewards of a practice that thrives!

The control is *within you* to get beyond your comfort zone and do new things to reach the people who need to see you. The control is within you to truthfully transform this stagnation in our profession into a personal state of creativity and giving through the best of your talents.

We can be the little kids with lemonade stands. We can break free of the constraints of managed care's and our own constraints. This chapter will provide you with a cornucopia of ideas on how to get focused, set your goals, overcome personal barriers, and follow through to achieve your practice success.

OPTIMIZING YOUR PRACTICE GROWTH

Gaining Perspective

Imagine that you are standing next to a huge wheel that is the same size as you are. It is made of thick metal and very heavy. Your goal is to get the wheel moving and build up momentum so it eventually will keep rolling with little effort.

Your first pushes do nothing. The wheel only begins to rock a little with all your effort pushing hard against it. Finally, you get it to roll a tiny bit. A few more pushes and it starts to rock backwards and forwards. After quite a bit of time, it actually starts to move forward. It rolls very slowly at first. You eventually succeed in making it go one full revolution.

A full cycle of marketing your practice can take a long time. If you are looking for a quick fix, you will not find it. One revolution may take as little as one year, but for many, it will often take 3–5 years. If you are already an established therapist in your community and are comfortable with large-scale projects, such as media work, you may see your practice expand more quickly. But a new therapist may need to put in much more initial time. The good news is that once you get it rolling consistently, most of your slight taps will keep it moving, with little effort on your part. Keeping up the commitment, energy, and hope is one of the biggest challenges that therapists face in being successful with marketing.

Time Management Skills

When you are building your practice with the goal of maintaining it for the long run, you will realize that it takes an incredible amount of vision and time. To set all the steps in motion, you will need to set aside periods of time to build and execute your plan. For many people, the flexible hours of private practice can create time difficulties, especially if you need to (or want to) put other priorities ahead of your practice building. It can be even tougher to stay on track if you split your time between your practice and other jobs, such as teaching, research, or a salaried position in another setting. Family joys and responsibilities also compete with your time. Remember that a major goal should be more quality time at home (Kolt, 1990). Let your practice development be a vehicle to take you there.

Set clear goals and work on them at regular scheduled times. Write them in your appointment book. Be sure to use a time management system or the project planner forms used in this book so you can stay on track.

Assessing Your Goal-Setting Skills

If you are not making satisfactory progress towards your goals, consider that one or more of the following may be occurring:

- You have not formed a clear practice vision and written it down.
- You have not broken it down into small subsets.
- You have too many goals.
- You have poorly developed time management skills.
- Your beliefs are not consistent with building your practice.
- You are setting unrealistic deadlines or work requirements to reach your goals.
- You have personal issues or responsibilities that are stopping you from reaching your goals.
- You procrastinate.
- You are immobilized by fear, anger, or something you have not resolved.
- You have difficulty accepting change.
- You spend too little time thinking and planning.

Comfort with Risk Taking

Without taking risks, technically excellent clinicians may find themselves out of business. Getting comfortable with change, learning new skills, and continuing to enjoy what you do for a living are skills that add up to an important combination of ingredients. With lots of fear and frustration out there in our ranks, you may need to put blinders on to stay true to your goals. Courage is not eliminating fear; it is managing the fear you have, and continuing to stay on course to achieve your predetermined goals.

Practice Development Consultants

Sometimes a practice consultant can serve as a coach or a mentor. If you are new to practice building or you are developing skills out of your range of experience, a consultant can be quite useful. He or she can help you refine your ideas, set clear and realistic goals, design tracking systems, and keep you motivated. Many consultants work on a national basis, and your consulting meetings can take place in person or over a long distance. Distant clients can effectively work via phone sessions with supporting fax, mail, and E-mail follow up. When choosing a practice consultant, be sure that you are getting a person that can really help. While no one can guarantee results, the following considerations will help you find a good practice consultant. A good consultant will do the following:

- Assess the developmental stage of your practice. This will help you see what developmental milestones you are immersed in. Newly licensed clinicians, seasoned professionals, and relocating therapists all have different challenges and needs (Lawless, 1995).
- Review your progression. By reviewing the number of new clients, income, marketing history, and other key variables, your

consultant can feed back to you a summary of your practice progression to date.

- Define your dream. The most fulfilled and successful small business owners have a dream. When you connect with the purpose of building your practice, you will find yourself in the flow of creativity and exponential growth. Your motivation will be high!
- Set realistic goals. By integrating your practice progression and your dream, you can set realistic goals that are ethical, consistent with your specialty and your unique personality, and aligned with your personal and career goals.
- Create a one-year business and marketing plan. Your new practice goals can be translated into a comprehensive plan. The foundation of each step in your practice development plan should be based on the previous step. As time progresses, you will develop momentum, increased visibility, and begin realizing your goals.
- Teach specific skills needed to reach your goals. You will be learning new skills, such as how to do effective networking, seminars, or workshops, writing for the public, organizing a health screening, working with the media, or countless other projects. Your consultant should be able to help you in all phases or give you resources of other people or organizations who can.
- Set up simple business tracking systems to assess your progress. All practice goals should be tied to easy-to-use measuring tools that provide regular feedback. The sooner you can see that you are on target or falling behind, the less effort will be required to adjust your course.
- Serve as a coach and mentor during the stress of stretching out of your comfort zone. Embracing change and taking risks is often accomplished with more ease and success when you have someone pacing you and believing in you (Kolt, 1983). A good practice consultant is a motivator. He or she is someone whom you respect and trust, as they encourage you to step into new levels of growth.
- Be ethical, professional, flexible, and allow you to set the pace. Although a consultant is not engaging in a psychotherapeutic relationship with you, he or she should be sensitive to your vulnerability and your trust in their expertise. Issues of confidentiality regarding your practice should also be defined and discussed. A written policy statement should be signed by both parties to clarify expectations, roles, goals, and the specific business arrangement.
- Familiar with the psychotherapy profession. A consultant must have a clear understanding of both the ethics and the sensitivity of the psychotherapy relationships and clientele. A consultant unfamiliar with health-care projects will have difficulty

understanding some of these issues. Even a consultant with an MBA or one who has worked with building dental or chiropractic practices may not have a clear understanding of the unique issues of the psychotherapy profession.

Remember that your consultant is helping you promote yourself in your community. You must feel that the vehicles you are developing are comfortable for you and meet your personal and professional ethical guidelines.

- Be flexible and allow you to set the pace. A practice consultant should respect you finances, time available for practice development projects, and timeline schedule to reach your goals. Your should feel free to hire a consultant for a comprehensive plan or on a per-project basis. A consultant should structure projects that respect your other personal and career commitments.
- Will make themselves obselete. Your consultant should help you create a practice-building template that you can continue to use and adapt on your own, for the rest of your career. After you go through one complete cycle of practice building with a clinical specialty, you will absorb the comprehensive series of steps to achieve practice growth. You do not need to use a practice consultant indefinitely.

COMMON QUESTIONS ABOUT GROWING YOUR PRACTICE

"But I am a generalist . . ."

For newcomers to practice development, the concept of developing a "market niche" from one of your clinical specialties may seem odd. The step-by-step process from vision, to business goal setting, to creating a one-year marketing plan, to assessing its success, and finally setting advanced practice development phases, can be laid out if you have narrow and specific goals.

"Writing down my practice goals is not really necessary."

Actually, writing them down is an important key to your success. When learning something new or embarking on something that you feel apprehensive about, there are many opportunities to abandon your goals. If you say, "I don't have time right now," or, "But, I know what my goals are. I know the direction I want my practice to go in general," you may eventually be saying, "Marketing doesn't really work, I tried it." "All of these plans overwhelm me!" "Being a psychotherapist is not what it used to be . . . I think I might retire and do something else."

Start somewhere, anywhere. Here are two examples.

What is one *realistic* practice goal that you think you can achieve? Do you know what your average fee per hour is? If not, find out by taking the last month's expected client income and divide it by the number of clients you saw. Do you like the figure? Do you want to change it? What would be a good target date? What do you want to tell your current clients?

Is there a new clinical specialty that intrigues you? Look over the list in chapter 2. How can you get more training in the area within the next 3 months? How would you tell people that you are taking clients in this area? Where can you learn how to develop a specialty brochure?

"I've been in the field for 25 years. I don't like the idea of marketing."

If you are a seasoned practitioner, you have several advantages. You are confident in your clinical skills and you are known in your community. Remember that promotional projects are not about *you*. They are an opportunity and a responsibility to educate the public. You are not marketing yourself but the *service* you provide.

"I just received license. I don't know a thing about private practice. How do I know if this is really for me?"

Congratulations on a job well done! If you can get through graduate school, get all of your supervised hours in, and pass the licensing exam, you can accomplish a lot! Stay in that spirit and start building your ideal plan. It doesn't matter if you aren't completely sure what you want your practice to be like. It is much easier to alter your course than to start the initial momentum going. Look for role models. Adopt ideas from others.

Your advantage is that you don't have to abandon old ways and retool your practice. You do not have to complain about the "good ol' days" and how private practice used to be. Your energy can stay clear of this negativism. Keep the student work ethic going and plow away at the business aspects of your practice. You will find yourself moving forward.

"I'm working in a community agency and I'd love to transition into private practice. What is good plan?"

Start slow and smart. Rent an office on a per-hour or half-day basis to conserve your money and keep your options flexible as you build. Decide how much money you need to be consistently making in order to give up your job on a full time or half time basis. Then set small, realistic financial goals in terms of the number of clients and revenue per month that you need. When you reach your goals consistently for at least 3 months in a row, consider taking the plunge and putting in your resignation. Be sure that you have a full-year marketing plan in place to carry you through the first several unpredictable months that follow. A smart business owner also accumulates extra "emergency money" reserves in case their income progression is unexpectedly unstable.

"I am an introvert, shy, afraid of public speaking, and I hate networking. I don't think I will enjoy this."

There are many vehicles that do not put you out in front of the public. Are you a good writer? What about joining a group practice with internal marketing already set up for you? Review the list in chapter 3. Just because you haven't liked doing something before doesn't mean that, with proper training and support, you can't learn to master it, as well as enjoy it now. Have you considered hiring a practice consultant to help?

AFFIRMATIONS TO HELP YOU STRETCH AND GROW

Another vehicle to get you up and keep you motivated is to use affirmations. When your mind "rehearses" the feelings, behaviors, cognitions, and pleasures of success, you will find yourself more enthusiastic about reaching your goals. This is another opportunity to tailor skills that you teach your clients and practice what you preach. This is particularly useful when you are moving into new or "uncomfortable" territory while you stretch and grow as a business owner.

Affirmations for Writing Articles and Books

Writing for the public is very different from writing within our field. Using professional jargon will often tend to make your audience lose interest. Terms that are commonplace for you can stop the clear flow of communication with the public. Remember that writing is an opportunity to educate the public about the value of your work. Use the opportunity to develop rapport, touch them, and help them learn and grow from what you have to say. Work to develop a writing style that flows and takes them out of a logical, left brain, defended mode. Help them feel a sense of trust and connectedness with you. You may find that this helps them feel more courageous so they can pick up the phone and call you.

Use the following affirmations that fit for you or develop your own:

The conceptualization of my ideas flows quickly:
My writing takes people on a journey.
My introductions are good pacesetters and mood setters.
My words have rhythm, punch, and flow. . . . My readers are rolled and tossed by the melody.
I leave them with the opportunity to feel, experience, and discover.
Light writing looks easy—so does ballet.

My writing is tight and flowing.

I write with personality and style.

Writing comes quickly to me.

I easily add humor and visual images that add life to my writing.

I am a successful author.

Every day, I shorten and tighten what I write.

I love to write and touch people's lives.

My writing unlocks the process of those who read my work.

I am a successful guide for others.

My endings are rich and wonderful, and they make people want to stay and linger.

PUBLIC SPEAKING

Speaking in front of the public is very different from giving a seminar or speaking at a professional conference for your peers. If you are fresh out of school and have recently defended your thesis or dissertation, be very aware that the public does not relate well to research or psychological terminology. Imagine that your dentist or accountant explained things to you in a way that their peers would follow with ease and interest. Do you think that you would, too?

The following affirmation can help you ease into a speaking career. Use the affirmations that apply to you or create your own.

Sample Speaking Engagement Affirmations

I prepare for my speeches well. I know my order, transitions, and concepts.

I trust and let go when I speak.

I am at my best when I speak; my posture is tall. I am eloquent.

I have enthusiastic and dynamic energy.

My speeches take people on a journey.

My introduction is a great pacesetter and mood setter.

My voice has rhythm, punch, and flow. The audience is rolled and tossed by the melody.

I have compassion for my topic and my audience and it shows.

I easily have humor and style.

My speaking unlocks the process of my audience.

I empower others through my work.

I leave them with the opportunity to feel, experience, and have a discovery.

My endings are rich and wonderful, and people want to stay and linger.

Twelve Ideas to Transform Public-Speaking Anxiety into Success

Most people find their anxiety is reduced when they are able to replace their fears with solid information. Yet for some, the issue of discomfort during a speaking engagement must be confronted head on to overcome it. Fear of public speaking is one of the most powerful fears. The best ways to overcome it are the following:

1. Only accept a speaking engagement on a topic that has meaning for you and you care about.

2. Don't accept any assignment that is outside your area of expertise.

3. Do your homework and be thoroughly prepared. Only accept an engagement that will take place with plenty of time to design your presentation and be sufficiently prepared.

4. Write your own introduction and give it to the person introducing you several days ahead of time. If you feel that they are representing your knowledge and special skills in a light that makes your feel important and confident, you will have a great start.

5. Go through a guided visualization for several days before you are scheduled to speak. Imagine the perfect audience that is captivated by what you have to say. They respect you and appreciate you. They will leave knowing that what you have said has changed their lives.

6. Imagine yourself feeling exhilarated! Confident! And actually enjoying the electric energy. Imagine yourself getting many new clients because they were seeking someone to assist them and your words gave them the confidence to begin.

7. Use of visualization and relaxation techniques paired with public speaking can be a good starting point. Develop positive cognitive self-statements and affirmations to add to your professional growth. Continue to listen to your practice audiotape so you are familiar with the topic through other mental pathways.

8. Focus on ways to make speaking to larger groups energizing. Get familiar with what actors, musicians, and other performers know. Discover the enjoyment of the electric energy of a crowd.

9. Move away from fear or ego gratification. Create a self-perception of competence while being humble, and let your message pass through you.

10. Add mental prompts such as overheads and slides to help you feel in control and create comfort.

11. Remember that the public will be viewing you as an expert. You can be introverted or shy in your personal life but you can be an excellent speaker if you remember that you are in control when you are speaking. They will be coming to your presentation to hear you. They want to learn from you. They will not have your knowledge base. Let that create security for you.

12. Prepare, prepare, prepare—and then let go.

Defusing Troublemakers

The old saying, "You can't please all of the people all of the time, but you can please some of the people some of the time; is true with public speaking, too. At some point you will meet up with an audience member that challenges you. The first thing to realize is that what hecklers say has nothing to do with you. They could be angry, envious, or need to monopolize time to satisfy their own need for control or ego gratification. Stay in control, strong, and appear unaffected by their comments. Learn how to redirect the topic when you see a new direction to go in.

If you become a regular speaker, you will find that there are often one or two people in an audience that may interfere with your presentation. They may want to appear smart and go "on and on" in a direction that takes you off course. In that case, let them know that you would be happy to talk to them about the subject further on a break. But right now, you want to stick to the information you are presenting. You will gain the respect of your audience, and they will be thankful that their time is not wasted by comments that are off track.

Sometimes you may encounter a person who has issues with authority. They may question what you say and challenge the foundation of your ideas. Remember that you are on *your turf,* so go ahead and defend your point of view. Again, mention that their ideas may be interesting, but you would be happy to talk to them on a break or at the end as others came here to hear your information. Many people in an audience have seen others challenge the speaker before so this is not new to them. Do not assume that they think anything is wrong with your ideas. Most people in your audience will appreciate you putting such a person in their place. Then they can go on and benefit from the rest of your presentation.

Seven Ideas to Boost Attendance When Registration Is Low

If you have invested a great amount of time or money in your seminar preparation, a low turnout can present a big psychological blow. But you still will have a job to do. If you are making the jump from local or regional to national seminars, your costs and preparation time will undoubtedly increase. Here are some tips to defray the tension or financial loss if your preregistration numbers are low:

1. Don't get frozen by fear! You are learning, and everyone who achieves success goes through tough experiences along the way. The people who become truly successful are the ones that get through these times. They keep going forward until they ultimately achieve their goals.

2. If anyone calls you for information, encourage him or her to sign up right on the phone. Even when people are truly interested at that time, other competing things can stop them from making the final commitment.

The biggest one is procrastination. Sometimes it is money. I would recommend that you get credit card payments over the phone when they call, if you can.

3. Talk to your hotel contact and see if you can downsize the room. Your contract will have a cutoff date when you must pay the full amount, no matter what. If you can work with him or her now, you may be able to get a smaller room and save money.

4. I always recommend a room that is full and feels (comfortably) packed. It implies interest in the seminar, success, and increases the perceived value. If you cannot reduce the room size, study the space and see how you can make it seem more intimate. Consider removing unneeded chairs, arching the chairs you will use in your presentation, or put fewer chairs in each row with a wider isle.

5. Think about having your friends not go to a "dress rehearsal," but add their ten bodies to the real event. Let them in as complementary guests.

6. Get all of your possible "complementary guests/colleagues/friends" lined up for the date. Perhaps offer it at a substantial discount to special groups. Contact organizations or schools and inform them about the opportunity as a field trip.

7. Whatever happens in the attendance realm, remember that your topic and your information is needed, important, valued, and worth pursuing.

A SUMMARY ON PRACTICE DEVELOPMENT

Have the Courage to Follow Your Heart

In these final pages, you will have the opportunity to examine all that you have learned about building a practice:

- The changing profession of psychotherapy
- Our need and responsibility to educate the public
- Your unique practice goals
- Your assets and blocks to practice success.

Now is the time to take action and begin the next phase of your practice development.

- If you are in graduate school, there are many important things that you can do now that will contribute to the success of your future practice.
- If you work in an agency, managed care company, teach, or work in any other paid position, you can begin now to prepare to enter your own private practice.

- If you are moving to a new community, what you have learned in the preceding pages will build your practice, if you begin to take action now.

Start with small, discrete steps to ensure that your plans match your real needs as well as desires.

> *Nothing in the world can take the place of Persistence. Talent will not; nothing is more commonplace than unsuccessful men with talent. Genius will not; the world is full of educated derelicts. Persistence and Determination alone are omnipotent.*
>
> —Calvin Coolidge

EXERCISE: BECOMING A SUCCESSFUL PRACTITIONER

In these final pages, you will identify your unique assets as well as roadblocks to practice success. This three-part exercise will also help you make plans to improve your progress towards your goals.

Part 1: Fifteen Attributes of a Successful, High-Volume Practitioner

Check off the ones that apply to you:

____   1. I have *specific* and *written* practice goals.

____   2. I maintain a low-anxiety lifestyle.

____   3. I am optimistic about the future of my profession.

____   4. I enjoy life.

____   5. I am physically relaxed and take good care of my health.

____   6. I am energized, alert, and focused.

____   7. I have simple systems in place to run my practice efficiently.

____   8. I am open to change and growth.

____   9. I am confident in my ability to build my practice.

____   10. I operate out of the highest standards of ethics and integrity.

____   11. I feel comfortable with money issues.

____   12. I am willing to step out of my comfort zone to reach my practice goals.

____   13. I am willing to invest my time and energy for 1–3 years to make my practice grow.

____   14. I feel a sense of civic responsibility to use my skills to improve my community.

____   15. I embrace the fun, playfulness, and rewards of being a small business owner.

Part 2: My Personal Blocks to Reaching My Full Practice Potential

Look psychodynamically at your personal history. Also examine the issues, values, and life decisions you have made that may get in the way of your reaching your practice potential.

Place a check next to the ones that apply to you.

___ Insecurities centering around _____

___ Fears stemming from _____

___ Difficulty seeing myself "out there" in the community.

___ Fear of failure

___ Fear of success

___ Fear of being sued if I am too visible and take risks

___ Focusing on anger at managed care and not my goals

___ Burnout

___ Being cynical about my clients, my community, etc.

___ Being cynical about my profession and where it is going

___ Feeling sad or guilty that I am spending too much time away from my children

___ Feeling sad or guilty that I am spending too much time away from my significant other

___ Feeling bad that I am not making the money I that want to make

___ Fear of doing something embarrassing in a public speaking or media forum

Part 3—I have or Will Consider

Place a check next to the ones that you are willing to commit to trying:

___ Accept that my profession is changing and that I can adapt

___ Reduce the anxiety, depression, or burnout in my life

___ Begin an exercise program that will reduce stress and increase my energy

___ Reframe practice development as a fun and creative project

___ Go into my own therapy to break through my barriers

___ Reassess my career values and goals to determine if psychotherapy is still the right profession for me

___ Form a local practice development support group to brainstorm and support each others' practice goals

___ Hire a practice development consultant or coach

___ Take continuing education classes or workshops in practice building

___ My other plans to mobilize myself include _____

ASSIGNMENT: HOW HIGH WOULD YOU DREAM . . . IF YOU KNEW YOU WOULDN'T FAIL?

Setting Your Dreams into Action

1. Write down your practice goals for the next week. Read them at the end of the week and see if you are on track. If not, analyze why.

2. Then write down your goals for the next month and do the same. Are there any consistent patterns that hold you back? How can you address them? Are there some interesting opportunities that seem really good?

3. Now write down the practice goals that you want to achieve within the next year.

REFERENCES

Preface

Bennet, T. (1993, June). *Survival in the '90s: A practice management workshop.* Symposium presented at the Meeting of the San Diego Psychological Association, San Diego, CA.

Chapter I

American Psychological Association (1987). Model Act for state licensure of psychologists. *American Psychologists, 42,* 696–703.

Astin, H. S. (1969). The woman doctorate in America: Origins, career, and family. New York: Russell Sage.

Black, J. D. (1949). A survey of employment in psychology and the place of personnel without a Ph.D. *American Psychologist, 4,* 38–42.

Haber, S., Chang, F., Hornyak, L., & Lubin, L. (1998). *Breast cancer: Talk to someone who can help.* [Brochure]. Washington, DC: American Psychological Association.

Kolt, L. (1982). *The influence of women career role models on the self-concept and role conflict issues of women in male-dominated professions.* Unpublished doctoral dissertation, California School of Professional Psychology, San Diego, CA.

Kolt, L. (1996). *How to build a thriving therapy practice: Today and into the 21st century.* Presented at the Kolt Leadership Group Seminar, Newport Beach, CA.

Lindskoog, D. (1998). *The ideas of psychology: Reclaiming the discipline's identity.* Washington, DC: Howard University Press.

Mancuso, J. (1998, September). The entrepreneur's quiz. *Spirit Magazine*, pp. 29–31.
Peters, T., & Waterman, R. H. (1982). *In search of excellence*. New York: Harper & Row.
Rabasca, L. (1998). Think of marketing as a responsibility. *APA Monitor, 29 (10)*, 38.
Seligman, M. (1998, August). *Presidential welcome*. Annual convention program of the 106th Annual Convention of the American Psychological Association, San Francisco, CA.
Strickland, B. (1988). Clinical psychology comes of age. *American Psychologist, 43 (10)*, 104–107.
Watts, P. (1996). Are we becoming a soulless profession? *The California Psychologist, March*, pp. 15–16.

Chapter 2

Glider, C. (1995). Niche marketing: Helping patients cope with infertility challenges. *Psychotherapy Finances, 21 (12)*. (Available: Ridgeway Financial Institute, Inc., 13901 U.S Hwy 1, Suite 5, Juno Beach, FL 33408.)
Kolt, L. (1997a, January). A new market niche: Infertility is fertile. *Practice Management Monthly*, p. 6.
Kolt, L. (1997b, June). Baby boomers as a market niche. *Practice Management Monthly*, p. 7.
Kolt, L. (1997c). Building an infertility practice—An untapped market niche. *The Independent Practitioner, 17*, 154–157.
Kolt, L. (1998a). Breast cancer marketing tips. *The Independent Practitioner*, Winter, pp. 17–21.
Kolt, L. (1998b). Meeting the demand for cardiac psychology. *The Independent Practitioner*, 29(10), 140–142.
Kolt, L., Slawsby, E., & Domar, A. (1999). Infertility: Clinical, treatment, and practice development issues. In L. VandeCreek & T. Jackson (Eds.), *Innovations in clinical practice: A source book*. Sarasota, FL: Professional Resource Press.
Morrissey, M. (1996). Helping couples cope with infertility challenges. *Counseling Today*. (Available: American Counseling Association, 5999 Stevenson Avenue, Alexandria, VA 22304–3300).
Rabasca, L. (1998). Help for infertile couples: A growing practice niche. *APA Monitor, 29 (10)*, 39.

Chapter 3

American Psychological Association. (1996). *Talk to someone who can help*. Washington, DC: Author. p. 1
Bryan, C. A. (1997). Frequency of family meals may prevent teen adjustment problems. Press release, APA Public Affairs Office.
Fizel, D. (1997). Pathological internet use: Psychologists examine who is hooked and why. APA Public Affairs Office, press release during the APA Annual Convention, Chicago, IL.
Kolt, L. (1996a). Let your holiday spirit bring in client referrals too—Practice Builder Column, *Practice Management Monthly*, November.
Kolt, L. (1996b). Behavioral Healthcare Tomorrow Annual National Convention. *Psychotherapy Finances 22*, (10), 9.
Kolt, L. (1999). A positive model for client satisfaction surveys. In L. VandeCreek & T. Jackson (Eds.), *Innovations in clinical practice: A source book*. Sarasota, FL: Professional Resource Press.
Rabasca, L. (1998). Think of marketing as a responsibility. *APA Monitor, 29 (10)*, 38.

Chapter 4

Derby, K. (1997). *How to communicate your message—from sound bite to guest spot.* Paper presented at the 105th Annual Convention of the American Psychological Association, Chicago, IL.

Gilligan, C. (1982). *In a different voice: Psychological theory and women's development.* Cambridge, MA: Harvard University Press.

Goleman, D. P. (1997). *Emotional intelligence: Why it can matter more than IQ.* New York: Bantam Books.

Gray, J. (1992). *Men are from Mars, women are from Venus: A practical guide for improving communication and getting what you want in your relationships.* New York: Harper Collins.

Gray, J. (1997). *Mars and Venus in the bedroom: A guide to lasting romance and passion.* New York: Harper Collins.

Gray, J. (1998). *Men are from Mars, Women are from Venus: The Game.* Mattel, Inc. El Segundo, CA 90254, U.S.A.

Gray, J. (1998). *Mars and Venus starting over: A practical guide for finding love again after a painful breakup, divorce, or the loss of a loved one.* New York: Harper Collins.

Sheehy, G. (1984). *Passages: Predictable crises of adult life.* New York: Harper Collins.

Sheehy, G. (1995). *New passages: Mapping your life across time.* New York: Random House.

Strunk, W., & White, E. B. (1979). *The elements of style* (3rd ed.). Boston: Allyn & Bacon.

Western Psychological Services. (1997). *The Ungame.* Available from Creative Therapy Store, 12031 Wilshire Boulevard, Los Angeles, CA 90025-1251, 800-648-8857.

Chapter 5

Anheuser-Busch, Inc. (1997). *Family talk: How to talk to your kids about drinking.* [Brochure, item #003-887, rev.]. St. Louis, MO: Author, Available: 1-800-359-TALK.

A strike voted by teachers. (1996, February 1). *San Diego Union-Tribune,* p. 1, sec. 1.

Bike helmet safety: Children's lives are saved with bike helmet use. (1998, July 12). *San Diego Union-Tribune,* Parade Section, p. 3.

Cantor, D. (1998). Public education campaign ready response team and brochure project integration. [on-line]. Available: *D1V42@LISTS.APA.org.*

Clark, C. (1996, February 1). Hearty Sarah recovering so fast she may face more surgery soon. *San Diego Union-Tribune,* p. 2, Sec. 1.

Erickson, E. H. (1975). *Life history and the historical moment.* New York: Norton.

Erickson, E. H. (1982). *The life cycle completed: A review.* New York: Norton.

Nizer, L. (1961). *My life in court.* New York: Pyramid Books.

Walker, L. (1998, August). *Conversation hour: From* Time *to tabloids, psychologists, celebrities, and the media.* Presentation at the 106th Annual Convention of the American Psychological Association, San Francisco, CA.

Walker triggers shock wave: Battered women's champ is now O. J. defender. (1995, January 29). *Denver Post,* p. 1, sec. 1.

Chapter 6

DeLeon, P. (1999). *Legal and ethical issues in behavioral telehealth.* Presentation at the 52nd Annual California Psychology Association Convention, San Diego, CA.

Chapter 7

Anatomy of a practice sale (1997, November). *Psychotherapy Finances, 23.*

Kolt, L. (1996a). *Business and marketing training manual.* La Jolla, CA: Author.

Kolt, L. (1996b, May). Are you headed for private practice? Part I. *The Inkblot,* p. 1.

Kolt, L. (1997, January). How will you pay off your student loans. *The Inkblot,* p. 1.

Maheu, M. (1999). *Malpractice and risk management.* Paper presented at the APA Midwinter Convention, Palm Beach, FL.

Chapter 9

Kolt, L. (1983). *Influences on career and personal identity.* Paper presented at the Association for Women in Psychology Annual Convention, Seattle, WA.

Kolt, L. (1990, December 7). House in order. *San Diego Daily Transcript,* p. 13.

Kolt, L. (1996, September). What holds *you* back from building a thriving practice? *Practice Management Monthly,* p. 6.

Lawless, L. (1995, January/February). Helping therapists take charge—More and more clinicians are hiring practice consultations. *The Networker,* p. 73.

ADDITIONAL RESOURCES

ORGANIZATIONS

American Psychological Association (APA)
750 First Street, NE
Washington, DC 20002-4242
Publication: *The APA Monitor*
Publication: *Directory of Experts:* Writers editors, and researchers for newspapers, magazines, wire services, radio, television, and specialized newsletters and journals are invited to call upon the practical and scientific knowledge of the APA members listed in the directory.

APA Division of Psychotherapy (DIV. 29)
3900 East Camelback Road, Suite 200
Phoenix, AZ 85018-2684
Phone: (602) 912-5329
Publication: *Psychotherapy Bulletin*

APA Division of Independent Practice (DIV. 42)
919 W. Marshall Ave.

Phoenix, AZ 85013
Phone: (602) 246-6577
E-Mail: div42apa@primenet.com
Publication: *Independent Practitioner*

APA Division of Media Psychology (DIV. 46)
Division Services/APA
750 First Street, NE
Washington, DC 20002-4242
Phone: (202) 336-6013
E-Mail: axs.apa@email.apa.ora
Publication: newsletter editor: jea905@aol.com

The Brochure Project—APA Division's 29 and 42 Project
The Brochure Project is a joint venture between APA Division 29 (Psychotherapy) and 42 (Independent Practice). For a free sample or more information on the brochures call 1-602-246-6768.

American Psychological Association of Graduate Students (APAGS)
750 First Street, NE
Washington, DC 20002-4242
Phone: 202-336-6014
E-Mail: APA65@APA.org
   The APAGS started in 1988 and has grown to 40,000 student affiliate members. It provides newsletters, scholarships, a voice in APA policy, reduced health insurance, and helps students better understand the profession of psychology that they will enter in the future. Members include graduate and undergraduate students.

American Counseling Association (ACA)
5999 Stevenson Avenue
Alexandria, VA 22304-3300
Phone: 1-800-347-6647
Website: http://www.counseling.org
Publication: *Counseling Today*

American Association for Marriage and Family Therapists (AAMFT)
1133 15th Street, NW, Suite 300
Washington, DC 20005-2710
Phone: 202-452-0109
Website: http://www.AAMFT.org
Publications: *Journal of Marriage and Family Therapy* and *Practice Strategies*

American Cancer Society
1599 Clifton Road NE
Atlanta, GA 30329
Phone: 1-800-227-2345
Website: http://www.cancer.org

American Society for Reproductive Medicine (ASRM)
1209 Montgomery Highway
Birmingham, AL 35216-2809
Phone: 205-978-5000
Website: http://www.asrm.org/
E-Mail: asrm@asrm.org
The ASRM is a nonprofit multidisciplinary organization promoting the study of reproductive disorders.

National Association of Social Workers
750 1st St., S.E., Suite 700
Washington, D.C. 20002-4242
Phone: 202-336-8216
Website: http://www.naswdc.org/

The National Coalition of Mental Health Professionals & Consultants, Inc.
Box 438
Commack, NY 11725
Phone: (516) 424-5232
E-Mail: NCMPC@aol.com
Website: http://www.No ManagedCare.com.

RESOLVE
1310 Broadway
Somerville, MA 02144-1731
Phone: (617) 623-0744
E-Mail: resolveinc@aol.com
Website: http://resolve.org
A nationwide education, advocacy, and support network with branches in many cities.

BOOKS, PERIODICALS, AND OTHER MATERIALS

American Psychological Association (1996). *Talk to someone who can help APA campaign kit.* Washington, DC: Author.

This three-ring binder is available to selected APA members and local psychological associations to share market survey information and teach promotional skills to enhance the field of clinical psychology. Although the information is useful, it is only available to psychologists.

Esteb, W. (1992). *A patient's point of view—Observations of a chiropractice advocate.* Colorado Springs, CO: Orion Associates.
Chiropractors have been entrepreneurial for years, long before it became acceptable for attorneys, medical doctors, and psychotherapists. Some of their ideas are appropriately transferable to psychotherapy.

The book covers useful topics centering on the theme of seeing your practice from the patient's point of view. Useful topics include training support staff to provide good customer service, helping the patient perceive quality, understanding what patients want, and how to handle the important first visit.

In contrast, a large portion of the book is directed to a profession that is quite different from psychotherapy. Yet the overlap centers around how to think effectively and creatively in understanding your clientele, knowing what they want, and how to reach them.

Family Therapy Networker: A Magazine for Mental Health Professionals
7705 13th Street, N.W.
Washington, DC 20012
Phone: 202-829-2452
E-Mail: ServiceFTN@aol.com

Kolt, L. (1996). *Business and Marketing Training Manual for Therapists.*
La Jolla, CA: Author.
Laurie Kolt, Ph.D.
1030 Pearl Street, Suite 3
La Jolla, CA 92037
Phone: 858-456-2005
E-mail: LJKOLT@aol.com
This niche marketing and business development manual assists clinicians in mastering sound business skills to build a profitable and enjoyable practice. Provides step-by-step training to develop marketing plans, brochures, networking strategies, speaking engagements, becoming a community expert, etc. Many samples, forms, and worksheets to build and track practice goals are included. This flexible practice template can be uniquely applied to building any specialty in any part of the country.

How To Build a Thriving Infertility Practice:
Kolt Leadership Group
1030 Pearl Street, Suite 3
La Jolla, CA 92037
Phone: 858-456-2005
E-mail: LJKOLT@aol.com
Includes professionally developed promotional materials, introductory letters to doctors, networking strategies, seminars (marketing, speech notes and handouts), sample infertility practice brochures, a community article to publish, media ideas, marketing plan, and business tracking forms and 300+ research abstracts. (2 bound volumes, over 300 pages).

Infertility Mind/Body Education: Clinicians who are interested in receiving more information about mind/body medicine can contact Harvard Medical School, Department of Continuing Medical Education at 617-632-9530. The Mind/Body Medical Institute, along with Harvard Medical School, offer a 7-day training program three times per year to health care professionals.

Kolt, L. (1997). *25 Essential Forms for an Efficient, Professional, and Ethical Practice.* La Jolla, CA: Author.
Kolt Consulting
1030 Pearl Street, Suite 3
La Jolla, CA 92037
Phone: 858-456-2005
E-Mail: LJKOLT@aol.com
Multiple forms include a set of practice management forms (PMS), forms for clients and therapist forms. Design annual marketing plans and analyze your practice growth. Also includes policy statements, intakes, insurance forms, treatment planning, confidentiality, releases, patient satisfaction surveys, termination forms, faxes, checklists and others. Includes originals to photocopy and on disk.

Levinson, J. (1993). *Guerrilla marketing.* **New York: Houghton Mifflin.**
Jay Levinson's book is full of creative information that many small business owners can use. Most of the material would need to be translated to be applicable to the therapy industry.

The National Psychologist Independent Newspaper for Practitioners
6100 Channingway Blvd., Suite 303
Columbus, OH 43232

Phone: 614-861-1999
E-Mail: natpsych@aol.com
An independent newspaper intended to keep practitioners up to date on practice issues.

The Journal of Marketing for Mental Health, Hawthorne Press, Inc., Ed Winston, W., Binghampton, NY
Written in the 1980s, this journal may be out of date, but useful in providing perspective in how the thinking in our field evolved regarding marketing.

McAfee VirusScan
3965 Freedom Circle
Santa Clara, CA 95054
Phone: 408-988-3832
Website: http://www.nai.com
Excellent software to detect and clean your computer of any viruses. Available at most business supply and computer software stores.

Peoples, D. (1988). *Presentations plus.* New York: John Wiley and Sons, Inc.

Psychotherapy Finances
P.O. Box 8979
Jupiter, FL 33468
Phone: 561-624-1155
Website: www.psyfin.com
Newsletters and books to help psychotherapists develop their practices.

Snell, M., Baker, K., & Baker, S. (1997). *From book idea to bestseller.* Rocklin, CA: Prima Publishing.

Stine, J. (1997). *Writing successful self-help and how-to books.* New York: John Wiley and Sons, Inc.

INDEX

255